Rethinking Leadership

Leadership, corporate responsibility and management ethics underline the human centered paradigm in the complex world of today. One major issue in management is impact on people. This book relates to the outcomes of human interaction within and beyond the borders of an organization. It discusses what motivates moral behavior at the individual and the collective levels, how morality is engrained in markets and how it is deployed in business processes and stakeholder relations. The book shows that human centered management is built and consolidated in four complementary dimensions: ethical, social, economic and institutional. It emphasizes that moral managers and moral markets are essential for business sustainability.

Rethinking Leadership covers ethics development from its origin to help managers understand and confront the 21st century's increasing challenges and disruptions. Its clear narrative and cogent examples bridge scholars and practitioners, with distinctive examples on how to implement human centered management and how to teach the subject to executives.

The author has 30 years of business experience in developed and developing countries and 20 years in academia in the US and in Europe, which provides solid background to effectively and affectively discuss the topic from the multiple angles.

Roland Bardy is Executive Professor at Florida Gulf Coast University and owner of BardyConsult in Mannheim, Germany. Born in Vienna, Austria, he earned his BSc from the Vienna University of Technology, his MBA from the Vienna University of Economics and his PhD from the University of Heidelberg. Dr. Bardy worked at BASF, the German multinational chemicals manufacturer, from 1970 to 1999 and took up teaching in 2000 in the US and Europe, including positions at Emory University and the Austrian Association of Purchase and Logistics.

Human Centered Management

The purpose of this book series is to re-position people to be at the center of organizations, the economy and society. Using management as the common denominator, the ultimate goal is to perform a paradigm shift from the entrenched approaches of the industrial past to a human centered methodology which is convergent with the needs of people and organizations in the constantly changing interconnected world that frames the new Knowledge Society.

The challenges that management is facing when dealing with human development, active participation, responsible leadership, financial accountability, and social responsibility issues can only be understood and solved through the cross-fertilization of ideas from different disciplines. Better integration between management, psychology, neuroscience, economics, education, business, and others needs to happen to accrue the benefits. The reason is simple. Global conditions create increasingly complex problems that can be highly disruptive. Solutions require approaches that build resilience through embedding multidisciplinary models that are effective in building productive organizations, transparent markets, sustainable economies, and inclusive societies.

Maria-Teresa Lepeley, Principal Editor
Maria-Teresa is an educator and economist. After a career in academia, she founded the Global Institute for Quality Education (GIQE) to respond to the challenges in achieving sustainable quality. She designs GIQE's programs and projects and delivers them worldwide, connecting networks of sustainable quality innovators and problem solvers.

Roland Bardy, Associate Editor
Roland Bardy is Executive Professor of General Management and Leadership at Florida Gulf Coast University, USA. He is also owner of BardyConsult in Mannheim, Germany.

Rethinking Leadership
A Human Centered Approach to Management Ethics
Roland Bardy

www.routledge.com/Human-Centered-Management/book-series/HUMCM

"Anyone who has a leadership position of whichever kind will immensely benefit from what the book exhibits on ethical thought, on moral practice and on responsible management."

Ambassador Andrew Young, Atlanta

"*Rethinking Leadership* is a simply awe-inspiring treatise on the future of management. Dr Bardy makes a very compelling case for moral leadership to regain employee, investor, and societal trust of the organization."

Jagdish N. Sheth, Charles H. Kellstadt Professor of Business,
Goizueta Business School, Emory University, Atlanta

"In the networked society, new types of interaction and collaboration require a new focus on their moral implications. Bardy's book clarifies the moral dimensions of interactions and is timely and compelling."

Charles Wankel, Professor of Management at St. John's University, New York

"*Rethinking Leadership* provides a systematic analysis of morality and ethics, as well as the social, economic, and institutional perspectives that are part of, and tied to, leadership and the management of an organization and its people. In his text, Dr Bardy offers a knowledge-based analysis of these complex and multifaceted concepts and presents it in a rational, easy to read, methodic fashion. The reader can easily understand how ethics and morality interface with leadership and human centered management to produce the 'moral leader'!"

Arthur Rubens, Professor Emeritus, Florida Gulf Coast University, Fort Myers

"Humans have been very good in creating societal complexity, but they have been less good in creating the organizational conditions under which this complexity can effectively be addressed. This requires an interdisciplinary, human centered approach to leadership that does not shy away from complex issues and the multifaceted approaches that are needed to deal with them. In this book Roland Bardy combines a solid understanding of practice with a variety of theoretical perspectives that can support more ethical behavior of corporate leaders. A good start to rethinking what it takes to be a responsible leader."

Rob van Tulder, Professor in International Business,
Rotterdam School of Management at Erasmus University Rotterdam

Rethinking Leadership

A Human Centered Approach
to Management Ethics

Roland Bardy

Routledge
Taylor & Francis Group

LONDON AND NEW YORK

First published 2018
by Routledge
2 Park Square, Milton Park, Abingdon, Oxon OX14 4RN

and by Routledge
711 Third Avenue, New York, NY 10017

Routledge is an imprint of the Taylor & Francis Group, an informa business

British Library Cataloguing-in-Publication Data
A catalogue record for this book is available from the British
Library

Library of Congress Cataloging-in-Publication Data
Names: Bardy, Roland, 1942– author.
Title: Rethinking leadership : a human centered approach to
    management ethics / Roland Bardy.
Description: Abingdon, Oxon ; New York, NY : Routledge,
    2018. | Includes bibliographical references and index.
Identifiers: LCCN 2017056039 | ISBN 9780815364610
    (hardback) | ISBN 9781351107174 (ebook)
Subjects: LCSH: Leadership. | Management—Moral and ethical
    aspects. | Business ethics.
Classification: LCC HD57.7 .B366135 2018 | DDC
    658.4/092—dc23
LC record available at https://lccn.loc.gov/2017056039

ISBN: 978-0-8153-6461-0 (hbk)
ISBN: 978-1-351-04696-1 (ebk)

Typeset in Bembo
by Apex CoVantage, LLC

Contents

Foreword

Rethinking Leadership: A Human Centered Approach to Management Ethics is an apt title to put forth in our current business epoch. One wonders whether much leadership has been thought out on an ethical plane to begin with, though. This book is very useful in its consideration of the ethical, social, economic and institutional perspectives of human centered management. These are connected through the concept of multi-stakeholder dialogues, based on reciprocal stakeholder engagement and promote collective learning as they uncover shared meanings and relational responsibilities. Successful multi-stakeholder dialogues sidestep conflicts and misunderstandings. The book discusses the building blocks of knowledge-based multi-stakeholder dialogues that leaders use to come to a common understanding on moral issues associated with their decision-making. A critical success factor that is presented is having a clear-cut philosophical concept combining ethical, economic and social considerations. The building blocks of the knowledge base to be developed are based on ethical leadership, trust building, morality, self-interest, entrepreneurship, sustainable development, social interaction and combining multi-stakeholder dialogues with ethics initiatives and organizational approaches to social issues. In handling such issues, the book aims to transcend the theoretical and be action oriented.

The beginning of human centered management, as the book says, is defining what a business leader understands by "ethical values," by spreading this understanding throughout the organization and by setting examples. Only on that base, human centered management can be implemented by developing corporate ethics codes.

The culmination of this important volume is its putting forth of principles-based business ethics education. It advocates holistic programs that integrate personal and interpersonal goals, societal objectives, and the elements of sustainable development. It entails shifting from a mechanistic mindset to a dynamic perspective. It is explained how leadership and morality should be taught together since in real life they have to be applied together. The book aims to connect to practical aspects of business by having human centered management produce meaningful outcomes in: developing leadership capacity, constructing moral character, systems thinking, fostering role models of ethical behavior for the workplace and beyond, and extending ethical stakeholder relationship management to all of an organization's constituencies. This volume will help clarify for you how to join morality and the free market through an ongoing dialogue and engagement with stakeholders in the development of a moral consensus.

Charles Wankel, Ph.D.,
Professor of Management, Tobin College of
Business, St. John's University, New York

Preface

This book connects the topics of leadership, corporate social responsibility and business ethics/management ethics with the human centered paradigm. While there are many studies on how leadership, social responsibility and ethics impact corporate performance, the impact of leadership on people and society and the reciprocities therein have not been researched as thoroughly. The book aims to bridge this gap. It intends to answer questions about what motivates moral behavior, whether morality can be embedded in rules of the markets, how people-to-people relations are governed by leadership within and beyond organizational boundaries, how business ethics influence business processes, stakeholder relations and how knowledge is built and managed.

The author has chosen the term "management ethics" to be part of the book title and not "business ethics." For one, the book is about "human centered" management, which connects to how people deal with each other and thus focuses on the issue of relations between persons, and second, it is not just businesses that need to be managed responsibly but other institutions as well. "Management ethics" occurs in the title of a book by Norman E. Bowie and Patricia H. Werhane (Bowie and Werhane 2004), and the book articulately emphasizes the unique ethical obligations that guide manager-level decision-making. Bowie has been an important voice in the ongoing debates over ethics in business, and even though the last title written by him reverts to "business ethics" (Bowie 2013), his reasoning is that a manager's moral imagination anywhere should be stimulated beyond mere compliance. An alternative denomination would be "managerial ethics." This term has as well been used for book titles, in particular for highlighting that ethics in business should be related to what has been called the *psychology of morality*, that is, the intrinsic personal reasoning that drives decision-making (see, e.g., Schminke 2010).

This book is carefully selecting a content that should attract the interest of executives at all levels in corporations and other institutions, of policymakers, and of people who design and organize executive education. They will greatly benefit from the insights offered by this book. The book will be useful to both an academic and a practitioner audience. It will help the practitioner to understand the philosophical foundation of ethics and morality. It is the opinion of the author, who has a business background of 30 years and then took up teaching 17 years ago, that management education very often leaves philosophical groundwork out of the curriculum. In addition, leaders in office rarely have the time to dig into the journals or papers that provide insights into this groundwork. The author believes that his book can fill the void. He also believes that managers who wish to deepen their conception of ethics will accept that they need to delve deeper into its philosophical foundation, because otherwise their knowledge on the subject will remain superficial and their actions will lack a proper underpinning.

The conception and the outline of the book are governed by the following ideas:

> There may be organizational and philosophical differences in how institutions regard governance and ethics, but it is imperative for their managers to develop moral behavior that focuses on people inside and outside their organizations. Being pragmatic in management practices and decision-making, especially in light of the ongoing challenges in highly interconnected markets, is definitely compatible with social responsibility. There is no real dilemma of weighing ethics against effectiveness – on an individual or a communal level – because the criteria for decision-making are always contributed through interaction. For the practitioner, this explains why *good ethics* means *good governance*. It also means good cost control through minimizing risks, avoiding fines, court-imposed remedies and criminal charges, reducing operational costs by properly handling environmental and workplace issues, avoiding loss of business, and enjoying greater access to capital. Management ethics is the challenge of ensuring that the enormous entrepreneurial energies released by today's free-market global economy end up by conserving society and not destroying it. This will only happen if people, not profits or share price or greed and selfishness, are at the heart of reasoning.

The author wishes to add a personal note on why he chose "human centered"/ "management ethics" and how this relates to what he experienced in 30 years of business life. Lessons on ethical leadership and humanistic management come from a large variety of sources, of which personal experience has the strongest effect. For a young manager, when leaders are examples of ethical behavior, the lessons are strong. In the author's case, he was privileged to work in BASF, the German chemical multinational, for 30 years since 1970. He could then recognize the value of good leadership as a matter of fact. Early on in his career, he and his colleagues looked up at the CEO and the chairman as true mentors with a leadership spirit that encompassed charisma, participatory management, and exemplary behavior. Later on, the young managers developed a more critical view on the successors of those "giants." But if it was not the same level of admiration, it was yet sincere respect.

By the time when the group of young colleagues were also becoming leaders, concern for people had to get into their focus. The author became an executive with leading responsibilities at an early age, when he had to supervise 180 persons in BASF's subsidiary in Argentina. He then recalled Geert Hofstede, the first Dutch scholar who identified the differences in leadership among national cultures (Hofstede 1980). Hofstede clustered Argentina in a cohort of countries where Individualism, Power Distance, and Masculinity dimensions rank high. So, participatory management, collective decision-making, and caring for others (associated with "Femininity" by Hofstede) were highly uncommon. But the type of inclusive management practiced by the author worked quite well in this environment. This was a learning experience in effective leadership, the theory of which would now be called transformative and transactional.

After retiring from BASF, the author took up a teaching track. Then he realized that what he taught to his students was inspired from experiences he had gained in his business management career. One peak event in the author's business of management training was a symposium on Peter F. Drucker's 100th birthday. The event was held in Vienna, Drucker's hometown, and the author's as well, where he was invited to do a presentation. For this, he and his co-author delved deep into Drucker's thoughts on ethics (Bardy and Rubens 2010) and realized that what they saw in Drucker's writings has been standing practice in BASF all the time.

Another experience has added value to the author's perception of what is ethics and how to teach it. A former CEO of BASF invited him to join the Wittenberg Center for Global Ethics, an American-German alliance founded, among others, by Andrew Young, a veteran civil leader, former US Ambassador to the United Nations, and Mayor of Atlanta; and Hans-Dietrich Genscher, Germany's longest-serving foreign secretary (www.wcge.org). The Wittenberg Center pursues a philosophy that links ethics, entrepreneurship and economic principles under the conception that morality in the economic system offers the necessary conditions for business to operate freely and to the benefit of all who are in that system. For this to be attained, the Wittenberg Center postulates that rules be in place which define modes of action that are permitted in conducting business, and these rules require moral criteria and a system of incentives. Then any firm in this economic system can act and move within these rules, setting strategies for business performance and business goals. A complement to this is to assume that those who follow the rules are rewarded by the market forces and those who break them are punished. This "system-justifying assumption" has begun to become accepted, at least, by business school students (Jost et al. 2003). The Wittenberg Center hopes that this will shape future managers' cognition and behavior.

One last personal note: the author has joined a working group of UN-PRME (the United Nations Principles for Responsible Management Education initiative), whereby he expects that he can contribute insights from his business and teaching experience. With more than 332 signatories, the PRME is probably the most solid initiative to inspire responsible business education globally. But, even though PRME has been around for 11 years as of 2018, some of the very renowned academic associations on business ethics, like the Society for Business Ethics (www.sbeonline.org), founded in 1980, have yet to get fully involved with this practitioner organization. This may be an indication of the ongoing need for amalgamating theoretical and practical viewpoints on the theme. This book intends to be a part of that effort.

Introduction

Leadership has been defined in terms of traits, behavior, motivation, interaction patterns, role relationships or occupation of an administrative position. Most definitions reflect the assumption that it involves a process whereby intentional influence is exerted over people to guide, structure and facilitate activities and relations in a group or organization. Gary Yukl, who has studied the phenomenon for more than three decades, suggests that leadership is "the process of influencing others to understand and agree about what needs to be done and how to do it, and the process of facilitating individual and collective efforts to accomplish shared objectives" (Yukl 2010, p. 26).

One viewpoint that Yukl emphasizes is that leadership occurs only when people are motivated to do what is ethical and beneficial for the organization – but he admits that leaders will more often than not attempt to merely gain personal benefits at the expense of their followers, and that, despite good intentions, the actions of a leader are sometimes more detrimental than beneficial for the followers (Yukl 2010, p. 23). This raises the question of whether there is a divisive difference between leadership and management – with the obvious conclusion that there is an overlap between the two. The overlap will be wider or narrower depending on the person who executes the position. One definition which shows this best is by viewing *management* as an *authority relationship* directed at delivering a specific routine, with *leadership* being a *multidirectional influence* with the mutual purpose of accomplishing real change (Rost 1991). But as has been pointed out by Bowie and Werhane (2004), there is an additional issue that comes into view when looking at who manages a manager. A manager typically works for another, and even top managers serve as *agents*, for the stockholders of a business or for the elected officers in a public administration entity. This will often draw conflicts of interest because almost every management decision has an effect on a manager's personal situation.

Whichever way we look at leadership or management, it is always about relations between humans. Management as an authority relationship produces accomplishment of routines. While this is brought about through the interaction of humans, a management focus is more on outcome and not on the nature of this interaction. This overlaps with what we may call autocratic leadership, where a decision is made by an authoritarian manager. From there, a continuum leads through consultation and joint decision to participative leadership and delegation. However, a distinction must be made between overt procedures and disguised ones, as sometimes what appears to be participation may only be deception (e.g., when a manager solicits ideas from others but ignores them when making a decision; see Strauss 2001). This would indicate that the person acts on false pretense. That person does not act morally, which brings us to the nexus between human interaction and morality. The common term applied to this is *unethical*, a term that is found throughout the academic literature and in practitioners' presentations. What is meant, though, is immoral behavior. As will be set out in the following, the terms of *ethics* and *ethical* should rather be applied to the reasoning for morality and moral. Consequently, this book will use the expression of *moral* and *morality* when talking about the nature of human interaction. Also, this book uses the term *human centered management* rather than *human centered leadership*, first because it wants to appeal to business executives at all levels, and second because when managers interact with people morally, they automatically move away from just applying compliance towards what is the essential essence of leadership, *human orientation* ("encouraging and rewarding individuals for being fair, altruistic, friendly, generous, caring and kind to others"; Kabasakal and Bodur (2004, p. 569).

The human centered paradigm is about leading in a manner that respects the rights and dignity of others (Ciulla 2004, speaking of human centered leaders). Leaders are per se in a position of social power. So when they use their social power in the decisions they make, the actions they engage in, and the ways they influence others (Gini 1997), they exercise human centered management. Six key attributes that appear to characterize human centered management/leadership have been identified in the literature, and this intersects with *ethical leadership* (an overview is given by, among others, Resick et al. 2006). The six key attributes are character; integrity; ethical awareness; community/people-orientation; motivating, encouraging and empowering; and managing of accountability. For any manager or executive to develop these attributes, he or she must become aware of their primordial importance – this can be learned and thus should always be taught first in a curriculum of any business school or university. Only then will all strives to develop leaders or *positive leadership* (Cameron 2012) make sense.

There is an additional aspect in the behavior-related perspective, and this regards the attempts of a leader to shape the moral behavior of others. With that in mind, Brown et al. define "ethical leadership" as the "demonstration of normatively appropriate conduct through personal actions and interpersonal relationships, and the promotion of such conduct to followers through two-way communication, reinforcement, and decision-making" (Brown, Treviño, and Harrison 2005, p. 120). Here, the employees' perceptions of what followers infer on good or bad behavior from the leader's conduct are taken into account as well. Still, while influencing others and setting good examples are prominent traits of *leadership*, the notion of *ethical* demands a more concise definition than just *normatively appropriate*. For one, complying with norms is just one perception; appropriate conduct towards others also entails the capacity for empathy and reciprocity, a sense of fairness and the ability to harmonize relationships, and the "internalization of others' needs and goals to the degree that these needs and goals figure in one's own judgment of behavior, including others' behavior that does not directly relate" (De Waal 2006, p. 168). On the other hand, the enumeration just given only specifies *how* people should behave, which means to behave *morally*, and not *why* they should or will behave that way. The question of *why* is the subject of what philosophers call *ethics*, that is, the study of the grounds of human beliefs and actions. Morality covers the *how* question: what are the principles that govern, what are the actions that display appropriate behavior?

One way to exhibit the distinction between morality and ethics is to differentiate between the capacity to act intelligently and the grounds of beliefs/actions, which is the source of reason. When stating that "intelligence is the ability to learn about the world, to learn from experience, to make new connections of cause and effect and put that knowledge to work in pursuing one's ends" (Korsgaard 2006, p. 113) we are with *how* to behave. Reason, by contrast, looks inward and asks whether actions are justified by motives or inferences from a person's beliefs (*why* does the person behave in a specific way?). Moral standards/morality would then define how to relate to people, and ethics would then demand that "we treat other people as ends in themselves, never merely as means to our own ends" (as per one postulate of the 18th-century German philosopher Immanuel Kant; Korsgaard 2006, p. 101).

All the definitions and postulations given previously are in some way monistic. But there is a systemic perspective in what this book calls *human centered management*, as it intertwines ethics, social aspects, the economic perspective and a relation to institutional concepts. Human centered management is a system as an integrated whole that is not the algebraic sum of the components, but an entity in itself, that needs to be converted into the object of analysis from all its perspectives (Jiliberto 2004). Thus, interpreting one perspective only, as is often done, weakens the systemic aspect and subsequently fails to identify relationships with problems in other fields. In accordance with the author's objective and purpose for this book, we will start with the systemic dimension in the discussion of how to look at leadership and morality. From there we will develop the ethical, social, economic and institutional perspectives. Finally, the book concludes with a view on how ethical leadership concepts should be implemented and taught. The organization of the book, then, can be depicted as follows:

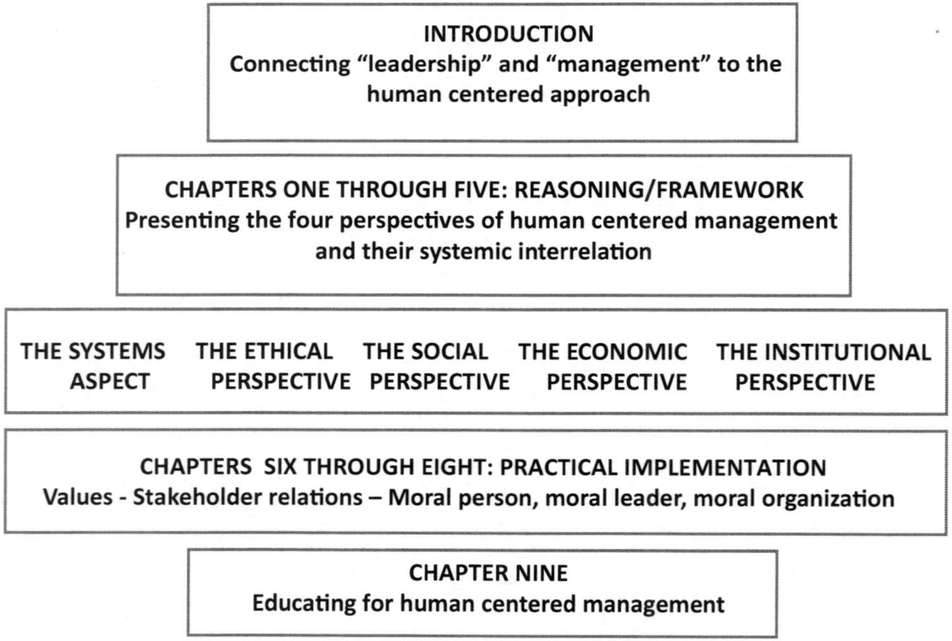

INTRODUCTION
Connecting "leadership" and "management" to the human centered approach

CHAPTERS ONE THROUGH FIVE: REASONING/FRAMEWORK
Presenting the four perspectives of human centered management and their systemic interrelation

THE SYSTEMS ASPECT   THE ETHICAL PERSPECTIVE   THE SOCIAL PERSPECTIVE   THE ECONOMIC PERSPECTIVE   THE INSTITUTIONAL PERSPECTIVE

CHAPTERS SIX THROUGH EIGHT: PRACTICAL IMPLEMENTATION
Values - Stakeholder relations – Moral person, moral leader, moral organization

CHAPTER NINE
Educating for human centered management

Exhibit 0.1 Organization of the book

Chapter 1

The four perspectives of human centered management

A systemic interrelation

This chapter will lay the foundation of what may be called a *framework* for delineating human centered management. Human centered management is determined by a systemic connection between various perspectives, and the intention here is to focus on this set of combinations. As will be seen, intertwining management and the human centered paradigm is much more than just a two-way relationship. It is a systemic approach that needs to combine ethics, social relations, economic effects and institutional conceptions. It is necessary then to embrace all these interrelations in order to validate the analysis. Systemic interconnectedness is an entity in itself, and it is to be studied on its own (Jiliberto 2004). So here, in order to attain a characterization of human centered management, the systemic view combines the ethical, social, economic and institutional perspectives. In the following these perspectives are briefly presented, and their interrelations are illustrated. The four perspectives will be dealt with more extensively in Chapters 2 through 5.

The four perspectives influence each other within a systemic interrelation as illustrated in Exhibit 1.1, and this sequence of mutual effects and feedbacks is a system of its own.

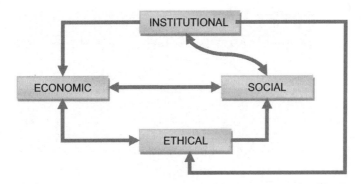

Exhibit 1.1 Interrelations between the ethical, the social, the economic and the institutional

Source: Author

This portrait of interconnectedness presents multiple impacts: ethical reasoning motivates social relations; it has an effect on the economic outcomes of any decision made by a leader or a manager, and it shapes the way the institutions work in a society – be they educational, legislative or judicial bodies. Conversely, institutions may inspire the ethical reasoning of decision-makers; they may frame the structure of economic activities and of societal organization. The mutual impacts continue with the interlace of social and economic occurrences and of social and institutional arrangements.

With this construct of combined perspectives, the framework given by this book differs from other setups of management ethics, which follow a pure stakeholder approach (like Bowie and Werhane 2004) or a moral principles framework (like Schumann 2001). Both moral principles and stakeholder relations are integrative parts of the multi-perspective framework as well, but the systemic dimension treats them as parts of a larger holistic entity.

1.1 The four perspectives

The combination of ethical, social, economic and institutional perspectives within the topic of human centered management makes this a complex phenomenon. Complexity is inherent in ethics issues, as they tend to be represented by different viewpoints of different people, and they are often conflictive and prone to ending up in dilemmas (Krebs, Denton, and Wark 1997; see also Poliner, Shapiro, and Stefkovich 2016, who present dilemma situations faced by educators).

This makes the phenomenon of human centered management attractive for systems theory and systems thinking. It sounds logical that the perspectives would be regarded as elements of the *system* of human centered management, influencing one another within this entity and exerting a combined effect on other systems (an organization, a group of stakeholders, groups of a society, etc.). But while social interaction in general has long been the subject of systems thinking, with, for example, the work of Niklas Luhmann in Germany (see Luhmann 1995) and of Talcott Parsons in the US (see Parsons 1980), the systemic aspect of leader–follower interaction has not been dealt with extensively. There is a massive body of empirical research in leadership effectiveness, but it is based on a one-way relationship; what comes closest to the morality issue is research on fairness in leadership (van Knippenberg, De Cremer, and van Knippenberg 2007).

The four perspectives will now be briefly presented within a concept that connects them to each other. This concept is multi-stakeholder dialogues. There are multiple facets in these dialogues which distinguish human centered management from routine stakeholder management. This is why after the first presentation of the four perspectives the multi-stakeholder dialogues concept will be laid out before discussing the perspectives in more depth. Multi-stakeholder dialogues, apart from being a management practice based on reciprocal stakeholder engagement, rather than on unilateral impulses for organizational control (Heugens, van Den Bosch and van Riel 2002; see also Gray 1989), have also been employed to evaluate scientific/technological advances for social/ethical and ecological risks and benefits. They promote collective learning as they uncover shared meanings and relational responsibilities. By engaging in dialogue, it is argued (Burchell and Cook 2008), ethical obligations and responsibilities are being co-constructed. The process of dialoguing with multiple partners, as it entails ethics and socio-economic considerations, requires a moral foundation as will be shown in section 1.2.

1.1.1 The ethical perspective

Leaders who acknowledge that there are universal principles that govern human behavior beyond written rules and codes act morally by nature. They abide by ethical principles in all the decisions they make, even though the outcomes of the actions they take may not always be uniform. Strict uniformity would concur with what is called universalistic ethics, meaning that an action is morally right or wrong under similar circumstances, irrespective of place, time and sociocultural context. However, *universal* does not mean *absolute*, because there maybe justifiable exceptions. This is often criticized as a casuistic position. For the casuist, the yardstick by which to measure the morality of actions is the circumstances[1] surrounding the person committing the action at the time that it is committed. When circumstances, place and time vary, one should not refrain from applying a different judgment. This casuistic stance turns its attention to individual cases and to debating the relative merits of choosing a solution to a specific problem from among a number of alternatives. Leaders often find themselves in situations like this, as their moral judgment usually has to incorporate economic and social considerations.

One outstanding management scholar who recognized this interrelation early on was Peter F. Drucker. While his casuist view on ethics earned him a number of negative critics (Schwartz 1998; Klein 2000), it was from the cognition of multiple perspectives that Drucker took business ethics very seriously and developed a clear position on business morality. The social perspective in business morality was one of his foremost concerns.

1.1.2 The social perspective

All decisions made by a leader eventually have a social consequence; therefore, the impact of human centered management on society is about benefitting and advancing the condition of people. The impact of business leaders on society at large has gained increasing prominence, both in management literature, which analyzes, interprets and also reinvents this relationship, and in practice, with many individual cases of exemplary performance.

Also, a considerable number of academic and professional associations that pursue real-life dissemination have been set up, such as Business in Society LLC (http://businessinsociety.net), the Academy of Business in Society (www.abis-global.org) and the Caux Round Table (www.cauxroundtable.org), to name just a few. All are connected to and some of them are co-founders of the Principles for Responsible Management Education (PRME) Initiative, which is the first organized relationship between the United Nations and business schools, with the PRME Secretariat housed in the UN Global Compact Office (www.unprme.org). This development has created a new range of concepts attempting to redefine and broaden business' responsibilities with respect to society and introducing the idea of corporate citizenship as a core metaphor (Smit 2013). Citizenship, nowadays, needs institutions in order to fully develop, which is why the fourth perspective of conjoining leadership and morality is about institutions. Markets are the foremost institutions that are relevant for businesses, so the economic perspective is presented here before the institutional.

1.1.3 The economic perspective

There are two aspects to this perspective. One is the reverberation of moral behavior in a leader's environment, which for business leaders means the markets. This aspect includes the impact of human centered management in business, which is discussed in detail in section 4.1.4.

The other aspect is the question of whether the economic model of capitalism promotes moral behavior or not. The most common definitions of capitalism include private ownership of the means of production, voluntary exchange of labor and goods, and competitive markets (e.g., Heilbroner 2008). The moral feature of voluntary exchange (or free markets) and competition is human freedom. But there are three contingent features (Homann 2006b):

1   Markets are built on a systematic feedback mechanism where buyers determine preferences through purchasing patterns.
2   Responsibility is clearly set in open markets. When a product or service is not acceptable to consumers, the producer has to adapt it to meet the needs of buyers.
3   Competition ensures innovation of goods and services as the imperative for providing effective solutions to problems and ensuring that they are rapidly disseminated.

Human freedom is a determinant, thus, for being able to choose between alternatives. This is a precedent for morality: morality is unattainable unless human beings have the freedom to choose between alternative actions or products without external coercion. Therefore, capitalism, which is free ownership in a market where labor and goods are exchanged freely, and prices are defined by supply and demand, is inextricably a system that maximizes human freedom.

The system cannot *guarantee* that all members of society behave morally. But as capitalism is conducive to free will, it naturally *promotes* moral behavior to the greatest extent possible, in contrast to an economic system where the decision-making power is concentrated in one central entity that also defines what is good or evil.

When the people of a community or country can exert their decision-making power, they will eventually opt for a capitalistic system, and it is this system that can easily adapt to the many diverse cultures of the world (Meltzer 2012).

As an additional note on freedom of choice, it should be emphasized that in order to make a moral decision (i.e., one that aims at doing good), people/leaders need to have the mental capacity to discriminate. The German philosopher Immanuel Kant (1724–1804) called this attribute *reason*. One of the criteria he gave for assessing morality was that an act is performed not for a particular outcome but for the sake of *goodness itself*. What would this mean in business life? Yukl (2010, p. 334) gives an excellent example to illustrate *goodness itself*:

> In the 1970s river blindness was one of the world's most dreaded diseases, that had long frustrated scientists trying to stop its spread in developing countries. A potential cure for the disease was discovered by researchers at Merck. The new drug Mectizan would cost over $200 million to develop. And it was needed only by people who could not afford to pay for it. When Roy Vagelos, the CEO of Merck, was unsuccessful to get governments of developing nations to pay for the drug, it became obvious that Mectizan would never make any profit for Merck. Nevertheless, Vagelos decided to distribute Mectizan for free to the people whose lives depended on it. Many people in the company said the decision was a costly mistake that violated the responsibility of the CEO to stockholders. However, Vagelos believed that the decision was consistent with Merck's guiding mission to preserve and improve human life. The development of Mectizan was a medical triumph and it helped to nearly eradicate river blindness. This humanitarian decision enhanced the company's reputation and attracted some of the best scientific researchers in the world to work for Merck.
>
> (Useem 1998, cited in Yukl 2010)

Vagelos followed what George W. Merck had enunciated 25 years earlier: "We must never forget that medicine is for people. It is not for the profits. Profits follow, and if we have remembered that, they never fail to appear" (Gibson 2007, p. 39). Now, if *reason*, according to Kant, leads to performing an action not to attain a particular outcome but for the sake of goodness itself, this implies that an additional outcome (the profits that follow, as stated by George W. Merck) is accepted as *reasonable*.

R.E. Freeman further developed Kant's profit theory, coining the term *Kantian Capitalism* and relating Kant's ideas on who has to benefit from an action to stakeholder theory (Evan and Freeman 1988). This directly connects Kant's reasoning about goodness with the modern theory of the firm embedded on value creation as the highest business objective, with profits not an end but an effective result (Laffont 1975).

Kant's philosophy is discussed in section 2.2.1 to highlight the importance of his theories on morality, as they are crucial for a human centered business ethics agenda and for an ethics-based stakeholder relationship framework.

1.1.4 The institutional perspective

This perspective is based on two aspects. One is the influence that moral leaders exert on institutions (with business associations being closest to business leaders although business leaders might also have an effect on other organizations, e.g., political institutions), and conversely, the motivation a leader receives from institutions.

The other aspect is that institutions are agencies with the power to deploy moral norms across organizations. This concept has been called *ethics of institutions*, and its basis is that a competitive market economy founded on capitalist principles and practices is sustainable with a carefully devised institutional system enabling everyone to pursue individual interests (Lütge 2005).

Institutional ethics distinguishes between actions and conditions of actions. This distinction was initially made by Adam Smith, who, besides being the "father" of free market economics, was a moral philosopher by training. In his first writings (e.g., *The Theory of Moral Sentiments*, published in 1759), he introduced a systematic differentiation between actions and conditions of actions, pioneering the idea of a link between competition and morality. His argument is that morality, which incorporates the idea of the solidarity of all, is the essential element in the conditions or the *rules* by which markets work; the members of the market act in a way that respects the actions of others. Only under these preconditions can competition be effective and foster productivity. Adequate conditions for the actors direct competition to an optimal level of advantages and benefits for all people. As the rules are the same for everybody, no one can exploit a situation where another behaves morally – everybody is induced to behave morally. This also gives an input for the discussion on whether *moral managers* or *moral markets* are more effective in mobilizing all the advantages of capitalism, which will be further explored in section 2.2.3.

The institutional perspective is directly related to issues of corporate social responsibility (CSR), maintaining that a corporation is an institution within society that has to deploy moral behavior towards other members of that society.

There are numerous organizations worldwide that offer recommendations on fostering CSR. Many of them are member-driven organizations where committed leaders work together on principles for moral governance. One example is the International Chamber of Commerce's *Nine Steps to Responsible Business Conduct*, which are directed to companies of all sizes including small and medium-sized companies (www.iccwbo.org/products-and-services/

trade-facilitation/9-steps-to-responsible-business-conduct). And leaders who understand what human centered management is will, conversely, shape the outcome of those organizations. Chapter 3 gives a wider picture of CSR.

In that context it is worth paying attention to developments in China, where institutional ethics constitute a central focus of political philosophy. This raises questions such as "What is a good institution?," "What should a good institution be like?," "How is such an institution possible?" and "What is the value of a good institution?" Typically, what Chinese ethicists ask for is to uphold the historicist mode of thought, that is, traditional philosophies such as Confucianism and the standpoint of the unity of substance and form (Zhaoming 2007).

1.1.5 The four perspectives and the human centered paradigm

All four perspectives of the human centered management paradigm focus on human beings. The *ethics perspective* is a humanistic concept, where the term *humanism* stands for both an emphasis on the value of human beings (*people-centered*) and on critical thinking over acceptance of dogma (reason-centered rationalism and empiricism). The *social perspective* deals with relations between human beings and between individuals and society. The *economic perspective* is about activities that are designed and delivered to meet and serve human needs, and the *institutional perspective* considers agencies that are set up to promote well-ordered human coexistence.

Relations between human beings in a society are at the core of ethics. The focus of ancient philosophies was always on the role of a person in society and his or her contribution to the improvement of the community. The leading examples are Plato, son of powerful politicians in ancient Athens, who laid down his central theses in his work *Republic*; and Aristotle, the educator of the Macedonian prince who was to be Alexander the Great, with his treatise titled *Politics*. So, from its beginnings in ancient times, ethical reasoning has always connected the individual and society.

Institutions arose in modern societies whose structures are much more complex and pluralist than those of ancient Greece. They need agencies that ensure that all members of a society, and especially the less fortunate, partake in progress and prosperity. Institutions exist to serve humans. And this also applies to any economic undertaking. Human beings pursue economic goals as a matter of survival, so human activity is embedded in business activity, which should make it self-evident that the economy and all businesses serve human needs.

While this has been a canon of philosophers and economists for centuries, there have also been conspicuous examples to the contrary – of greed, maltreatment and manipulation of human beings, corruption and misuse of power. And all this happens in spite of remarkable writing about business morality by eminent academicians and practitioners and severe punishment by law for transgressions. However, many successful attempts have been made to reduce the chances for fraudsters to get away unpunished, for example, through the US Securities and Exchange Commission (SEC). The SEC created a pertinent website, which it even named after Bernie Madoff, who was sentenced to 150 years in prison for deceiving hundreds of investors (www.sec.gov/spotlight/secpostmadoffreforms.htm). And German lawmakers substantially expanded the scope of what was considered commercial bribery in German criminal law in the aftermath of the Siemens scandal (Primbs and Wang 2016).

But an important question remains, why do people act immorally, even though most are aware of their guilt in harming other people, and even though they probably know that they will be found out in the end? In the long run, ethical, social, economic and institutional norms will prevail, as this book intends to show. Prevalence of the "good" requires perseverance in dialogue between stakeholders, who then all benefit from the correlation between the ethical, social, economic and institutional perspectives of human centered management. This is the topic of the next section.

1.2 Interrelating the four perspectives through multi-stakeholder dialogues

There is more to systemic thinking[2] than merely determining interrelations. In organizational development theory, which has made extensive use of systems thinking, organizations are viewed as open systems that interact with their environment. Katz and Kahn (1978) have set up a model that interprets organizational interrelations in terms of input, throughput/transformation and output (see Exhibit 1.2). The model factorizes the environment of the organization: the elements, both tangible and intangible, of the external environment are input into the organization, and the results of the output into the environment are fed back into the organization. This contributes to the functioning of the system and a boundary is created that goes beyond the organization.

We can draw an effective parallel from this model to the combination of the four perspectives that conjoin leadership and morality. The ethics perspective could be expressed as an input into the *throughput* of moral behavior and moral decisions that consider human and societal concerns in parallel with what is needed to achieve political or business objectives. Output is the impact on society, with the economy and institutions as the *environment* that helps to develop ethical reasoning shaped by exemplary leadership based on moral behavior.

This mutual influence works through intensive communication. Effective communication is essential to enhance the results of a leader's actions and to promote how institutions can inspire ethical reasoning of decision-makers. Effective communication is a necessary condition for optimizing transmission of knowledge.

The stakeholder relation theme is distinctly engrained in the human centered paradigm. In the definition by Carroll (1996, p. 74), who was one of the

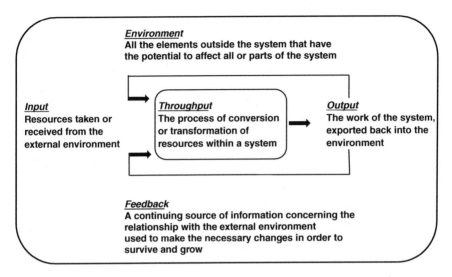

Exhibit 1.2 Katz and Kahn Open System Model

Source: Katz and Kahn (1978), p. 78

first to relate stakeholder relations to ethics, a stakeholder may be thought to be "any individual or group who can affect or is affected by the actions, decisions, policies, practices, or goals of the organization." But human beings need not be conceived as "isolatable, individual entities . . . who have separate wills and desires which are constantly colliding" (Buchholz and Rosenthal 2005, p. 138, p. 141). If the community of stakeholders and business is seen as nothing more than the sum of its parts, the end will be irreconcilable tension. We need to find a different way that would lead to unity.

Effective unity between people – stakeholders in our context – arises in a form of action and thinking that does not fragment the whole and proclaims *implicate order* (Bohm 1980). The term was coined by Bohm in the field of quantum theory; in the context of organizations, the argument is that nothing binds individuals and institutions together except self-interest; so the solution starts by making all parties aware that taking account simultaneously of economic performance and its social aspects will serve common as well as individual interests. This philosophical stance has been called "American pragmatism." It rejects the view of individuals as atomic, separable, isolated units and sees the individual as inherently social. It builds a bridge from the Greek philosophers' notion of ανθρώπος ξώον πολιτικόν ("man is a political being"),[3] and it holds that individuals consider others in the development of their conduct, and in this way, a common content is developed that provides a community of meaning.

A prominent representative of American pragmatism is John Dewey, who wrote extensively about morality and democracy. In his words,

> to learn to be human is to develop through the give-and-take of communication an effective sense of being an individual distinctive member of a community; one who understands and appreciates its beliefs, desires, and methods, and who contributes to a further conversion of organic powers into human resources and values.
>
> (Dewey 1984, p. 332)

This closely relates to stakeholder relations and stakeholder communication.

1.2.1 Communicative action in societal relationships

This subsection looks at the prerequisites for transmitting and grasping knowledge on morality issues and on the dualism of social aspects and economic performance. It builds on what was said previously about the influence of institutions on motivating human centered management and on the reverse effect of moral leaders on institutions.

The first prerequisite is to achieve consensus in a situation in which all participants are free to have their say, which is the epitome of Habermas's *discourse ethics* (Brand 1990). Habermas's philosophical paradigm recognizes that knowledge is fundamentally dependent on relations between subjects. Knowledge is by definition a *construct* to be agreed on by the parties involved, based on mutual understanding, that leads to "shared sensing" (Hannerz 1992). And it is only after the creation of mutual understanding that action can be undertaken.

Habermas argues that most people and organizations tend to engage in *strategic action*, based on egoistic achievement of specific outcomes and where success is judged by the efficiency of influencing the decisions of rational opponents (Habermas 1982). This hypothesis contrasts with communicative action that is oriented towards shared understanding, where partners in an interaction set out, and manage, to influence each other, so that their action is based on *motivation through reason* (Brand 1990).

Effective communicative action needs to include Seyla Benhabib's (1993) call for an extension to Habermas's paradigm. Benhabib adds another purpose of moral discourse: she calls it *achieving a reflective position of reversibility*. This is an empathetic ability to put oneself in another's shoes, which is necessary to achieve a moral point of view (Daboub and Calton 2002b). Benhabib shifts attention away from procedures for achieving purely rational agreement and towards the need to create and sustain practices in which reasoned agreement becomes *a way of life*. She maintains (see Benhabib 1993, p. 337) that there are just two principles by which moral claims of dependent stakeholders receive legitimization, which are:

- The principle of universal moral respect: recognizing the right of all human beings capable of speech and action to be participants in a moral conversation.

- The principle of egalitarian reciprocity: within such conversations, each person has the same symmetrical rights to various speech acts, to initiate new topics and to ask for reflection about the presuppositions of the conversation.

This approach enables decision-making in a pluralist context among a diversity of stakeholders without giving priority to any when they endorse different or even conflicting cultural and moral frameworks (Doorn 2009). This is the context that is regularly found when leaders, especially in business, explore the impacts of their decisions on the community and institutional environments of their firms and on society in general.

Furthermore, effective communications leading to the achievement of moral objectives need to consider that all relationships are subject to three critical issues: agreement, congruency and accuracy. Grunig and Hunt (1984) give a definition of these terms along the following lines:

- Agreement refers to the extent that organization and stakeholders are able to identify a common situation and recognize the validity of the other party's concerns.
- Congruency represents a status where the perception of one party is influenced by the mental model of the other party. Full and open exchange of information is impossible unless the other party's values, knowledge and interests are acknowledged, accepted and "assumed."
- Accuracy derives from the perception that congruency may or may not be a fair reflection of the stakeholders' true values and beliefs. The accuracy relation indicates the veracity of the organization's perception of the interests of the stakeholders. To the extent that the organization's perception closely correlates with the stakeholders', the organization has a more solid base for developing an effective communications strategy. Less congruent and less accurate perceptions lead to less effective communications.

Effective relationships, whatever their type, require operational learning and communication skills, including reflection, inquiry and advocacy (Isaacs 1999), wherein (see Simcic, Brønn, and Brønn 2003):

- The objective of reflection is to become increasingly aware of the thinking and reasoning processes that distinguish between actual "data" and abstractions.
- Inquiry engages the communicating parties in a joint process of understanding the thinking and reasoning of each other, from where statements and conclusions can be advanced.
- Advocacy is the process of communicating one's own thinking and reasoning in a manner that makes them visible to others.

A prudent facilitator of a dialogue seeks a proper balance between inquiry and advocacy, avoiding one-way communication as much as feedback overflow. What should be achieved here is "organizational listening competency" (Burnside-Lawry 2010).

Organizational listening competency is another element of success in conducting multi-stakeholder dialogues. When encounters of stakeholders are prone to produce conflicts and misunderstandings, mastery of listening skills ranks ahead of negotiation skills (Gable and Shireman 2005). This brings us to the building blocks for knowledge-based multi-stakeholder dialogues that leaders use to reach common understanding on moral issues related to their decision-making. Since most societal relationships have an economic underpinning – although one may very well uphold the ethical position that our lives are not measured in dollars (Allaway 2005) – stakeholder-dialoguing is exemplified here in the business environment.

1.2.2 The building blocks for multi-stakeholder dialogues

This section is guided by the views of German business ethicist Karl Homann. In the context of businesses and the very widespread relationships towards their environment, Homann proposes that ethics be reformulated in terms of economic methodology (Homann 2006a). He draws a parallel between ethics issues and problem structures in economics which are determined by conflicting interests of interactive partners. Homann's methodology will be further discussed in section 2.2. Here, it may suffice to note that his approach connects to the topic of stakeholder dialogues as these also encompass relationships between morality and economic advantage.

Any stakeholder engagement and all communication processes need to be prudently and carefully prepared. It is not enough merely to request a dialogue between societal groups and institutions. Outcomes that meet moral standards will only be produced when it is known who the relevant stakeholders are and whether their claims are legitimate, how to talk to them, and how such dialogues are to be organized in a democratic way (Belal 2002).

A variety of *engagement mechanisms* have been described in the literature (Friedman and Miles 2004; Kaptein and van Tulder 2003). Some scholars have even proposed generic strategies for stakeholder management (Savage et al. 1991) and general communication models for talking to different constituencies (Crane and Matten 2004). But rarely do we find this linked to Habermas's discourse ethics, whose outlines were exposed previously. Habermas's model should be taught in management courses, at least in principle, as it lays down a textbook recipe for executing proper stakeholder dialogues.

Stakeholder engagement is not just an effort to synchronize the relationships between a business organization – or any other institution – and its constituencies and where the communication process can be managed as one-way (Andriof 2001; Foster and Jonker 2005). A more effective approach is to build a framework that gives stakeholders a role where they feel that it is *they* who allot the firm a *social license to operate*. For this, the firm must build two-way relationships where the interests and concerns of all parties are taken into consideration and decisions are made in the light of those – often conflicting – interests and concerns (Bendell 2000).

The conceptual approach, methods and responsibilities entailed in a genuine stakeholder communication must be prepared and promulgated through a collective effort by the management team that will execute the business purpose, the representatives of all stakeholders and the facilitators of the stakeholder dialogue.

A critical success factor is a clear-cut philosophical concept that combines ethical, economic and social considerations. This holds true especially for multi-stakeholder dialogues where aggravating effects have to be taken into account. For example, cultural differences may have such an effect, as they often pose a noticeable barrier to common understanding and arriving at a consensus. It is crucial to move away from a narrow definition of *ethics* that covers only the obligations the institution owes to stakeholders and the obligations that stakeholders owe to the institution. The ethics that govern stakeholder dialogues must strive to balance the full variety of stakeholders' values. This requires a format of *organizational learning* where the organization comprises all participants in the dialogue (Payne and Calton 2002; Daboub and Calton 2002a), with the overall objective of securing trust and a *level playing field*.

The building blocks of the knowledge base to be developed are based on:

1   Ethical leadership and governance; trust building; social responsibility; effective articulation of ethics and economics;
2   Morality, self-interest and the markets;
3   Entrepreneurship, development and collaboration: fostering the spirit of business;
4   Foundations of sustainable development;
5   Social interaction: acts and modes of cooperation and the rule-finding discourse;
6   Combining multi-stakeholder dialogues with other standardized ethics initiatives, such as predefined codes, norms and procedures; organizational approaches to social and/or environmental issues;
7   Fundamental learning and communication skills in conflictive environments: reflection, inquiry and advocacy.

This list could also be pertinent to the curriculum of a business school or business course because its building blocks refer to universally accepted subjects. Unfortunately, many still assume that subjects such as ethics and communication can be learned by *osmosis* (Carnevale 2000; Rao and Sylvester 2000).

All the items of the list have their base in a proper understanding of communicative action in societal relationships and could demonstrate what may be regarded as success factors for fruitful multi-stakeholder dialogues. But many business school materials, even those in schools that focus on organizational behavior and culture and value, tend to be theoretical and not action oriented (Ashkansay, Wilderrom, and Peterson 2000). On the other hand, books on the topic of general cultural consulting only offer a random path (e.g., Reeves-Ellington 2004).

A *level playing field* puts each stakeholder into the same position while accepting that not all stakeholders have the same level of importance. Ranking this importance was developed by Mitchell, Agle, and Wood (1997), who categorize stakeholders by three attributes:

1   Power: the ability to get others to do what they otherwise would not do (along the lines of Weber 1947).
2   Legitimacy, which refers to the mandate of the stakeholder – its right to exercise its powers in relation to the claim on the firm.
3   Urgency of a stakeholder claim, which refers to the need to expedite the process of stakeholder interaction.

By combining these attributes in various ways, four types of stakeholders can be distinguished (see Wartick and Wood 1999, p. 113):

•   Long-term core stakeholders who share the attributes of legitimacy and power, but not urgency (e.g., shareholders);
•   Stakeholders who share the attributes of power and urgency, but not legitimacy, and tend to become violent or coercive radical action groups;
•   Dependent stakeholders whose claims are legitimate and urgent, but who lack power (e.g., secondary stakeholders);
•   The immediate core stakeholder group which combines all three attributes, thereby making it mandatory for managers to properly manage the stakeholder relationship with this group as first priority.

1.2.3 Frameworks for preparing and conducting multi-stakeholder dialogues

Stakeholder participation and involvement have been recognized for several years as crucial factors in the context of sustainable development issues (see, for example, van Tulder and van der Zwart 2006), and multi-stakeholder standards have emerged for these issues with considerable potential for effective consensus building, knowledge sharing and interest representation (Fransen and Kolk 2007). Yet the literature is recognizing that currently there is a lack of specificity of the multi-stakeholder concept, and it suggests refinement of multi-stakeholder standards (Fransen and Kolk 2007).

There is no general *tool kit* for addressing multi-stakeholder dialogues, even in the advanced discussions on environmental issues, and much less when dialogues take place in a foreign environment unfamiliar to firms that go

international. Specific formats have been promoted only for high-level dia-
logues, for example, by the Secretariat of the United Nations in creating the
NGO Coalition on Sustainable Development in 1997, through various initia-
tives at other UN-organizations, and with the 2011 UN Department of Public
Information publication "*NGO Conference on Sustainable Societies – Responsive
Citizens*" (UNDPI 2011). Another example is Rupert Brown's 2001 textbook,
Group Processes: Dynamics Within and Between Groups, which does not address
communicative and ethical issues. Likewise, the *Consensus Guiding Principles*
of the Canadian National Roundtable on the Environment and the Economy
(NRTEE), first published in 1993, and the United Nations Environment and
Development Forum (UNED) *Methodological Framework on Multi-Stakeholder
Processes*, by Minu Hemmati (2001), are primarily directed at instrumental procedures. More recently, the WHO *National e-Health Strategy Toolkit* lists recommendations for stakeholder engagement which also encompass ongoing
monitoring and evaluation (WHO and ITU 2012).

For a framework to be generally applicable it should comprise the following
steps (see Benson and Dodds 2010):

- *Process initiation*: scoping, identifying a core coordinating group, locating
  the issues to be addressed, identifying a clear timeline and milestones;
- *Mapping key issues and actors*: connecting topics and actors, establishing a
  system by which stakeholder groups can select or elect representatives,
  choosing the language and terminology used for the dialogue, approaching
  possible facilitators, examining potential confrontations and so forth;
- *Preparing the dialogue*: producing position papers based on stakeholders'
  input developing sharing information rules, agreeing on principles to
  guide the facilitators' work;
- *Conducting the dialogue*: ensuring a comfortable physical atmosphere, assigning experienced rapporteurs to document the session, deciding on the
  admission of observers;
- *Follow-up*: establishing expected outputs, such as a facilitator's summary, an
  agreement report or a set of recommendations to keep records, ensuring
  that the final document is accepted by all stakeholders and communicated
  to their constituencies in de-briefing, and agreement on media coverage.

Benson and Dodds's catalogue reads like a text from a project management
course. It is undeniably important to have good command of state-of-the-
art techniques in this field. It is more effectively applied when the stakeholder community is clearly identified, and all members understand and
accept the general objectives and the "rules of the game." Nonetheless, a
different approach is necessary to address the challenges that leaders face in
effective communication, where an initial consensus cannot be expected and
where the communicative potential for including the majority of possible
stakeholders has yet to be developed. To take a practical case, the leadership

challenges discussed here are centered on the example of a firm that is investing in a developing country:

> A business organization that plans to invest in a developing economy where
> it has not had any activity before must cope with multiple challenges and
> the inherent uncertainties of a new business environment. Even where mul-
> tilateral or bilateral agreements on foreign trade and investment are in place,
> which may be considered as a robust base for the undertaking, in reality
> direct international investment involves considerable amount of risk. There
> is no doubt that trade agreements (TAs) are an imperative and have brought
> substantial progress in decreasing discrimination on access to resources and
> markets, and they have great potential to protect foreign investors from host
> governments' lack of international experience (UNCTAD 2011). But TAs
> are not a perfect solution to minimize risk.
>
> No coverage at all or very scant coverage is found in any international
> agreement on non-equity (contractual) modes of activity, which constitute
> an important part of the cross-border engagements particularly when a
> foreign firm sets out to prepare the ground for a new investment project
> (Dunning and Lundan 2008; Lundan and Mirza 2011). Additionally, local
> institutions in the developing country are often unable to assess the ben-
> efits of international direct investments, such as the contribution to the
> local tax base, employment creation, increase in wages (Khanna and Yafeh
> 2007), and technology and knowledge transfer. These shortcomings frus-
> trate efforts to identify stakeholder interests (Jensen and Yakovleva 2006),
> and they also have an impact on the firm's capacity to negotiate with public
> authorities (Conway 2011).
>
> From the institutional perspective, the inefficiencies of public agencies
> in developing countries are the subject of widespread criticism sustained
> by numerous research studies (e.g., Abed and Gupta 2002). Increasingly,
> attempts have been made to improve performance and eradicate corrup-
> tion. They have been led by the Anti-Corruption Network for Transition
> Economies of the OECD Directorate for Financial and Enterprise Affairs
> in Paris (www.anticorruptionnet.org). But persistent deficiencies remain at
> regional and local levels, identified by Bardy and Massaro (2013) as:
>
> - inadequate public institutions and conflicting objectives with local
>   authorities;
> - low productivity and low standards of staff performance; lack of tech-
>   nical and management expertise, e.g., in maintenance of machinery
>   and equipment;
> - inefficient employee-recruitment practices based on patronage
>   instead of skills and capacity;

- excessive bureaucracy delaying decision-making and obstructing the issuance of permits, licenses;
- civil servants' lack of responsibility and commitment to performance and quality standards;
- high levels of corruption and embezzlement.

Dealing with and trying to solve these challenges is a primary mission for international business leaders who wish to contribute to improving the local business climate and to open business opportunities that require foreign investment to foster economic growth and social growth.

Social development and growth that is focused on education and healthcare are essential to raise the standard of living in developing countries, many of which are drawing benefits from foreign business and direct investments as they contribute to creating jobs and expand national demand and supply. For the social effect of direct investment in developing countries to be successful, the investors will have to exert a moral influence on the people and institutions with which they partner.

An analogy can serve to illustrate why it is a moral duty of foreign investors to exert a positive influence on business partners and society in their host country: the Maastricht Principles on Extraterritorial Obligations of Nation States in the Area of Economic, Social and Cultural Rights. The Maastricht Principles were adopted by the International Commission of Jurists, a group of experts in international law and human rights, in the town of Maastricht, the Netherlands, in 2011 (De Schutter et al. 2012). The principles uphold the axiom of non-intervention set forth by the International Court of Justice, which forbids all states to intervene directly or indirectly in the internal or external affairs of other states. But they acknowledge that internationally recognized human rights – such as those included in the Universal Declaration on Human Rights – impose limits on state sovereignty, and such matters cannot be exclusive to the national jurisdiction of the territorial state. States that are in a position to influence the conduct of non-state actors, such as businesses or civil society organizations within the jurisdiction of another state, should exercise such influence in accordance with the Charter of the United Nations and general international law, in order to protect economic, social and cultural rights (Kirshner 2015). The ability to influence is not limited to legal action; it may include various forms of reporting or social labeling and referencing to human rights-based conditions in procurement schemes. This is where the analogy comes in: by adopting means and measures of this kind, enterprises can remedy any deficiencies of their institutional stakeholders.

There are many examples of business firms with human centered management that set the path for a type of stakeholder involvement aiming to provide value, not only to their customers and suppliers but to the business community in general. They are often destined to exert influence on public institutions and local authorities in a host county. Kolk, Van Tulder, and Kostwinder (2008) present outstanding examples, with Unilever, Shell, Chevron and ABN–AMRO taking the lead. Partnerships like this are a special form of stakeholder engagement, as they mostly provide support to underserved parts of a society. They are also common in the pharmaceutical industry, with an effect that is comparable to Merck's resolution to freely give away the river blindness drug that was referred to earlier.

Partnerships to improve healthcare can start on a much lower level, for example by simply encouraging the use of soap for handwashing in developing countries. This was pursued in the early 2000s by three big soap manufacturers (Colgate-Palmolive, Unilever and Procter & Gamble) which joined in the initiative *Health in Your Hands*, founded by the World Bank's Water and Sanitation Program, the US Agency for International Development, UNICEF and the London School of Hygiene and Tropical Medicine. This program advanced fastest in Ghana under the title *Truly Clean Hands* ("Hororo Wonsa" in the most common local language of this country). This was a national handwashing initiative that reached almost all districts in the country (Curtis, Garbrah-Aidoo, and Scott 2007). The roles and responsibilities of the partners are summarized in Exhibit 1.3 (where *Private Sector* and *External Support Agencies* would also include civil society organizations).

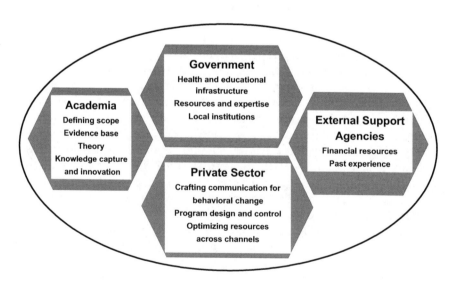

Exhibit 1.3 Stakeholder roles in a private–public partnership on health issues
Source: Adapted from Curtis, Garbrah-Aidoo, and Scott (2007)

Partnerships like these have long-lasting effects on public policy and institutions that reach beyond the borders of the business community where they were applied because other enterprises also benefit from improved efficiency.

In any case, public institutions have to be viewed as primary stakeholders considering that they have or will develop contractual relations with the foreign business organization, similar to relations established with other cohorts of the society including co-investors, customers and suppliers.

While primary stakeholders (the transactional stakeholders in the definition by Wartick and Wood 1999) are the main responsibility of the firm (Clarkson 1995), support must also be sought from secondary, non-transactional stakeholders in the community that interfaces with the organization.

Local communities are commonly regarded as secondary stakeholders, who do not directly influence the economic activities of a firm but indirectly have influence on or are influenced by the firm. Secondary stakeholders, apart from local communities, may also include local media, trade unions, competitors, analysts, environmental activists, and supervisory bodies set up by coalitions of non-profit organizations.

The importance of specific government institutions and supervisors may shift, depending on the process of stakeholder involvement, and, likewise, the importance of local communities may increase or decrease. Other external stakeholders are the "natural environment" and "future generations," which may come into play when groupings are formed that represent the interests of the biosphere and of the generations to come.

To exert a moral impact on an institution or any other stakeholder, a business leader must not only have excellent communicative skills and outstanding arguments, but he or she must also be personally committed to the ethical foundation of leadership behavior and business behavior. What that foundation should convey to all stakeholders is that businesses (especially large international or multinational businesses) have to assume responsibility to halt or diminish any potentially negative economic, social and environmental impacts of their business activity.

The discussion about corporate social responsibility has placed businesses at the center of an often hot and spirited debate about what "rights" businesses can expect to enjoy in society and what "duties" society can reasonably expect businesses to perform. But what needs to be emphasized are the ethical underpinnings. If business leaders actively partake in the CSR discussion and in deliberations about what ethics are and how they are practiced and deployed in the organization, then they must engage in understanding its philosophical attributes. It has been said that "concepts which are the bread and butter of management" have direct, but often ignored philosophical foundations (Joullié 2014, p. 198; see also Joullié 2016; De Borchgrave 2006; Small 2004). The following chapters intend to reveal aspects of management that are embedded in the philosophical dimensions of ethics, economics, societal[4] and institutional relations.

Notes

1 Often, these circumstances are deemed to be culture, ethnicity or geographical location. This relativism, or relativistic ethics, argues that different groups of people ought to have different ethical standards in their respective societies. The question is whether a norm can properly be described as "ethical" unless it is understood as having cross-cultural validity. Within the purpose of this book, a further discussion on relativism and universalism is not needed. In praxis, moral reasoning and decision-making are always context-specific, and it does not make a difference if it occurs in, let us say, the US or the UK or in China.

2 The author has refrained from using the term "systemic morality" because this has been applied to a totally different concept by Goodpaster and Matthews (1982). They employ the term to denote that a pure capitalist approach to business ethics places morality, responsibility and conscience in the role of the invisible hand of the free market system. A discussion on the moral aspects of free market capitalism follows in section 2.2.2.

3 Some clarification regarding the basic ideas of Greek philosophy on morality will be given in section 2.2.

4 The author uses the term "societal" for features that are often denominated by the word "social." "Social," in the context of philosophy, is about characteristics of individuals rather than about groups. "Societal" is about issues that concern society. The terms are often used interchangeably elsewhere, but for this book the author wishes a clear connotation.

Chapter 2

The ethical perspective

2.1 Introduction: morality, ethics and principles

Morality is commonly described as discerning what is right or wrong, and defining the practices and rules, written and unwritten, that are intended to guarantee responsible conduct and behavior among individuals and groups. The aim is to maintain or enhance the common good. That same definition is very frequently used for ethics. If we take the example of one prominent source (Kidder 2003, p. 63), the notion of *ethical* also translates to what would be termed *moral* when it comes to behavior and conduct. There is no remedy against this interchangeable usage of ethics and ethical with morality and moral, and this is deplored by even the most well-known encyclopedias, such as *The Cambridge Dictionary of Philosophy* (Deigh 1999). However, this book will try to differentiate: morality is about doing good, while ethics[1] is about *why* we do good, that is, about the criteria under which the rules for doing good (for what is good and what not) are determined and selected. These criteria then transform into the categories for evaluating the structure of modern societies (see Lütge 2005).

The issue is not just theoretical: moral conduct cannot be performed without a foundation; it has to be based on principles. And in practice, leaders who act on principles will be in a much better position to make their followers understand moral conduct than those who just abide by rules.

Comprehending principles-based leadership requires an appreciation of what is meant by principles in this context. When the concept of principles-based leadership was introduced by Stephen R. Covey in the 1980s (he used the expression *principle-centered leadership*: see Covey 1989), quite a few management principles had been in place for a long time, but they merely described determinants of managerial activity:

> The principles of management . . . are the means by which you get things done to others . . . the activities that plan, organize, and control the operations of the basic elements of people, materials, machines, methods, money

and markets, providing direction and coordination, and giving leadership
to human efforts, so as to achieve the sought objectives of the enterprise.
(Carpenter, Bauer and Erdogan 2009, p. 11)

Here again, we have a two-level phenomenon like morality and ethics. Achieving the objectives of the enterprise is the operational level, and one level up are the guiding patterns, which are overriding principles like natural laws that go without saying and are absolute. They are manifest in the form of values, ideas, norms and learning, but while these manifestations may be subjective and internal to an organization, the overarching principles from which they derive are objective and external, no matter what the conditions of an organization.

According to Covey, four such overarching principles are core in professional and personal life: security, guidance, wisdom and power (Covey 1989, p. 20). Each of these refers, in essence, to the relation of the individual with himself or herself or with others – and they are recast in the workplace through the quality of being worthy of trust (at the personal level), trust (at the interpersonal level), control (at the managerial level) and alignment (at the organizational level). The human centered paradigm connects closely with these elements of leadership, as they all focus on interactions between people.

If we wish to build a strong foundation for moral principles, we need to dig deeper. We need to uncover the prerequisites for apprehending how these principles can turn into guiding patterns for human centered management. One prerequisite is the agenda set by the philosophy of ethics; another is the logic that engrains morality and competitive behavior in the capitalist society; and the third is the cognizance of how these two translate into practice.

Dealing with the philosophy of ethics is becoming a fundamental subject for leaders and managers. This is on the grounds that it develops managerial wisdom, deepens one's understanding of the complexity of management life, and improves creative and critical thinking skills (Chia and Morgan 1996; Small 2004). This was true throughout history. Going far back, we find Marcus Tullius Cicero (106–43 BC) saying that anyone who wants to become a leader should embrace philosophy (Schütrumpf 2014). The words of this Roman statesman, lawyer and member of the senate were taken literally by one of the Roman emperors, Marcus Aurelius (r. AD 161–180). Marcus Aurelius's *Meditations*, written between 170 and 180, are still revered by many as a literary monument to a philosophy of service and duty, describing how to find and preserve equanimity in the midst of conflict (Grant 2011). We do not know of any other emperor or king, Roman, German, British or French, who was his like. However, some of the early US presidents were; Fornieri (2014) contends that Abraham Lincoln's political genius is best understood in terms of a philosophical statesmanship that united greatness of thought and action, one that combined theory and practice, and displayed six dimensions of political leadership: wisdom, prudence, duty, magnanimity, rhetoric and patriotism. So any contemporary leader who sets a good example by applying philosophical wisdom is in good company.

The next section is an excursion into the philosophical background of our topic, which might help to arouse more interest among leaders and future leaders to study ethical reasoning.

2.2 The prerequisites: setting an adequate philosophical agenda

An agenda for morality in leadership, one that appeals to practitioners, cannot be construed without considering how the view on what a leader is has evolved over time. Let us go back, first, to the admirals of the Roman Empire's navy, whose stance was *navigare necesse est, vivere non est necesse* ("navigating the ship is of the essence, human lives are not").[2] Fifteen hundred years later, Niccolò Machiavelli committed to paper what were his reflections on the nature and effective exercise of power. The ideal Machiavellian leader exercises power in the service of the security, glory and expansion of his reign. Machiavelli does not argue that in normal circumstances one should abide by current morality and only resort to *immoral means* when they are needed to preserve the state. What he states is that these measures are quite normal and are a regular condition of political life. Machiavelli's The Prince was written in 1513 for the instruction of the Medici, who ruled Florence at the time, but it has become one of the best-known essays in the history of political philosophy (Machiavelli 2001). Machiavelli's ideas about power and leadership, though rooted in a specific time and place, have also been reformulated and reinterpreted to apply to power exerted by contemporary business executives (see, e.g., Galie and Bopst 2006; Ciulla 2013).

Machiavelli's writings were a reaction to what had been upheld by Christian philosophers such as Thomas Aquinas (1225–1274) (see Fathers of the English Dominican Province 1952), that questioning obedience to those in authority was immoral because God had given them power. Machiavelli's leaders acquire power by virtue of their abilities and through the skillful application of knowledge, control and the capacity to win (war), and their goal is "to create and maintain a strong and well governed social whole" (Galie and Bopst 2006, p. 237).

Following the perceptions of Macchiavelli, Thomas Hobbes (1588–1679) defines the power of leadership to be "the present means for achieving some future apparent good and thus defies the notion that what is good can be authoritatively known" (Friedrich 1961, p. 3). But even if Hobbes sets out from a position which claims that morality, i.e., defining what is good or evil, depends on the nature of one individual (leader), and as he or she changes, good things may become evil and evil things good – with which Hobbes gets to the point that morality should in the end be dependent on the happiness both of the individual and of others (see Frost 2008). From the insights of Hobbes, subsequent theorists of the 1700s and 1800s started to embrace a view that replaced purely egoistic motivation by the quest for outcomes that are more altruistic, like utilitarianism or duty-based reasoning (known as *deontism*, from the Greek word *deon* for duty). Utilitarians deem that an action is good if it benefits the greatest amount of people, and deontists deem that an action must be ruled by consequent moral judgment on the actor.[3]

The rise of the utilitarian principle did not really have an immediate impact on leadership behavior because the prevailing type of governance in the 1700s and 1800s was absolutism; likewise, the posture of the Roman admirals was adverse to what had been developed by the Greek philosophers of the time. Aristotle (384–322 BC) claimed that acting bravely alone is not sufficient for a leader to have normative moral and political weight (Nussbaum 1992; Burger 2008). Moral virtue, according to him, encompasses courage, temperance, justice and prudence. And even though this scheme was taken up and elaborated further by prominent Christian philosophers such as St. Augustine and St. Thomas Aquinas (see, e.g., MacIntyre 1988), Machiavelli's portrait of the prince seems to have been the predominant leadership model throughout the centuries. If we look at four contemporary business leaders and what they have said about leadership, we still find an authoritarian posture in one of them (Bardy 2002):

Jack Welch (General Electric), stressing speed, simplicity and confidence:

> "Create a vision and relentlessly drive it to completion!"
> "Have self-confidence and self-assurance – be critical!"
> "Make the customer drive the corporation!"
> "Sustain integrity and live with the law's letters and spirit!"

Helmut Maucher (Nestlé), stressing keeping the company alert:

> "Select and recruit people who have a broad span of interest and who can understand the overall context … as they rise through the organization."
> "Every leader should be asking: What do I add?"
> "My biggest worry is that they'll think they know all the answers."

Juergen Schrempp (DaimlerChrysler), stressing personal involvement:

> "I am the architect of this global automotive company and I want to see it through."
> "I will consult the committees and then I will take a decision."
> "I wish to demonstrate that what I've said … comes to fruition."

Reinhard Mohn (Bertelsmann), stressing the rules of sociability:

> "Society must integrate and reward."
> "Shared values allow freedom."
> "Open dialogue is better than formal discussion."
> "Exercising one's rights requires discipline."
> "Society is governed by reliability."
> "Society must teach sociability."

In each of these statements, the emphasis lies on very different aspects of leadership. This may be due to the different personalities and abilities of the four leaders, but there is more. Leadership research has focused on leaders' abilities for a long time, trying to demonstrate what causes successful leadership: energy, intelligence, dominance, self-confidence, sociability, openness to experience, task-relevant knowledge and emotional stability, to name the most important (see Yukl 2010). What can be seen in the statements of those four leaders is that authoritarian characteristics are just but one of the features.

While from the Roman admirals to Machiavelli's prince to Juergen Schrempp's autocratic, even narcissistic leadership at DaimlerChrysler (Oesterle, Elosge, and Elosge 2016), there has not been much substantial change, having other models besides authoritarianism would mean that nowadays we have a significant range in the notion of what leadership should be. What has also changed between the time of the Roman admirals and today's understanding are the contexts: philosophy and society are intimately intertwined today, and the individualism that prevailed in past centuries is now but one track of philosophy. The other change in context is the prevalence of an economic footing in all that relates to modern life. This was recognized as early as 1905 by Max Weber in his famous study *The Protestant Ethic and the Spirit of Capitalism*. Weber writes:

> The capitalistic economy of the present day is an immense cosmos into which the individual is born, and which presents itself to him, at least as an individual, as an unalterable order of things in which he must live. It forces the individual, in so far as he is involved in the system of market relationships, to conform to capitalistic rules of action.
>
> (Weber 1905/1976, pp. 54–55)

These two present-day societal and economic contexts of ethics and philosophy in general will be presented in what follows.

2.2.1 The societal context

History shows that in spite of Aristotle's call for balancing courage, temperance, justice and prudence and in spite of the early Christian philosophers' moral teachings, and contrary to utilitarianism and deontism, the figure of what constitutes a leader was much like the Machiavellian prince until well into the 1800s. For Aristotle, the answer to the question of what is the essence of life was to serve others and to do good. And Cicero noted that "Men were brought into existence for the sake of man that they might do one other good" (cited in Trompenaars and Voerman 2009, p. 6). The centuries that followed the fall of the Roman Empire well into the beginning of the Enlightenment did not take up this viewpoint. There were the great 5th-century writings of St. Augustine, who demonstrated the need for moral action (see, e.g., Loriaux 1992), but they did not motivate the leaders of his time or afterwards. It was not before the French Revolution and similar societal movements on the European continent as well as the drawing up of the US Constitution that changes came up. Still, one century before that time, it was the English philosopher Thomas Hobbes (1588–1679) who claimed that a moral leader should in the end pursue not just his own contentment but that of others, too. This may sound unfamiliar because Hobbes's theoretical work is mostly seen to be an attempt to defend philosophically the power of the English king and the general structure of the English monarchy.

Hobbes's writings must be judged from the historical background. His texts were written during the English Civil War, which broke out in 1642 when Hobbes lived in France in the company of the exiled royalists, and his theory of civil government is influenced by what he saw as a political crisis resulting from the war. Hobbes compared the state to a monster ("Leviathan," which is the title of his most famous work published in 1651) composed of men, created under pressure of human needs and dissolved by civil strife due to human passions: "Were it not for political community, people would have to fear death, and lack both a commodious living and the hope of being able to obtain it" (cited in *Stanford Encyclopedia of Philosophy*, 2014, entry "Hobbes's Moral and Political Philosophy"). Political community, as Hobbes means it, would then arise from "people acceding to a social contract and establishing a civil society under the auspices of a sovereign authority (the king), to whom all individuals in that society cede some rights for the sake of protection" (Hobbes 1651/1996, p. 117).

Hobbes's development of what has come to be known as *social contract theory*, that is, justifying political arrangements by agreements made among suitably situated rational, free and equal persons, has laid the ground for subsequent work in political philosophy ever since his death. While his own conclusion was that we ought to submit to the authority of an absolute sovereign power, his philosophy gives an answer to the question of what holds human societies together. And it is all about leadership when he argues that people seek protection under royal authority, because he also upholds that this authority is legitimate only when it can effectively protect those who have consented to obey it; political obligation ends when protection ceases (Peacock 2010).

The core of Hobbes's social contract theory, which is still of relevance today, is that this contract establishes (ethical) norms in order to fulfill the interests of all members of a society – which straightly connects to the human centered paradigm. From there, we also have a clear path to bring the ideas of Immanuel Kant into modern conditions: people constrain themselves – autonomously, but collectively – by rules, for the sake of greater benefits. The condition for this is the consent of all others. And it does not matter if they constrain themselves under the authority of a ruler or under the authority of commonly accepted rules. But before looking at this Kantian *autonomy* and how it relates to other contemporary features of Kantian philosophy, the utilitarian approach needs to be examined as it is somehow positioned between the contractarian and the rules-based approaches.

The utilitarian school of thought, though mostly ascribed to Jeremy Bentham (1748–1832) and John Stuart Mill (1806–1873), was originally founded by Richard Cumberland, an English clergyman (1631–1718) who argued that humans, by nature, are not wholly selfish but basically altruistic. For the theological utilitarians, promoting the happiness of others was necessary because it was approved by God (see, e.g., Albee 2014). For Bentham, it is about the consequences of an action: the welfare of a group – of society – determines if an action (the decision of a leader) is good or bad. This, then, takes on the tinge of relativity: goodness and evil become qualities of acts or decisions relative to the situation in which they are performed. Consequentially, the measure of good has to be in terms of "the greatest good of the greatest number." So, one must ask of a decision if it will bring the greatest good ("utility") to the greatest number of individuals.

Businesspeople feel most at home using the ethical foundation of utilitarianism (Cavanagh 2006), as it focuses on results: when utilitarianism evaluates actions on the basis of their outcomes or consequences (hence the term *consequentialism*), it considers any action that would result in the greatest net gain for all concerned parties to be the right, or morally obligatory, action. This comes close to the modern term of stakeholder orientation. And just as there are criticisms of stakeholder theory (e.g., that because of the many different and competing interests or the diffuse utterance of interest someone must have the power to prioritize, which may jeopardize fair treatment of all interests), there are also criticisms of utilitarianism: it ignores justice, it may instigate favoritism, calculating utility is self-defeating, consequences of decisions for all that they affect are inherently unknowable and so forth. But the moral foundation of utilitarianism will certainly always remain a helpful guideline for ethical decision-making.

Finding a helpful guideline for ethical decision-making was also the objective of Immanuel Kant. His answer is the categorical imperative, where categorical means unconditional: "Act only according to that maxim whereby you can, at the same time, will that it should become a universal law" (Kant 1785/1993, p. 30).[4] To some extent, this arose from his dissatisfaction with utilitarianism, the popular moral philosophy of his day, believing that it could never surpass the level of hypothetical imperatives. Kant argued that when a utilitarian says an action is wrong because it does not maximize good for those involved, this is irrelevant to people who are concerned only with maximizing the positive outcome for themselves. Consequently, hypothetical moral systems cannot be regarded as bases for moral judgments against others, because the imperatives on which they are based rely too heavily on subjective considerations (Rachels 1999).

Very often the categorical imperative is viewed as a philosopher's rewording of the moral standard that is considered to be universal: the Golden Rule.

This rule can be found in all major religions and teachings of wisdom. Shermer (2004, p. 25 f.) enumerates 20 sources, from Leviticus 19:18 in the Holy Bible to *La Morale Anarchiste* of Peter Kropotkin (1889/2006). The Golden Rule expresses the idea of reciprocity, although often in a negative way. For instance, the fundamental text of Hinduism, the *Mahabharata*, states: "This is the sum of duty: do not do to others what would cause pain if done to you" (see Suchanek 2008). A more colloquial version is "Don't do things you wouldn't want to have done to you." The positive formulation can be found, for example, in the Holy Bible at Matthew 7:12: "Therefore all things whatsoever you would have men do to you, do you even so to them."[5]

Kant's reasoning, however, is not about reciprocity. Rather, the categorical imperative is an attempt to identify a purely formal and necessarily universally binding rule on all rational agents. The Golden Rule, on the other hand, is neither purely formal nor necessarily universally binding. It is *empirical* in the sense that applying it depends on providing content, such as "If you don't want others to hit you, don't hit them." Also, it is a hypothetical imperative in the sense that it can be formulated, "If you want X done to you, then do X to others." Kant feared that the hypothetical clause, "if you want X done to you," remains open to dispute (Flew 1979). He wanted an imperative that was categorical: "Do X to others." Hypothetical was not what Kant was about: he knew he needed empirical facts to make moral judgments. This is why his ethical theory can be applied to issues in the real world, as agreed upon by almost any practitioner and most contemporary philosophers, while the Golden Rule cannot (Herman 1993; Stroud 2002).

The problem with the Golden Rule is, stating it bluntly, as Albert Carr did almost 50 years ago (Carr 1968, p. 155), that so long as you accept (or you have to accept) that others treat you in an immoral way, it seems as if you are allowed to treat them immorally as well. In the business world, where being faced with promises that are not kept and being deceived is not uncommon, wouldn't the Golden Rule mean that it is morally acceptable to deceive and cheat on one's own side as well? By contrast, Kant's stance shows that Carr's view is morally wrong because it is contradictory: if all members of a society made promises without an intention to keep them, promises would never get made. And no one would enter into an agreement if he or she believed the other party had no intention of honoring it.

It is the expectation that promises are honored which holds a society together – as is the prospect that one may possess private property and transfer it. These two principles are also fundamental to any *social contract* by the definition of Thomas Hobbes. They are sustained by all moral theorists, from David Hume (1711–1776), a contemporary of Kant, to Friedrich August von Hayek (1899–1992), whose 1944 book *The Road to Serfdom* is said to have been lying permanently on the nightstand of George W. Bush. Bush awarded the Presidential Medal of Freedom to Hayek in 1991. *The Road to Serfdom* is about the "Errors of Socialism," and von Hayek used this as the subtitle of the last book he wrote (*The Fatal Conceit*; Bartley 2011).

If we just take the two criteria mentioned previously (fulfillment of promises and property rights), we can easily understand why the socialist systems in communist countries fell apart when their regimes fell. With the two principles, we also have an answer to what might be the "social glue" or moral capacity that the citizens of a society have for keeping their society stable. But, as the fall of communism has shown as well, in our times the economic conditions also impact the stability of a society. This has given rise to an attempt at rethinking ethical concepts through applying a methodology that is used in economics. The approach that was developed by Homann (2006b) deviates from Kant's emphasis on grounding moral norms and rules in *reason*. Instead, it favors an *economic* grounding of moral rules and looks at calculations of advantage and disadvantage. Before discussing this concept in section 2.2.3, we need to explore what theory has in place to connect the societal level to the individual level of ethical rationale.

2.2.2 Societal and individual rationales

Moral philosophy assumes, as we have seen, that the "social contract," encompassing the principles of property rights and of honoring promises, ensures responsible and moral behavior of the members of a society towards each other. From there, moral philosophy looks at the motivations for moral behavior that are intrinsic in an individual. This will be considered here through Kwame Anthony Appiah's reflections on the five modes of response underlying moral sentiments (Appiah 2008, pp. 126 ff.). They all relate to business life. The first mode is compassion, or the *concern mechanism*, where individuals intrinsically aim to minimize suffering of others. The second mode is reciprocity, which combines fairness and gratitude. The third has to do with attitudes such as respect and contempt; they are attuned to status in social groups. The fourth is anchored in an individual's capacity for disgust, e.g., for open violations of social order, and the fifth is about belonging to a community – the in-group/out-group distinction.

Anyone working in an institution and reaching out to stakeholders will confirm that these five modes of morality are densely interwoven in management life. They should induce managers to act morally. But management in real life also tells us that there is fraud and conspiracy, negligence and disrespect, to name just a few features of immoral behavior. Just as there are moral managers, there are also those who act irresponsibly – and on the corporate level there are those that act with social irresponsibility (Lange and Washburn 2012). Society will have to find a way – and has indeed found it, as will be set forth at the end of this section – to ensure that these wrongdoers get reprimanded, more or less automatically, by the markets in which they commit immorality.

There are two other individual-level motivations for moral behavior (which may also influence the behavior of society as a whole), and they are spirituality and culture. Both offer guidance on personal responsibility and service to others. The issue of culture will be dealt with in Chapter 3. At this stage, a quick glance will show what the world's major religions reveal about responsibility to others – the *spiritual dimension*. The word *spiritual* means relating to the spirit rather than the material. The question must be asked, when increasing numbers of people are describing themselves as spiritual while at the same time not identifying with any particular religion (Saad 2013), whether religion and spirituality exist separately. But let us first look at the foremost teachings of the five world religions addressing morality.

Christian tradition uses the language of the duty to love one's neighbor to speak about responsibility to the other. The Ten Commandments from the Old Testament delineate basic guidelines for human action and set out the particulars of the duty to love one's neighbors by prohibiting murder, adultery, lying, stealing and envy of a neighbor's property. In the present-day Catholic Church, Pope Benedict XVI and Pope Francis have spoken at length about this duty. In his encyclical *Deus Caritas Est*, or *God is Love*, Pope Benedict describes how love of neighbor flows from love of God, and how this love is the fulfillment of justice (Pope Benedict XVI 2005, 1, 8, 18, 28–29). With regard to Protestant denominations, the common view as expressed by Mark A. Noll (2011, p. 5) is that "the message of salvation . . . encourages believers in self-sacrificing service to fellow humans." This reaches way beyond altruism, which does not necessarily have a faith base, as will be clarified when exploring the meaning of self-interest within the context of the *moral market*. But while self-sacrifice may go to extremes that cannot be expected in circumstances of daily life, sacrificing one's personal convenience to the benefit of a someone less fortunate is (hopefully) commonplace among Christians.

Both the Roman Catholic and the Protestant religions have a say in business ethics: Weber's *Protestant Ethic and the Spirit of Capitalism* (1905/1976) has been mentioned already. The counterpart is Catholic Social Thought. The social teaching of the Catholic Church is guided by four permanent principles, which are the common good, solidarity, subsidiarity and respect for the human being (US Catholic Bishops 1996). From there, a list of imperatives has been listed that all revolve around the attainment of providing justice to humans in society (see Hornsby-Smith 2006, pp. 104 ff.):

1   The economy exists for the person.
2   All economic life should be shaped by moral principles.
3   A fundamental criterion for any economy is, how are the poor faring?
4   All people have a right to the necessities of life.
5   Working conditions should be decent.
6   People have the responsibility to work.

7 The free market has clear advantages, but governmental supervision is needed to preclude abuses.
8 Society has a moral obligation to pursue economic justice.
9 Workers and managers and owners are moral agents in economic life. By their choices they enhance material well-being and social justice.
10 We have a moral responsibility for the global economy.

This enumeration is human centered per se: humans are the object of what the teachings of any Christian church expound. It has been found, though, that Orthodox Christianity has a tradition that leans more towards the liturgical than the predicament (West 2002), and from there socio-economic teaching and the concept of the social responsibility of business, in particular, are considerably less developed in the Orthodox tradition than in Catholic or Protestant social thought (Lukin 2008). Nevertheless, in 2000, the Archbishops' Council of the Russian Orthodox Church published a document titled *The Foundations of Social Doctrine* (http://www.mospat.ru/chapters/conception), of which two sections, "Work and Its Fruits" and "Property," address economic questions.

Another document, specifying the papal doctrine further, is *The Code of Ethical Principles and Economic Rules*, which was passed at the Fourth Global Russian Peoples' Council (published in *Pravoslavnaya Beseda Journal* 2/2004). Both documents are regulatory, including passages such as "The Church grants its blessing to any work/professional activities that serve the good of people, if the work does not contradict Christian moral standards," and "it is God's commandment to those who work to take care of those who, for whatever reason, cannot provide for themselves – the disadvantaged, sick, foreigners (refugees), orphans and widows – and share with them the fruits of one's labor" (Fourth Global Russian Peoples' Council, p. 2).

In **Judaism**, the theme of deep, internalized responsibility to others is strongly present all over. There is one passage in the book of Leviticus (19, v. 18) – "And you shall love your neighbor as yourself: I am the Lord" – where, "neighbor" can be understood as meaning "fellow citizen," implying that love and consideration ought to be shown to those in one's own community. While once this passage may have referred to only those who belong to the Jewish community, this has developed over time to include all human beings, regardless of their religion or community of origin (Lipinski 2007, p. 227). In business transactions, Jewish dealings, for example in the diamond world, are often concluded with the words "*Mazal oubracha,*" which is "luck and blessing." More specifically, merchants risked being outcast if they did not honor a contract.

Islam emphasizes responsibility to others by both stressing "good" conduct towards neighbors and travelers and also making charitable giving a religious obligation (Sardar 2007). In the *Hadith*, which is a set of sayings of and stories about Mohammed and a major source of Islam's ethical teachings, there are several passages that stress the importance of justice and injustice to correct behavior: "Justice is the cause of righteousness and peace and of the existence of all forms of life in the world. Injustice is the cause of discord, dis-peace, destruction and ruin" (Sialkoti 1984, p. 78). But it was also found that traditional Islam is more "tribal" in the sense that responsibility to others largely focuses more on those within the Muslim faith than those without (Haidt 2012, p. 140).

Regarding the business world, Islam is often perceived to be an impediment to business, with the economies of most Muslim states underdeveloped and only five out of the Fortune Global 500 leading companies by market capitalization based in the Islamic world (Wilson 2006). Yet most of the contemporary philosophical writings are far from being antagonistic to business. For example, based on the Qur'an, which says in Q. 59:7, "so that this (wealth) may not circulate solely among the rich from among you," the prominent Islamic philosopher Hamidullah discusses the economic policy of Islam with respect to distribution. In his writing, he says: "Equality of all men in wealth and comfort – even if it is ideal – does not promise to be of unmixed good to humanity."

The logic of Hamidullah lies, first, with natural talents not being equal among all men, and, further, in the interests of human society: it is desirable that there should be grades in wealth, which gives the poorer the desire and incentive to work harder. On the other hand, Hamidullah goes on to point out that

> if everybody is told that even if he works more than what is required of him as his duty, he would get no reward and would remain as those who do not do more than their duty, then one would become neglectful, and one's talent would be wasted to the great misfortune of humanity.
>
> (Hamidullah, "The Economic System of Islam," p. 121, quoted in Islahi 2009)

Buddhism, in seeking enlightenment through the path to the end of suffering, identifies wisdom, morality and meditation as the three main divisions of this path. Within morality, one of the major goals or themes is right conduct, "which instructs that a good life should be one of selflessness and charity" (Smith and Novak 2003, pp. 38–39). In the words of the Dalai Lama, spiritual leader for the Gelukpa lineage of Tibetan Buddhism: "The realization that we are all basically the same human beings, who seek happiness and try to avoid suffering, is very helpful in developing a sense of brotherhood and sisterhood – a warm feeling of love and compassion for others" (Dalai Lama XIV and Piburn 1990, p. 16).

Hinduism is similar to Buddhism in its goal of liberation from suffering through a path to an end of reincarnation, and Hindu writings on responsibility and service to others define duties (*dharma*) for a person based on his or her station in life. An ancient text on *dharma* lists eight virtues: "compassion to all creatures, patience, lack of envy, purification, tranquility, having an auspicious disposition, generosity, and lack of greed" as well as "remembering a good deed and returning it with another" (Coward, Neufeldt, and Neumaier 2007, pp. 92–93). But there is another feature in Hinduism, which is the caste system.

The caste system has had a narrowing effect on *dharma* and has strongly influenced Hindu ethics. For centuries, responsibility and service to others was not meant to be applied to the lower castes. The Indian Constitution now prohibits discrimination based on caste, and the "untouchable" class has been abolished. Modern Hindu thought is increasingly focused on compassion and kindness across castes, not only within castes (Sharma 2005). This thought is supported in the sphere of economics by what the prominent spiritual leader of the Hindu faith, Prabhat Ranjan Sarkar (Shrii Shrii Anandamurti), called "Progressive Utilization Theory," a socio-economic framework that seeks the all-around welfare and happiness of everyone, with a clear expression of an equitable economy based on social contract and achieved through a progressive utilization momentum that strives to meet the basic necessities of all and to progressively improve the standard of living (Anandamurti 1994).

This brief enumeration reveals striking similarities between religions. So, it is quite logical that an effort has been made to draw up a minimal code of rules of behavior that all religions can accept. This was achieved in the project *Weltethos* ("Global Ethic"), initiated by the Swiss theologian Hans Küng (www. weltethos.org) and his *Declaration of a Global Ethic* (www.religioustolerance. org/parliame.htm). There are two streams of criticism of this project that was initiated in the early 1990s: one is from the churches that fear that centuries-old knowledge and traditions might fall into oblivion if there is just one common denominator; the other is that the project marginalizes people who are not religious. A "counter-project" that was established on this behalf is *Ethify Yourself* (http://ethify.org/en), a community promoting an ethical lifestyle and good working conditions based on principles such as prudence, balance, fairness, self-determination and justice. This brings us back to the question of how spirituality that is not based on a religion can define moral and ethical guidance. A good way to look at this in the context of business ethics is by viewing how this spirituality translates into workplace practice.

When organizations open up for a spiritual dimension, they make room for meaning, purpose and a sense of community. This would embody employees' search for simplicity, meaning, self-expression and interconnectedness to something higher (Marques, Dhiman, and King 2007). A growing number of organizations, including large corporations such as Intel, Coca-Cola, Boeing and Sears, were reported to have incorporated spirituality in their workplaces, strategies or cultures (Burack 1999). This may also extend beyond the borders of the firm. Some corporations incorporate spirituality into their strategies within the framework of corporate social responsibility. For example, the late Anita Roddick, founder of the Body Shop, was committed to contributing to the needy in the area of Glasgow, Scotland, through social responsibility projects. The projects were destined to solving the problems of high unemployment, crime rates and urban decay in the region. She invested a quarter of net profits back to the community to "keep the soul of the company alive" (Karakas 2010).

Howard argued in 2002 that the "explosion of interest in spirituality as a new dimension of management ... [was] probably the most significant trend in management since the 1950s" (Howard 2002, p. 230), but since then many other mindsets have arisen that embrace ethics, entrepreneurship, systems thinking, self-awareness and spirituality within the dimensions of management (Gretzel et al. 2014; Hörisch 2014). From *green spirituality*, which considers nature as having intrinsic value, deserving reverent care and sacred (Taylor, R.B. 2010), to *mindfulness*, which is linked to compassion and a sense of responsibility to others (Hamilton, Coulter, and Coulter 2015, p. 304), leaders can choose from a broad range of non-religious concepts for determining how to act morally and make their followers act morally. Non-religious is equal to having a secular worldview – that of the ancient philosophers, of the Renaissance humanists or the 19th- and 20th-century existentialists. Whichever belief it is, it belongs to public life, and what secularism does not mean is that the motivation for one's doings is his or her private matter: what counts is conscience, and it is conscience that "unites thinking persons and free peoples across ethnic, national and creedal lines" (Dacey 2008, p. 211).

Given this broad range of ethical concepts, why do people, and leaders in particular, still act immorally? Social psychologists demonstrate that the evolution of humans has always encompassed both cooperation (more successful hunts in the Stone Age, group protection from enemies, etc.) and rivalry (more resources for oneself and family, etc.), and that the direction taken in any given situation will depend on a complex array of variables (Tavris and Offir 1995, pp. 332 ff.).

The variable that is said to have the strongest influence is power. What is often referred to is the famous assertion of Lord Acton in 1887 that *power tends to corrupt and absolute power corrupts absolutely* (even though this assertion was originally directed towards suggesting that democratization reduces corruption; see Werlin 2007). The more general notion may also apply to corruptive structures in the business world such as influence markets, elite cartels, oligarchs, clans and moguls. The means and mechanisms to fight and eliminate abuse of power. Some of the positive evolvements regarding power will be studied in Chapter 6, which encompasses implementation of human centered management.

To end this section on societal and individual rationales, one last issue needs to be explored, and this is about why immorality happens at all.

Why are we immoral? Or, in the business environment, why do corporations act irresponsibly, such as cheating customers, violating human rights or damaging the environment? Or why do we often find people in the boardrooms who are destructive to their organizations, their employees, their countries and their constituents? These "toxic leaders" often "slip into paranoia and toxicity, frequently devote the lion's share of their energies to controlling their followers . . . instead of pursuing growth" (Lipman-Blumen 2006, p. 16). The answer, apart from the socio-psychological perspective mentioned earlier, lies with character. If we just reverse the components of what has been viewed to be the essential components of a good character since the times of Aristotle, we get cowardice instead of courage, recklessness instead of temperance, unfairness instead of justice, and unruliness instead of prudence. While seemingly these are opposites, it is a short step from acting out of self-interest to taking advantage of the vulnerability of others, from working for creating wealth to greed and the satisfaction of acquisitiveness, and from extolling the virtues of individualism to an uninhibited pursuit of gain or glory (Pellegrino 1989).

One might argue that selfishness leads to immoral behavior. But is it just about selfishness? Or should we rather ask about the standards of discriminating between good and evil? Most people shrug their shoulders hopelessly if asked, "What is unfair?" But there is an easy answer. Unfairness can be defined as violating the rules by which we have agreed to be bound in social relationships. And this is where the individual and the societal rationales concur: these rules need to be based on values that apply both to an individual and to a collective group. For the eminent American economist Paul Heyne (1931–2000), who posed the famous question "Are Economists Basically Immoral?" (Heyne 2008), these values are order, minimization of conflict, reasonable equity and the preservation of physical life. Disorder, maximum conflict and inequity are therefore the outcomes of immoral behavior. That applies to corporate life as well.

There are many answers to the question of why corporations act irresponsibly. One answer that is often given is that some people might have different moral beliefs and values at work from those they have at home – people have "multiple ethical selves" (Treviño and Nelson 2011, p. 149). We might also look at the influence of bureaucratic organizations on the value system of individuals, as was first done by Max Weber in the 1930s when he distinguished between actions that were guided by an *ethics of ultimate ends* (a translation of the German word *Gesinnungsethik*, which, however, narrows Weber's term) and an *ethics of responsibility* (*Verantwortungsethik*).

Weber had a positive view of organizational rigor (like in a bureaucracy), and although much can be said of bureaucracy's negative features, its effect on social order is recognized even in today's world of super-organizations. A contemporary argument, for example, is by Paul du Gay, who makes a compelling case for the continuing importance of bureaucracy and for the relevance of bureaucratic ethos (Du Gay 2000). This leads to another answer, which lies with the construct of corporate (social) responsibility.[6] The term has been used in many different contexts, but the underlying view stems from a negative discernment: since quite a few corporate activities do not comply with the normative beliefs of society, firms need to be criticized for low social and ecological standards, for price increases, or for the dismissal of employees. But it must be questioned if such activities can be declared per se as irresponsible (Jones, Bowd, and Tench 2009). The point is that there is a sliding scale from strong certainty to strong doubt about the factual validity of one particular corporate action being harmful to the parties affected by the action.

The proper avenue to access the question of what is irresponsible would be what has been called *provisional ethics* by the French philosophers Michel de Montaigne (1533–1592) and René Descartes (1596–1650). They made a distinction between knowledge and conduct. Both were theologians, and they attributed the power of full knowledge only to God, while acknowledging that humans do not possess sufficient intelligence to comprehend "how he leaves the free actions of men indeterminate" (Shermer 2004, p. 108).

Provisional ethics would offer a conditional ("provisional") agreement on what is right or wrong with a corporate action if the evidence and justification for the action allows clear judgment. The judgment remains provisional because the evidence and justification might change. Again, we have here a nexus between the individual (a corporate leader) and the societal (the normative beliefs): irresponsible action occurs when a corporate leader disregards, bends and neglects the beliefs of his or her constituency.

There is other reasoning on the defects of corporate legitimacy, which originates from the views of legal theorists: constitutional lawyer Joel Bakan (2004) has argued that the law constitutes the corporation as a dangerous psychopath, because, as he contends, it exclusively focuses on profits. Bakan, a Canadian law professor, became famous for the movie *The Corporation*, which he directed and which features evidence from critics of corporate behavior such as Noam Chomsky and Michael Moore presenting brutally dishonest investment brokers, corporation spies and other negative examples of corporate "psychopaths."

The term *corporate psychopaths* is used to describe "managers with no conscience who are willing to lie and are able to present a charming façade in order to gain managerial promotion via a ruthlessly opportunistic and manipulative approach to career advancement" (Boddy 2005, p. 30). Bakan's argument is that corporations benefit hugely from the legal fiction that they are persons, hence entitled to the legal rights of persons, even though their only duty is to follow the law (Achbar and Bakan 2003).

Bakan followed in the footsteps of Lawrence Mitchell (2001), a corporate law scholar, who compared the corporation to a "golem" that can never be called back (Mitchell 2001). By using the word golem, which stems from early Judaism and characterizes an animated anthropomorphic being that was magically created from inanimate matter, Mitchell wished to point out that man has created a monster eluding its own creator. In Mitchell's view, in order to avoid a firm becoming a golem, corporate law must give shareholders the exclusive right to elect or remove directors, the exclusive standing to initiate lawsuits on behalf of a corporation against any third party, and the exclusive ability to sell control of the corporation to the highest bidder. Interestingly, Mitchell comes up with the idea that managers are, at heart, "decent people; and, if left alone, they will use their powers responsibly" (Mitchell 2001, p. 13), and the problem of irresponsibility would thus have to be resolved by limiting shareholders' voting rights. Mitchell pleads for public-spirited deliberation within the corporation, and indeed there have been many positive evolvements in this direction since his critical writings, with US corporate governance structures moving slowly towards characteristics that include a higher degree of outside control (Cremers and Ferrell 2014). Nevertheless, this still leaves us with the issue that if it is not the managers, then it could be the stockholders who may stay out of control when acting irresponsibly.

At the end of this section we seem to have reached a conundrum: can neither the appeal to the individual nor the societal appeal prevent leaders from wrongdoing? And does the legal foundation for corporate behavior promote irresponsibility towards all other stakeholders over the profit for shareholder maximization directive? If so, could an economic appeal furnish a remedy? Is there a mechanism in the business environment that provides a means to automatically eliminate immoral behavior, i.e., to make managers and corporations both "do good" and "avoid bad"? It seems there is, because otherwise the managers at Enron and Siemens who cheated and bribed, and Bernie Madoff, who literally dispossessed investors, to name just three cases, would not have been taken to justice. And we can also find some philosophical argument for this, as will be shown in the following section.

2.2.3 Grounding moral theory in economic thought

When asking if there are market mechanisms that prevent or at least eliminate immoral behavior, the first theory that comes to mind is the *moral market*. The moral market construct (established by Boatright in 1999; see also Smith 2005; Dunfee 1999) leads away from the focus on the individual responsibility of managers towards a focus on the economic regulations that achieve ethical ends. We are *not* looking at formal regulations by laws and ordinances that minimize managerial discretion but rather at (informal) mechanisms that punish immoral behavior. With this, we proceed from the axiom that markets and competition ought to serve human beings, and this is moral, as it does good.

Competition and the market economy alone can guarantee and enhance the opportunities of all individuals for a better way of life. So business ethics in the market economy become, paradigmatically, the ethics of the social order (Homann 2006a). The question is not whether altruism or other non-advantage-seeking behaviors are anachronisms in a competitive environment, nor whether practice has proven that only self-interested behavior leads to beneficial economic result. The question is whether this *incentive- and advantage-based ethics* (Lütge 2005) provides both a theoretical and a practical framework that will encompass rules that ensure moral behavior. In practice, private business firms have increasingly taken on the role of corporate citizens by embracing the rights and duties of lawmakers and political actors. They have engaged in rule-finding discourses and rule-setting processes in which they actively cooperate with government and civil society organizations (Bardy, Drew, and Kennedy 2012).

The link between the economic and the ethical paradigm is advantage-seeking: if economics, in the general sense, is an "advantage/disadvantage grammar where advantages and disadvantages steer action and expectations" (Homann 2006a, p. 7), this holds true for ethics as well. Ethics and economics both explain and shape the results of interactions – more specifically, the aggregate results of interactions. Ethically significant results can never be introduced by an individual agent on his or her own; they are determined by the "rules," that is, the mechanisms governing the business and social environment, and by the incentives issuing from them. Thus, if moral behavior promises to be recompensed – in whatever fashion – individuals behave morally from self-interest (Homann 2006b). Business ethics, thus, is an ethics of conditions, of orders or of incentives.

This may turn out differently in crisis situations: Etzioni (1998) argues that when businesses with a moral culture run into difficulties, the deontological motive is more important than the economic motive. In times of economic hardship especially, this motive may prove more significant than the profit motive in the continued pursuit of corporate policies.

Emphasizing the importance of a carefully crafted balance between rights and responsibilities and between autonomy and order, Etzioni has provided broad empirical evidence that demonstrates that business leaders, to a large extent, feel they have a moral duty towards society. Subsequent empirical research has verified Etzioni's view that they are driven more by *intrinsic* motivation – a person's will to obey a certain moral norm because it is desirable in itself – rather than by *extrinsic* motivation – the will to adhere to a moral norm because it is instrumental in achieving another end, such as earning money (Graafland 2002).

We may also see Etzioni's thought as a symbiosis between utilitarianism and Kant's categorical imperative: subjugating utility to morality, that is, pursuing an advantage only if the means are moral would create a moral organization. And it would be in line with the argument that self-interest and the profit motive need not necessarily be in conflict with moral claims of conscience – an argument that goes back to Adam Smith's unique projection of moral philosophy (his *Theory of Moral Sentiments*) onto his economic writings (the *Wealth of Nations*).

In "updating Adam Smith on business ethics" (Wagner-Tsukamoto 2012; Stroud 2002), contemporary scholars point to three different perceptions of Smith's concept, in terms of (1) societal welfare (public good) as an outcome of economic activity, (2) the systemic codification of morality in institutional frameworks (e.g., business laws), and (3) the embedding of ethical reasoning in market transactions. What we have here concurs with the four perspectives that this book claims to be inherent in human centered management. So even though structures of society have changed since the era of Adam Smith, ethical concepts and categories have obviously not changed to a large extent.

There is, however, one aspect that has changed since the times of Adam Smith: while he recognized that ethics must govern both the competitive actions and the rules (the conditions) of competition, his view on the criteria that determine the rules of the game was necessarily limited to the common values of his society. Today, in the age of globalization, there is no a priori consensus on common values. This does not negate the need to achieve this consensus for a business entity[7] or for a business transaction, but on a global level the only "value" that secures stability is reduced to that of mutual advantages and benefits. This has been called *sociological economics* in the work of 1992 Nobel laureate Gary S. Becker (MacRae and Becker 1978).

Advantages, according to Becker, are simply monetary, financial or material advantages; they are everything that people consider beneficial (health, reputation, the good life, etc.). Monetary incentives themselves can sometimes crowd out intrinsic motivations for moral behavior. But advantages and incentives, if they are part of clearly defined rules, can govern moral behavior; therefore, the challenge for rule-makers is to establish rules that provide these types of advantages to all. Here we are looking at the institutional perspective again: the system will only work if there are institutions that ensure all parties to a market look for their advantage, that set the right incentives for dealing with the quest for advantages, and that are able to implement sanctions for enforcing incentive-compatible rules. The institution that best serves to guarantee all these assurances is the capitalist system of free markets.

The issue, then, is to engrain morality in capitalist society, or the other way round, to prove that morality is engrained in capitalist society because no other economic system can provide advantages to all members of the society.

2.2.4 Engraining morality in capitalist society

Capitalism is a social setting in which businesses can operate freely. The first view on morality in capitalist society must be one that defines freedom or liberties philosophically. The basic understanding is that a free society provides "unalienable rights" (a term that is used in the US Constitution) to all its members, and that these rights are, according to the definition of the English theorist and political practitioner John Locke (1632–1704), "life, liberty and property" (Locke, J. 1698/1988, § 131). While the US Constitution's "unalienable rights" are spelled out as "life, liberty and the pursuit of happiness," Locke's emphasis on "property" (for which the state, as he says, must give protection from its whole strength) implies the right of the society's members to use it, give it away or sell it. Property rights, thus, may deemed to be moral rights. And while property per se is no guarantee of happiness, happiness is, for at least most of humanity, unattainable without some property.

Locke took property rights to be essential for a well-functioning society (a "just" society). His view has influenced the establishment of legal frameworks on property in the Western world and, nowadays, beyond; and while he asserted that the state must give protection, he excluded government control on property or general restrictions to its use. With property rights being the basic support of the free society, the question then arises, how far do these rights go for the owners of property, or of businesses? The logical limit is the rights of others. This would be the principal rule of the game. So quite logically, from this end, but at the same time quite disputably, Milton Friedman's (1970) famous conclusion comes up with "There is one and only one social responsibility of business . . . to increase its profits so long as it stays within the rules of the game, which is to say, engages in open and free competition without deception or fraud" – a quotation from which the moral appeal placed in the second half of the sentence is often left out.

The Friedman doctrine is controversial, especially in hindsight and in view of the abuses of corporate power that happened in the many decades after Friedman's proclamation. But Friedman's view also holds that managers spending resources on social issues misuse their position as agents of the business owners. So since ownership rights need to be respected, this offers a way out of Friedman's dilemma: if business owners decide to assume social responsibility, they are justly exercising their role in society. Friedman's theory will be examined briefly in section 3.1.

Another fierce advocate of the free capitalist market, though less well known in the US and many other countries, was Ayn Rand (1905–1982). Her thoughts, however, are of a higher quality than Friedman's simplistic stance, as they are rooted in a philosophical concept. They deserve to be recalled here, because her philosophy, which she coined *objectivism*, considers laissez-faire, that is, unrestricted, capitalism as the only moral social system because only capitalism is based on the protection of individual rights and property rights (Peikoff 1991). She opposed *statism*, which she understood to include theocracy, absolute monarchy, Nazism, fascism, communism, democratic socialism and dictatorship. Ayn Rand knew what she was talking about, because before moving to the US in 1926 she lived in Russia and experienced the revolution and the brutal system that the communists erected.

The term *objectivism* is intended to express that the only means of knowledge is reason (as opposed to any "higher" ideology) and that rational self-interest is the objective moral code (as opposed to utilitarianism); thus, logically, unrestricted capitalism becomes the only objective social system. But one must not simplify. Ownership rights are but one element of capitalism with moral implications; there are also competition, command and change. We have here another systemic phenomenon: competition, defined for this context as the effort of securing a business by offering the most favorable terms, and command, viewed as the execution of power related to ownership rights, affect the changes that occur in a society. Clearly, command and competition are also interrelated. The opposite view on this is to fear that laissez-faire capitalism creates *market imperialism*.

Market imperialism would mean that money could buy anything, and a laissez-faire economy would invade every sphere of life, transforming every good into a commodity: it would "purchase state offices, corrupt the courts, exercise political power" (Walzer 1983, p. 120). And, indeed, in some post-Soviet countries market imperialism took on these manifest forms, displaying an extreme manner of pure profit seeking, which eventually has destabilized the markets. This only happened because of a total failure of comprehending what the role of the state ought to be. Going back to John Locke, the clear understanding must be that "free exchange must be protected by the state from its whole strength" (Locke 1698/1988 § 135). The state will guarantee this by providing proper institutions, rules, customs and traditions to the extent that the free market requires these guarantees to be able to sustain itself.

If the state provides well-functioning public institutions, this also guarantees freedom from economic oppression and ensures fair dealing in all market transactions. While we have to admit that this idealistic condition is not omnipresent, as markets spin out of control and unfairness is practiced deplorably often, we also see that remedies, both short and long term, are provided by institutions: the legal system, state supervision of, for example, the financial service industry, self-regulatory bodies of business associations and so forth. It is the moral framework provided by these institutions that prevents market capitalism and makes the capitalist system appealing to all members of society because it is beneficial to each and every one – it is *moral capitalism*. Again, is this just another idealistic condition? There is an answer to this question: moral capitalism *works*.

"Moral capitalism at work" (the title of an essay by Stephen B. Young, co-founder of the Caux Round Table;[8] see Young 2006) can be observed throughout the world in a myriad of cases that exhibit exemplary corporate behavior. They range from Unilever's and Chevron's partnerships with society that were mentioned earlier, to the initiatives of Grameen and Danone Foods providing affordable nutrition for malnourished children in Bangladesh, and of Microsoft and Google enhancing knowledge in developing countries (see, e.g., Prahalad 2010; Allison 2015; Peterson 2015). The model applied by Google is called "for-profit philanthropy," embodied by Google.org, a boundary-spanning entity managing an annual philanthropic budget of USD 2 billion (Kelly 2009).

We are witnessing the opening up of China and India, which has lifted hundreds of millions of their people out of poverty through the increasing employment opportunities afforded by these countries becoming the new manufacturers and service providers of the world. It is through this process that capitalism is shaping their living conditions and that capitalism is being shaped to the advantage of a previously underserved population. Because there still remain regions in Africa, Asia and Latin America that are economically underdeveloped, it is up to the major economies and the multinational firms to set the stage there for transformation and restructuring. With the power of the large firms involved, we often find that if the national institutions in a given country do not provide the optimal setting for moral business, corporations often perform a mediation function. Positive outcomes in this field will sooner or later stifle the anti-globalization movement, as evidence of a better way will eventually persuade most of the critics in the long run.

The essence of what has been called moral capitalism is about reconciling private interest with the public good). In line with this, Andrew Young, former US ambassador to the United Nations, coined the term *public purpose capitalism* (Sehgal 2010) to denote socially active public–private partnerships where the private sector would invest in public facilities, buildings and businesses. The concept had a tremendous success in Atlanta, where Andrew Young was the mayor from 1981 to 1989, and it was then transferred to Africa where the Southern Africa Enterprise Development Fund was founded in order to enhance social and infrastructure projects. The most recent application of the concept is in Haiti, where a similar Enterprise Development Fund is being built, which it is hoped will produce a sustainable economy after the earthquake disaster, and not just a relief economy aided through grants from abroad (Young 2010).

Serving society with a greater purpose (i.e., committed to making a difference in the world) *and* producing a reasonable profit certainly poses a challenge to business managers. Whether it is termed *sense-making business* or *integral business*, the drive to create organizations and careers that are both purposeful and profitable has not only become a "trend" (Whetten 2013); it seems that this is the only one option: managers and stockholders alike will only draw long-term wealth from their activities and from their holdings if their firms neither sacrifice social and environmental purposes for profits nor sacrifice profits for social and environmental purposes either. There are many examples of carefully crafted business models to achieve this (see, e.g., Osterwalder and Pigneur 2011). And firms that view society and their workers as the ultimate stakeholders are nevertheless highly profitable. Sisodia et al. (2014) call them "Firms of Endearment," and it has been shown that their share value has increased about ten times more than that of the S&P 500 companies over the 15-year period ending in 2014. Chapter 8 of this book will show more data on the issue.

The importance and the promulgation of the topic can be gleaned from several other denominations beyond "moral" and "public purpose": *conscious capitalism*, from Rajendra S. Sisodia (2011); *shared value capitalism*, from Michael Porter and Mark Kramer (2011); *creative capitalism*, from Bill Gates (2008); and *capitalism 3.0*, from Otto Scharmer (2010). There may be slight differences in where the concepts place their emphasis, but the focus and the objectives are all the same: assuring that financial wealth is not created at the expense of social, cultural, environmental, intellectual, physical and spiritual well-being; empowering people at all levels; and engaging their best contribution to serve a higher sense of purpose and thus making a net positive impact on the world. The main argument is that, because corporations take resources from society, they have a moral obligation to give back, although a few dissenters believe that if organizations voluntarily contribute to social causes they are misappropriating shareholder funds.

Two other terms should be looked at briefly in this context. The first, *welfare capitalism*, has been around for some time, while the second, *sustainable capitalism*, is relatively new.

The term *welfare capitalism* is used for two issues: one relates to a society that has a capitalist structure and where the government applies a wide range of welfare policies, for examples, in the countries of Scandinavia; the second meaning is the practice of businesses providing welfare services to their employees. Welfare capitalism in this second sense, or industrial paternalism, was practiced in industries that employed skilled labor and peaked in the mid-19th century. One protagonist was Robert Owen, who introduced one of the first private systems of philanthropic welfare for his workers in the cotton mills of New Lanark in Scotland and then transferred this scheme to New Harmony, Indiana, where he created a model cooperative.

In the early years of the 20th century, the Cadbury family of philanthropists and business entrepreneurs set up a similar model in their chocolate-making factory at Bournville, England, where loyal and hard-working employees were treated with great respect and given relatively high wages and good working conditions; Cadbury, even though nowadays often criticized for turning a blind eye on child labor (Mena et al. 2016), has pioneered pension schemes, joint works committees and a full staff medical service. Also in England, Lever Brothers (whose name is remembered in Unilever) built Port Sunlight in Wirral to accommodate workers in their soap factory. The model village could house a population of 3,500 and it had a cottage hospital, schools, a concert hall, an open-air swimming pool, a church and a temperance hotel. Lever Brothers introduced welfare schemes and provided for the education and entertainment of the workforce, encouraging recreation and organizations that promoted art, literature, science or music (see https://en.wikipedia.org/wiki/Welfare_capitalism).

The denomination *sustainable capitalism* was first used by Al Gore and David Blood to describe a "framework that seeks to maximize long-term economic value by reforming markets to address real needs while integrating environmental, social and governance (ESG) metrics throughout the decision-making process" (Gore and Blood 2012, p. 66). They suggest various key actions, including:

- Identifying and incorporating risk from assets that are not valued properly ("stranded assets"), for example, by attributing a reasonable price to carbon dioxide emissions or water. As long as this is ignored, stranded assets can cause reductions in the long-term value of particular companies and entire industry sectors.
- Integrated reporting by corporations on both their financial and ESG performance.[9]
- Aligning compensation structures with long-term sustainable performance in order to hold asset managers and corporate executives accountable for the ramifications of their decisions over the long term.

Those concepts may have a very optimistic feel, but the people who devised and employed them do not live in an ivory tower; they were and are close to business. They know that strong institutions are needed that deploy a proper balance between regulation and the freedom of corporations to decide on their own behalf; they know that institutional arrangements that are characteristic of certain welfare state regimes might well have unintended negative consequences; they know that excessive governmental restrictions on property rights, fiscal freedom and monetary freedom will impact entrepreneurial activity; and they know that exceptional leadership is needed to implement moral capitalism at state, industry and corporation levels.

Most leaders acknowledge that improved external controls are important in today's business environment, and they pursue strict compliance with regulation as this helps to bring "one's ethical house into order . . . and to reconcile ethical mandates and the individuals' personal wishes or values" (Schminke, Arnaud, and Kuenzi 2007, p. 173). But there are other enablers for human centered management as well.

2.3 Enablers of human centered management

People do not come into this world as born leaders, let alone as moral leaders. They have to learn about ethics and morality through proper education and mentorship and from personal experience. In this process, they will pass through three levels of moral development (see Kohlberg 1981): the pre-conventional level that anchors moral principles in narrow self-interest, fear of punishment and desire for reward; conventional morality, representing an emerging concept of self-identity in the framework of institutional community where morality is motivated by concepts such as being a good neighbor, community member or citizen and devotion to community norms and authority; and post-conventional or principled morality, which utilizes universal moral principles transcending community norms and is rooted in a conception of autonomy and moral objectivity (Gross 1995). Attaining this objectivity will enable a leader to stay firm in ethical decision-making.

Staying firm in ethical decision-making is often hampered by various stumbling blocks. One is the argument that the notion of ethics is by no means global, that it evolves according to time and culture, and that each individual, at a given place and at a given time, has a unique degree of ethics. Sociologists call this *situation-specific* (Annas 2006), and the main proponents of the situationist thesis (e.g., Doris 2002) base their views on psychology experiments such as the famous Stanford prison experiment of Zimbardo in 1971. This experiment will be briefly discussed here because it is deemed to be the most powerful example of how work roles can have substantial impacts on how we behave. There are prominent textbooks on business ethics (Crane and Matten 2004, pp. 134–136; Brenkert and Beauchamp 2010, pp. 44 ff.; Sekerka 2016, pp. 122 ff.) that argue that the experiment exhibits the stifling effect of a role assignment on individual morality.

The Stanford prison experiment was conducted in 1971 under the supervision of the Stanford University psychologist Philip G. Zimbardo, who assigned the roles of "prisoner" or "prison guard" to 24 healthy middle-class male students within an experimentally devised mock prison setting on the Stanford University campus. The projected two-week study had to be prematurely terminated when it became apparent that many of the "prisoners" were in serious distress and many of the "guards" were behaving in ways that brutalized and degraded their fellow subjects. In addition, the role-playing situation was beginning to influence virtually all those who operated within it to behave in ways appropriate to the characteristics of the prison setting, but inappropriate to their usual life roles and values; this included the research staff, faculty observers, a priest, a lawyer, ex-convicts, and relatives and friends of the subjects who visited the prison on several occasions (Zimbardo 1973).

Most workplace situations are quite different from the prison environment, but we do find situations in the business world where good people can be readily induced into doing evil to other good people within the context of socially approved roles, rules and norms, and even with institutional support. We also find situations where blind obedience to an authority may suffocate the values, beliefs and attitudes a follower normally holds and where a leader utilizes this purposefully.

Human centered management must be strong enough to withstand conditions close to those described previously, and this psychic and cognitive strength will have to be built on knowledge about the problem positions that relate to this context. There may be five problem positions that can lead to suppressing one's own morality: *obedience* to authority, *mood effects* that can be characterized as having been brewed by organizational culture, *conformity with a group* that prevents moral behavior, the *hurry factor* inhibiting people from stopping and being a Good Samaritan when that would be the right thing to do, and lastly, *deception*, when bending the truth seems to be more appropriate than telling the truth (April et al. 2010).

Awareness of these issues will not only enable a leader to challenge their outcomes; it will also generally lead to an increased perception of uncertainty and risk in business matters that involve moral decision-making. The moral perspective is but one matter in decision-making; it is, however, the one with the widest impact. When depicting what makes a great business leader, one all-embracing attribute was emphasized early on by Emory professor Jeffrey Rosensweig: being able to link people and profits. Rosensweig (1998, p. 203) goes on to list the following competencies of a truly global manager: broad education, multicultural sensitivity, integrity, embracing moral values, responsiveness, energy, interpersonal skills, command of information technology and fluency in several key languages.

Leaders who apply the capabilities identified by Rosensweig within a global system of free trade and coordinated international policies will set the path for "bringing hope – and not only hope but actual economic progress – to the billion or so truly indigent people on this planet. Business is, bar none, the best real hope of the poor" (Rosensweig 1998, p. 234, quoting from Michael Novak's 1996 book, whose title, *Business as a Calling*, truly indicates how corporate leaders should apprehend the human centered paradigm).

2.3.1 Enablers from within: Amartya Sen's capabilities approach to personal and social development

The capabilities approach was popularized by Amartya Sen (1985, 2000). Capabilities, according to Sen, are the alternative combinations of *functionings* an individual can achieve. For Sen, *functionings* denote the various attainments a person may value – varying from elementary issues such as nourishment and shelter to complex ones such as self-esteem and community participation (Sen 2000). The focus is not on collective outcomes such as, for example, justice, but rather on building individual competencies, and ensuring that people have the freedom to convert economic opportunities into outcomes they desire.

The capabilities approach is a normative proposition: what people can do and be – their capability-set – depends on the one hand on their resources and on the other hand on factors that affect their ability to use resources to achieve doing and being. The emphasis is on the extent of freedom people have to promote or achieve functioning they value. Progress, or development, or beneficial outcomes of human centered management occur when individuals have greater freedoms. With regard to moral capitalism, a primary evaluative role of the capabilities approach is to assess if this system has expanded human freedom, or what kinds of freedoms the system has expanded. In the context of human centered management, capabilities are the enablers from within the individual for deploying his or her resources. But there also is the systemic relationship to institutional, social and economic structures, because these (like the structures of a capitalist society) would expand an individual's capabilities.

2.3.2 Executing the philosophical agenda

The philosophical agenda of the moral perspective, as laid out previously, turns into action through leadership capabilities. They are the foremost enablers for discerning what is right or wrong, for defining the practices and rules, written and unwritten, that describe responsible conduct and behavior, for arriving at moral decisions and for enhancing the common good. One might think that when doing the right thing it does not matter how or why it was done, whether willingly or unwillingly, through fear of public opinion or for its own sake. But, in the words of the British essayist C.S. Lewis (1952, p. 74), "the truth is that the right actions done for the wrong reason do not help to build the internal quality or character . . . and it is this quality or character that really matters." It is the right reason – the philosophical agenda – that produces the right consequences. This agenda is fundamental to the very essence of how individuals set (moral) actions and make (moral) decisions. So, it is through the effects that we need to investigate how the agenda works. Two effects will be exhibited in the following sections: The impact of leadership on followers of a leader, and the impact on the business environment of a morally led enterprise. The effects on business performance will be shown in Chapter 4, which analyzes the economic perspective.

One striking comparison will be used here that steers us to the two effects that will be examined. This is the comparison between what guides an irresponsible corporation and a moral corporation (see Table 2.1).

In this comparison, under the heading of "moral corporation" are the standards developed by the Caux Round Table. The Caux Round Table is an international network of principled business leaders – leaders who follow moral principles. It was founded in 1986 at a meeting in Caux, Switzerland, by Frederick Philips, former president of Philips Electronics and Olivier Giscard d'Estaing, brother of former French president Valéry Giscard d'Estaing and founding dean of the INSEAD business school. The Caux Round Table Principles for Business were formally launched in 1994 and presented at the United Nations World Summit on Social Development in 1995.[10] The principles articulate a comprehensive

Table 2.1 What guides the irresponsible corporation and what guides the moral corporation

	The irresponsible corporation	The moral corporation
Ideal	Greed, disregard of others	Human dignity, stewardship
Principles	Maximize shareholder wealth irrespective of consequences to others	Respect for all stakeholders, including nature
		Sincerity, candor, truthfulness
		Abiding by rules, abstaining from and eliminating illicit operations
		Contributing to justice and social development; promoting free trade
Standards	Stock price, total compensation	Self-assessment of strategies
		Reflection for improvement of results
Stakeholder Benchmarks	"*Caveat emptor*" (buyer beware), concealment of liabilities, bullying suppliers, destroying competitors	Customer and supplier sovereignty, treating employees as moral agents, protecting owners' assets, giving back to the community

Source: Adapted from Young 2003, pp. 38 and 88

set of ethical norms for business, and they are recognized by many as the most comprehensive statement of responsible business practice ever formulated by business leaders for business leaders.

Many infamous effects of irresponsible leadership have been reported in the media – from criminal acts at Enron and Tyco and WorldCom, to name the most notorious cases in the US and which cost shareholders and customers billions of US dollars, to the Siemens bribery scandal and the Volkswagen emissions fraud. By contrast, the millions of honest and upright businesspeople do not make it to the news. Meritoriously, there are some newer business books that depict how firms can produce a positive effect on their constituencies. Three titles speak for all: *Connect: How Companies Succeed by Engaging Radically With Society* (Browne, Nuttall, and Stadlen 2015); *Everybody Matters: The Extraordinary Power of Caring for Your People Like Family* (Chapman and Sisodia 2015); and *Firms of Endearment: How World Class Companies Profit From Passion and Purpose* (Sisodia, Wolfe, and Sheth 2014). It would be redundant to enumerate the cases presented in these publications. In line with the agenda of this book, a more abstract presentation will be given here on the effects caused by leaders who follow principles like those exhibited earlier. "Abstract" does not, however, mean purely theoretical = they relate to experiences any practitioner will have had in his or her business career.

2.4 The effects

2.4.1 Reciprocities in human centered leadership

Leading is intended to affect other people's attitudes and behaviors. It goes without saying that human centered management is directed towards positive effects which would be an outcome of moral intention. However, we do not always see moral intentions in managers, and, worse, there are cases where supervisors motivate their subordinates to do wrong (the terms *supervisors* and *subordinates* are used here on purpose because good leadership/good management and *immorality*, as this book claims, should be mutually exclusive). The phenomenon of wrongdoing has been studied under the denomination of workplace deviance and organizational deviance. We may find acts directed against the company, such as sabotaging equipment, stealing and wasting resources, and some of it happens when employees experience leader abuse or lack of leadership support. Occurrences like these suggest that employees abused by their managers may retaliate by engaging in behaviors that harm the organization (Thau et al. 2009). This abuse of power may also be viewed as diverting the focus of leadership from the people to what the person in power wants the people to do (Erkutlu and Chafra 2013).

Abuse of power is the classic example of bad people doing bad things that produce negative effects. But negative effects may also be the outcome of good people doing bad things. There is a psychological background to this (see De Cremer and Tenbrunsel 2012; Tenbrunsel and Messick 2004): individuals often do not see the moral components of a decision, not so much because they are morally uneducated, but because they are unaware of the processes that lead them to their opinions and judgments. Ignorance and false beliefs about oneself can create errors in a manager's judgments concerning moral responsibility and in estimates of the effects a decision can cause. Carefully examining the overall effect of a decision would help to remedy theses errors. But it may be difficult to perform this analysis, above all when a manager works in a large organization where the decision-making process is complex and where organizational units may have conflicting interests. Here, "too many hands" are partaking in the processes and individual responsibilities are prone to get lost. This "Many Hands Dilemma" (Kaptein and Wempe 2002) may also occur when collective responsibilities get lost in joint efforts with external stakeholders. A solution for both the internal and external dilemma would be to portray a clear-cut business model that describes the division of work and the input/output at interfaces. This would allow to chart and to monitor the chain of effects.

Managers who strive for positive effects may just be motivated by their assumptions of duty. They may not be aware that there are two reasonings on duty: positive duty and negative duty. Negative duty is simply the idea that one ought not to cause unnecessary harms to other people. This could include causing physical harm or financial disadvantage or impediments of a career, or even lying and theft. There is the argument that on a view that is bound by negative duties: "we are free to pursue our interests and do as we wish, so long as our activities cause no harm to others" and "if we unnecessarily cause harms, we are responsible for them and owe redress" (Fairley 2006, p. 2 f.). Positive duty, on the other hand, requires that one provides help, even if she or he had nothing to do with the origins of the harm, and ought to improve the situation of those who are badly off (see, e.g., Singer 1972, in his seminal article "Famine, Affluence, and Morality"). Whether managers are aware or not of the difference will hardly determine their day-to-day decisions; and if the effect is positive, the nature of causation is irrelevant. It does count, though, when a decision needs to be justified.[11] But, it will be the effects of a decision on which the line of arguments for that justification will have to be based in the first place.

Effects, in the sense of what is to be achieved by a leader's or a manager's action, will come in a variety of manifestations – from improving a business process to changing customer or supplier relations. But there is more as we deal with human centered management/leadership with its focus on people. This is intrinsically what has been called *transformational*. The concept of transformational leadership was introduced by James McGregor Burns. He defined transformational leadership as a process where leaders and their followers raise one another to higher levels of morality and motivation (Burns 1978).

There also is the definition of *authentic leadership*, which refers to pattern of leader behavior that draws upon and promotes both positive psychological capacities and a positive ethical climate, to foster greater self-awareness, an internalized moral perspective, balanced processing of information and relational transparency on the part of leaders working with followers, fostering positive self-development (Walumbwa et al. 2008, p. 94). Another term, coined by Edwin P. Hollander (2012), is *inclusive leadership*, which highlights the role of followers as a key to effectiveness. There is a distinct reciprocity in each of these concepts: leaders who are aware of how they think and behave and of the context in which they operate are also perceived by their followers as being aware of the values, moral perspectives, knowledge and strengths of others.

Specific indications of leader–follower reciprocity (leader–member exchange) have been researched by Yukl et al. (2013) in their "Ethical Leadership Questionnaire." The questionnaire relates to four specific relationship-oriented behaviors (supporting, recognizing, consulting, delegating) and leading by example (which can be viewed as an indicator of integrity), and it asks the respondents to affirm or not a list statements on a Likert scale (see Exhibit 2.1).

The elements of this list indicate that leaders, when they express their true selves by setting examples of morality and by doing good, will not only achieve positive effects on their followers but positive feedback as well. Authenticity, in this respect, goes beyond acting in accord with one's own values, preferences and needs as opposed to acting merely to please others or to attain rewards or avoid punishments (Kernis 2003, p. 14) towards behavior that incites followers' personal identification with the leader. This is about building trust – a leader's

---

My boss . . .

---

1 shows a strong concern for ethical and moral values.
2 communicates clear ethical standards for members.
3 sets an example of ethical behavior in his/her decisions and actions.
4 is honest and can be trusted to tell the truth.
5 keeps his/her actions consistent with his/her stated values ("walks the talk").
6 is fair and unbiased when assigning tasks to members.
7 can be trusted to carry out promises and commitments.
8 insists on doing what is fair and ethical even when it is not easy.
9 acknowledges mistakes and takes responsibility for them.
10 regards honesty and integrity as important personal values.
11 sets an example of dedication and self-sacrifice for the organization.
12 opposes the use of unethical practices to increase performance.
13 is fair and objective when evaluating member performance and providing rewards.
14 puts the needs of others above his/her own self-interest.
15 holds members accountable for using ethical practices in their work.

Exhibit 2.1 Ethical leadership questionnaire

Source: Yukl et al. (2013), p. 46

capacity to cultivate follower trust will enhance his or her ability to direct followers — and about building *social capital*. With regard to trust building, it has often been said (see, e.g., Iles and Preece 2006) that interpersonal exchanges between leader and followers have the highest impact on trust as they bolster the followers' sense of being valued as important contributors. Equally important are contextual leadership behaviors that help followers to make sense of organizational structures, processes and policies (Hernandez, Long, and Sitkin 2014).

The topic of social capital building reaches much further: social capital is a widely discussed theme in today's economists' debate after Joseph E. Stiglitz and Amartya Sen took to exploring new indicators of economic performance and social progress beyond gross domestic product (GDP; Stiglitz, Sen, and Fitoussi 2010). They recommend measuring the strength of social connections and relationships to determine well-being in a society, an enormous task that is far from being completed (see, e.g., Dill 2016).

Among the first definitions of social capital were those that pointed towards the inner life of organizations, such as the conception of the American sociologist James S. Coleman (1988) who connected to the research of Oliver Williamson on the conditions under which economic activity is organized in firms or markets. His perception is of "social structures and resources both, internal and external to the organization, which allow us to facilitate responsible action and which are inherent to more or less institutionalized relationships of mutual recognition" (Maak 2007, p. 331). This type of social capital is the one that business leaders can build — they can enable and broker sustainable, mutually beneficial relationships to stakeholders within the corporation and beyond its boundaries. Creating stakeholder goodwill and trust will ultimately build trusted businesses in society.

It is a key quality of responsible leaders to act as weavers and brokers of this social capital. Some writers speak of a straightforward link to a beneficial effect: an "investment in social relations with expected returns in the marketplace" (Lin, Cook, and Burt 2001/2008, p. 4). Whichever concept is followed, mere *relations* will not suffice. The effort has to encompass *content* (a common mindset, a cognitive appeal), *structure* (network configuration and organization) and *momentum* (seizing opportunity, motivation and ability). One aim is certainly to achieve benefits — advantages and incentives, as said earlier, are drivers of moral efforts. But a responsible leader will also have to take account of the risks inherent in this social capital. They arise because of the complexity of multiple networks and might include inertia and low adaptability of a follower or partner who is overwhelmed by inclusion in the network; but there may also be feelings of exclusion, restrictions on the freedom to act and excessive claims by a stakeholder (Maak 2007).

Social capital building is one of the effects that human centered management of businesses has on the corporate environment. There are many other effects. This will be shown next.

2.4.2 The impact of human centered management on the business environment

Morally led enterprises affect their community directly. There is some empirical research, though not abundant, on the relationship between human centered management in a corporation and the firm's performance in its business environment. The starting point is connecting the firm's socially responsible actions towards the customer and supplier base, sustainable product design and so forth with financial performance (e.g., Waddock and Graves 1997; Stanwick and Stanwick 1998; Xueming and Bhattacharya 2006; Nelling and Webb 2009), and the methods that are applied are based on Freeman's (1984) classic model, which links financial performance to stakeholder relationship and firm strategy, either through a combined effect or through a moderating role of stakeholder engagement (Berman et al. 1999; see Exhibit 2.2).

Berman et al. (1999) tested the model and several variations of it on a sample of 1991–1996 data for 81 of the top 100 firms of the Fortune 500. For this period, they used the KLD (Kinder, Lydenberg, Domini) Socrates Database (www.library. hbs.edu/go/socrates.html), which is a socially screened, capitalization-weighted index of 400 common stocks (the Domini 400 Social SM Index) providing data on those firms' socially responsive actions.

Five measures were chosen: employee relations, diversity, local communities, natural environment and product safety and quality. The results indicate that

The Direct Effects Model

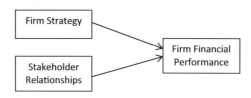

The Moderation Model

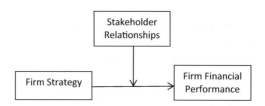

Exhibit 2.2 Strategic stakeholder management models

Source: Berman et al. (1999), p. 493

employee relations and product safety/quality have the strongest effect on performance – the business environment rewards these attributes the most.

More recently, Rais and Goedegebuure (2009) made an analysis similar to that of Berman et al. using empirical data for manufacturing firms. For the stakeholder perspective, they adapt a framework developed by Clarkson (1995) that uses a series of indicators for relations with customers, employees, suppliers, shareholders and communities. These were tested in a Likert-type questionnaire, which was answered by a total of 109 companies. The results confirm that managers tend to stay within their fiduciary duties: while they are trained to understand the meaning of responsibility in the context of business processes (finance, human resources, marketing, etc.), they also understand that they are held accountable for the results of their decisions. Therefore, they execute their obligations and responsibilities to customers, employees, suppliers and other important constituencies to the extent that this does not collide with the ultimate goal of producing shareholder value. It may seem that in view of the format in which the questionnaire was designed, the answers did not encompass activities beyond the instrumental ones. This would confirm that stakeholder theory is mainly about managing relations, but still, the moral disciplines of accountability and responsibility are engrained in this model implicitly.

Another type of analysis is reported by Choi and Wang (2009). Their research is based on surveying financial data on 518 firms from the S&P 500 or DSI 400 for the period 1991–2001, with the quality of stakeholder management being computed by scoring 'strengths' and 'weaknesses' across several areas of relations with groups that don't directly benefit from the firm's financial returns – that is, employees, customers, suppliers and the local community. The main findings are that when a firm performs well (above average for its industry), good stakeholder relations help sustain it for a longer period of time, and when a firm performs poorly, good stakeholder relations help it bounce back faster.

Apart from financial performance, reputation is another motivational factor which supposedly drives socially responsible business behavior. Research has been carried out on this (e.g., Graafland, Kaptein, and Mazereeuw 2010); according to this, executives perceive that responsible leadership will contribute to their reputation, especially in the cohorts of older executives who wish to be remembered as good businessmen when their career enters its last phase. But the question remains if there are public relations motives that outshine the intrinsic motive and how can one distinguish between public relation motives and real motives for moral leadership. If this were the case, though, the "cover-up," similar to "greenwashing" (i.e., just pretending to care for the environment), would certainly be short-lived. In this respect, all firms, and more than others, big firms, face considerable scrutiny from shareholders as well as from other stakeholders. Even a very strong and self-assured CEO cannot afford to jeopardize stakeholder relations.

Maintaining responsible stakeholder relations is not just a part of corporate social responsibility (CSR). It is an ingredient of human centered management. From another viewpoint, stakeholder relations may be seen as part of the firm's intellectual capital; therefore, research that studies the interaction between intellectual capital and firm performance also encompasses the aspect of (ethically conducted) stakeholder relations. A study that analyzes Australian firms (Clarke, Seng, and Whiting 2010) presents findings that are based on the Value Added Intellectual Coefficient (VAIC). VAIC was developed by Pulic in 1998 (Pulic 1998). Taking a stakeholder perspective, VAIC is offered as a measure of the efficiency with which a firm uses its physical, financial and intellectual capital to enhance stakeholder value. The index consists of the sum of three component ratios: human capital efficiency, structural capital efficiency (which includes both internal and relational capital efficiency) and capital employed efficiency (Nazari and Herremans 2007). In order to calculate VAIC, a firm's ability to create value added (VA) to all stakeholders must first be calculated. In its simplest form, VA is the difference between output and input. Human capital efficiency is then deemed to be VA divided by the firm's expenses for employees; structural capital efficiency is calculated as a residual by subtracting those expenses from VA; and capital employed efficiency would be VA divided by capital employed in the firm. There is no business ethics content here, but the approach points the way towards embedding efficiency into the concept of intellectual capital (and, as will be shown in the following, efficiency in a firm and in its relations to stakeholders is indubitably affected by moral behavior).

An earlier study that also used VAIC examined Taiwanese firms (Chen, Cheng and Hwang 2005) and found a weaker effect of intellectual capital on performance than reported in the case of the Australian firms. It may be concluded that firms and investors place greater importance on physical and financial capital than on human and structural capital in East Asian countries. This corresponds with what was said about cultural influence on behavior and ethics in the previous sections.

There are two more results that point in the direction of cultural influence. In the first, a much stronger effect of intellectual capital on performance was found in an analysis performed on the banking sector in Pakistan (Ur Rehman et al. 2012). All banks that participated in the survey had values of human capital efficiency that were higher than those of the other components of intellectual capital performance: 70%–80% of the value creation capabilities are attributed to human capital efficiency, but the interconnectedness with relational capital is demonstrated by the fact that the magnitude of structural capital efficiency follows suit, even before capital employed efficiency. One reason may be that the Islamic work ethic strongly affects employees' perception of attitudes and behavior and their impact on organizational culture and development of organizational citizenship behavior (Zaman et al., 2012). Not surprisingly, research carried out on the micro-finance industry in Uganda (Kamukama, Ahiauzu, and Ntayi 2010) also corroborates the effect of human capital on stakeholder relationships.

In all, businesses with ethical values at the core will successfully build trust and social capital with their stakeholders. A positive corporate environment is the natural result of an ethical and trustworthy corporate culture. In this reasoning, the interactions and relationships with suppliers, customers and other stakeholders will return positively to the firm, and the firm will be able to attract and retain good talent, which in turn increases human capital. With this, we are arriving at the social perspective of conjoining leadership and morality.

Notes

1 The word ethics comes from two Greek terms, *ethos*, which is "just behavior," and *itos*, which is "status of mind." This draws coherence between the exterior attitude and interior reasoning (Dherse and Minguet, 1998, p. 362).

2 The phrase was attributed by the Greek historian, biographer, and essayist Plutarch (AD 45–120), to Gnaeus Pompeius Magnus, a military and political leader of the late Roman Republic who commanded ships from Africa to Rome. When a great storm arose at sea, and the captains of the ships were reluctant to set sail, he led the way himself and ordered them to weigh anchor, shouting: "We have to sail, we do not have to live." This later became a motto of Roman admiralty. It is reported that the Italian dictator Mussolini, at a conference on aeronautics in Rome in 1923, modified it to *volare necesse est* ("We have to fly, . . ."; Wohl, 2005).

3 Utilitarianism and deontism will be presented more extensively in section 2.2.1, but an attempt to discuss this in academic depth would be beyond the scope of this book.

4 This is how Kant formulated his categorical imperative in the first place. He also worded it another form: "Act in such a way that you treat humanity, whether in your own person or in the person of any other, never merely as a means to an end, but always at the same time as an end" – a truly human centered perception. It will be dealt with in section 7.1 of this book, which shows how to apply ethics in labor relations.

5 Faith-based thinking will be explicated in section 2.2.2, which deals with the spiritual element of individual reasoning.

6 Corporate (social) responsibility is a section of the next chapter; the discussion at this point is only about how it relates to the approach of provisional ethics.

7 A common understanding on values is the precondition for a code of ethics in any institution as will be shown in section 6.1.

8 More on the Caux Round Table will be presented in section 2.3.2.

9 Detailed recommendations on this have been elaborated by the International Integrated Reporting Committee (see http://integratedreporting.org).

10 A substantial basis for the Caux Round Table Principles, in language and form, was provided by the Minnesota Principles, set up by the by the Minneapolis Center for Ethical Business Cultures together with a group of Japanese corporate leaders who contributed the concept of *kyosei*, which is "living and working together for the common good." It was this agglomeration of leaders from several continents which enabled worldwide recognition of the Caux Round Table Principles.

11 In a wider context, it is a positive duty obligation of international organizations or of powerful enterprises to protect economic, social, and cultural rights where a failed state maltreats its citizens. This would be the causation logic for the Maastricht Principles exhibited in section 1.2.3.

Chapter 3

The social perspective

The human centered paradigm, from a viewpoint that looks at the motivations for an individual to behave morally, is founded on the premises, values, beliefs and assumptions that were explicated in the previous chapter. When the individual connects to others or when a larger group of individuals acts collectively, these motivations will materialize through value-based social interactions. For management and managers, these are business interactions. In any society, everyone is a client, a supplier or a shareholder in some sense and is affected by business decisions and business structures. This applies to both moral and immoral outcomes of those decisions and structures. Quite a lot of media reporting focuses on bad outcomes, but this is not necessarily negative (even though one would wish more storytelling on good outcomes): members of a society often have a propensity to overlook events that do not concern them directly, and when media reports point out what is going wrong, this indifference will much less create an immoral atmosphere which spreads and eventually affect all members of a society. Leaders in businesses and in governmental institutions therefore not only have to work at disseminating principles of morality, but they also have to fight indifference towards their neglect. This is why the first section of this chapter, on corporate social responsibility, will look at how and why firms do both good and evil. The discussion begins by asking about the purpose of business.

3.1 Corporate social responsibility

Is the purpose of business just business? And is the responsibility of business just to increase its profits? Contrary to the now infamous words of Milton Friedman (1970) and his followers who still uphold the argument, it has become widely accepted that businesses do indeed have responsibilities beyond simply making a profit. At minimum, corporations take on those social responsibilities out of "enlightened self-interest," that is, they do so because it serves them well. They might be rewarded with more customers, whereas perceived irresponsibility might result in consumer boycotts; employees who are committed to moral values might be attracted to work for the firm, and these employees usually tend to be good professionals; and a community that feels that a firm positively contributes to society might become a stable and secure context for the firm in which to do steady business.

There is only one claim of Friedman's that everybody would go along with: it is people who do good and it is people who do evil. But when Friedman refers to the corporate executive as a person "in his own right" who "may have many responsibilities that he recognizes or assumes voluntarily – to his family, his conscience, his feelings of charity, his church, his clubs, his city, his country" but claims he cannot apply this type of "social responsibility in his capacity as businessman" (Friedman 1970, p. SM 18), how can Friedman seriously believe that a person can split up her or his "feelings"? Friedman resorts to the argument that the corporate executive must act as an agent for the shareholders. Now, if the shareholders' opinion counts and if they request the corporation to pursue a social cause, would the corporate executive have to oppose that? Would he have to tell them that a social attitude on their behalf will strengthen the "view that the pursuit of profits is wicked and immoral and must be curbed and controlled by external forces"? (Friedman 1970, p. SM 19).

To Friedman's credit, we have to acknowledge that the world has changed since he wrote his statement in 1970. There have been corporate scandals that may be taken as an evidence of executives acting without moral reasoning; there is globalization, which drives corporations to take account of underserved markets with frail consumers and to deal with underprivileged societies; and there is a worldwide network of data and information that detects and enables prosecution of corporate abuse wherever it occurs. Kofi Annan, when he was UN Secretary-General, called on the business community to support a Global Compact with society, a "contract" based on human rights, labor standards and environmental principles (United Nations 1999). And the joint World Economic Forum (WEF) and UN declaration of 2002 exhorted businesses to embrace a responsible business agenda, signed by 34 of the world largest multinational corporations (see World Economic Forum 2002).

The Global Compact was designed to encourage businesses to make a positive contribution to the social, economic and environmental well-being of the world's population. The title of the WEF and UN declaration shows that it is all about governance and morality: "Global Corporate Citizenship – the Leadership Challenge for CEOs and Boards" (World Economic Forum 2002). So, beyond the enlightened self-interest mentioned earlier, which may also be called a strategic motive, businesses have a wide array of guidance when it comes to arguing why and how to perform social responsibility. But a business leader will also have to look for justification from the inside: is there a business case for corporate social responsibility? And what are the visible outcomes? This issue will be discussed in the next section, together with two others. One relates to the question of how to distinguish between business ethics and corporate social responsibility, and the other is about the human centered facet of corporate social responsibility. It is not the intention of this book to replicate what has been said on corporate social responsibility in the vast body of scholarly papers and pragmatic writings. We are concerned here with the relevance of leadership and morality to the topic.

3.1.1 The business case for corporate social responsibility

The business case refers to the rationale that would support a business accepting and advancing the corporate social responsibility "cause." The primary question would be to determine what a business and the business community get out of corporate social responsibility and how they visibly benefit from engaging in socially responsible policies, activities and practices.

Returning to enlightened self-interest, the contention is that businesses ensure long-term viability by taking actions now (e.g., towards the community of neighbors of manufacturing facilities) that will be rewarded in the future (producing a healthy climate for debates about, e.g., impacts of facility expansion or of new manufacturing technologies). This would also pave the way for moving business ethics up to the level of public interest (Dorasamy 2010). A second argument is that favorable stakeholder relations will ward off government regulation, as businesses have a reservoir of management talent, expertise and capital that should be employed to solve social problems (arriving, e.g., at self-disciplined standards that fulfill society's expectations of business). Another justification is that being proactive on social problems (anticipating, planning and initiating) is more practical and less costly than simply reacting once the problems have surfaced (Carroll and Shabana 2010).

A different analysis, which focuses on specific activities and their outcomes, is based on Carroll's (1991) four-part definition of corporate social responsibility, which identifies four categories of responsibilities: economic, legal, ethical (moral) and discretionary/philanthropic.

1   With the **economic responsibility** of business being to produce goods and services that society desires and to sell them at a profit, the determination of profit resurfaces once more. But even Friedman had a moral perspective in mind with regard to profits when he claimed that engaging in activities designed to increase its profits is acceptable to a business "as long as it stays within the rules of the game, which is to say, engages in open and free competition without deception or fraud" (Friedman 1970, p. SM 120).

Drucker strikes a note that could be seen as balancing mere shareholder interest and the interest in maintaining the corporation for the benefit of all its stakeholders in the long run. He argues that profit performs three main functions: first, it measures the effectiveness of business activities; second, it provides a "risk premium" necessary for the corporation to stay in business; and third, it insures the future supply of capital (Drucker 1954/2006, pp. 76–77). The emphasis is on the long-term view. Balancing the social and economic responsibilities of the corporation will produce shareholder wealth in the long run; short-term profit maximization will not.

2   The connection of **legal responsibility** to the moral perspective is that laws and regulations constitute but one category of compliance and only partially fulfill the social contract between business and society. The other category is ruled by a society's common values. The debate is whether these, and how much, need to be codified, that is, whether a regulatory framework for corporate social responsibility should be created (e.g., De Schutter 2008). The opposing argument is that there is enough control by the markets (products and services market, labor market, finance market) to ensure that voluntary engagement in corporate social responsibility activities gets rewarded and failure to engage is penalized.

In the UK, a ministerial cabinet post was created in March 2000 designed to coordinate corporate social responsibility across government. Critics have argued that this might create conditions in which UK central government departments are compelled to engage with activities while at the same time it compounds the visibility of business activities (Turner and Fairbrass 2001). But so far, the UK government has abstained from even a light regulatory approach. This is pointing towards the borderline between legal and moral responsibilities.

3   **Moral responsibility** refers to a corporation's activities for promoting and pursuing social goals that extend beyond its legal responsibilities. The firm will identify the goals that are important to society or to different stakeholders in society. The importance of these social goals to society may be inferred from measuring how they are accomplished, and a firm will report how it is contributing to this achievement ("the outcome").

Achievements and outcomes of moral responsibility are the subject of social sustainability reporting. Some of this will be covered in Chapters 6 and 7, which deal with the implementation of human centered management. At this stage, reference will be made only to the Kinder, Lydenberg, Domini (KLD) social performance index that was mentioned earlier in connection with stakeholder management. The KLD index covers a wide scope: environmental, social and governance outcomes all together. Environmental issues include climate change, products and services, and operations and management; social issues include community, diversity, employee relations, human rights and product; governance issues include reporting and structure; and finally, controversial business issues include abortion, adult entertainment, alcohol, contraceptives, firearms, gambling, military, nuclear power and tobacco (Chatterji et al. 2009). An example of what the index can reveal about the human perspective is given in section 3.1.3.

4   Even though **discretionary/philanthropic activities** are the most voluntary of the four categories, the term *responsibility* applies as well. Engaging in acts or programs to promote human welfare or good will, such as making donations directed at education, community improvement, arts and culture and so forth may seem to be left to the discretion of the firm. But first, community relations are not a one-way street and community improvement gets its reward; second, historically, promoting arts and culture at locations that were far away from traditional cultural centers was necessary for attracting well-educated scientists and technicians to areas that may have been called "remote" – for example, when the chemical industry built production sites in the mid-1800s in Europe and in the US.

The philanthropic activities of the chemical industry from the 1800s onwards were (and are today) about improving competitive advantage through higher attractiveness as an employer; similarly, improved marketing and selling capabilities, or better relationships with governmental and nongovernmental organizations, will serve the purpose as well. The range goes beyond communities that are directly impacted by manufacturing, and this compares to the community partnerships of Unilever and Chevron that were mentioned earlier. Deutsche Lufthansa, to take another example, enhances its relationship with communities in which it operates by running a community-involvement program (Bruch and Walter 2005, p. 50).

In all, research on the topic has identified five main areas of business benefits (Weber 2008):

1   Positive effects on company image and reputation, which is influenced by communication messages. We have a human perspective here as well, since reputation builds on personal experiences and characteristics and includes a value judgment by people (Schwaiger 2004).
2   Positive effects on employee motivation, retention and recruitment. Apart from an impact from improved reputation, there also is a direct influence on employees as they might be more motivated working in a better environment or draw motivation from the participation in the firm's social activities, such as volunteering programs.
3   Cost savings: efficiency gains resulting from a substitution of materials in the implementation of a sustainability strategy, improved contacts with certain stakeholders such as regulators resulting in time savings, or easier access to capital (Epstein and Buhovac 2014).
4   Revenue increases from higher sales and market share, as consumers wish to reward firms that practice social responsibility.

5   Risk reduction or management, because social responsibility programs can also reduce or manage risks such as negative press or customer reviews and boycotts from civil society organizations.

Empirical research on the business case for corporate social responsibility has employed statistical analyses to account for the causality between social and financial performance. One example is a study by Philipp Schreck (2011), who studied differences between industries. The results indicate that there is a strong link between single stakeholder-related issues of corporate social responsibility and financial performance, even though they provide no evidence that there is a universal model for causality within these relationships.

Another way to look at outcomes is related to the concept of public goods. Defining and comprehending this concept is even more complicated than defining the concept of social capital. For the purpose of this book, it must suffice to state that public goods are those that are consumed by society as a whole and not necessarily by an individual consumer. Using public goods is open to everyone; no one can be excluded from using them, and their use by one individual does not reduce their availability to others (Morrell 2009, p. 543). They comprise infrastructure – from street lighting to flood control systems, availability of water and fresh air, access to knowledge, the education system, the legal system, the labor market, up to national security and all the political resources that enable free global trade. There is a simple logic that connects public goods to corporate social responsibility: as firms use public goods, they should have an interest in maintaining those goods and improving their quality if necessary. This is about "giving back to the community," which is what corporate social responsibility aspires to, and the outcome certainly is that the firm benefits from well-functioning public goods.

But it is not about outcomes only: corporate social responsibility relies on the involvement of the employees as the major stakeholders in its co-creation and implementation. From this human perspective, corporate social responsibility is a dynamic and developing process. Involving employees from the initiation stage of social activities will contribute favorably to the later stages. It goes without saying that a socially responsible organization will focus on its own people first when it comes to transfer corporate social responsibility from philosophy into action. In the early stages, employees will ask "Why corporate social responsibility?" and "What is corporate social responsibility?" Leaders who can give the right answers will successfully motivate their employees to take part in programs and initiatives directed towards the communities that surround their workplace.

A company offering a good example of involving employees in visible community engagement is the US building material retailer Home Depot, which has established numerous links with local communities through activities such as company-sponsored voluntary work to build playgrounds for children (Snider, Hill, and Martin 2003). Experiences like this will make employees receptive to policies of the firm that are directed towards, for example, convincing suppliers to improve their social standards, or educating customers to avoid excessive refuse. Employee involvement will contribute to preventing these initiatives from failing before they reach implementation, and it will broadly enhance the implementation process. When reaching a stage where employees are visible to third parties of as part of the firm's corporate social responsibility "brand," the firm will have created what Pursey et al. (2008) describe as an "authenticity bonus" – not as a result of public relation campaigns but because involving employees in its business matters has truly represented the firm's concern for its local political, economic, and social environment (Bolton, Kim, and O'Gorman 2011).

3.1.2 Which of the two ranks higher: business ethics or corporate social responsibility?

What is the relationship between the terms *business ethics* and *corporate social responsibility*? This can best be accessed by stating that corporations are a part of society and make a contribution to social life. Because of that, any discussion about corporate social responsibility includes not just the question of what corporations should do, but also where the limits of their responsibilities lie (Lin Hi 2008). This comes to the fore explicitly with corporations in the pharmaceutical industry. For many diseases in developing countries, the pharmaceutical industry does not provide (affordable) medicine. Furthermore, active pharmaceutical ingredients for life-threatening but rare diseases are mostly not researched by industry. But there are limits to spending for research, even in research networks and collaborations between universities and industry. There is a dilemma here: ethically, and following George W. Merck's statement referred to earlier ("medicine is for the people"), researching into all diseases would be the responsibility of industry. But business decisions taken by pharmaceutical firms have to depend on their financial potential. This imposes a limit to responsibility – and so we would have to say that *business ethics* reaches beyond *corporate social responsibility*.

Another solution might be derived from one practitioner-oriented definition of corporate social responsibility which states that it "addresses topics of business ethics, corporate social performance, global corporate citizenship, and stakeholder management" (D'Amato, Henderson, and Florence 2009, p. 2). In this definition, topics of citizenship and stakeholder management are instrumental by nature and less conceptual. So would the concept of business ethics be a part of corporate social responsibility, or would it be the concept that sets the stage for the other components to be deployed? A clarification comes from the *Stanford Encyclopedia of Philosophy*:

> Business ethics addresses the moral features of commercial activity. It examines the moral principles and the moral problems that arise in a business

environment. It applies to all aspects of business conduct and is relevant to the conduct of individuals and entire organizations.

(see Marcoux 2008)

A newer source goes even further:

> The landscape of business ethics is very vast and encompasses such concerns as corporate governance, reputation management, accurate accounting, fair labor practices and environmental stewardship to name but a few. . . . In fact, the field addresses the entire scope of responsibilities that a company has to each of its stakeholders: those who have a vested interest in the decisions and actions of a company, like clients, employees, shareholders, suppliers and the community. Business ethics refers to corporate offices and programs intended to communicate, monitor, and enforce a company's values and standards.
>
> (Pimple 2012, p. 762)

Thus, whichever way round, and whether one of the two terms *corporate social responsibility* and *business ethics* is ranged above or below the other, they certainly overlap and are often used interchangeably. There is no simple answer, as with the interchangeable use of the terms *ethical* and *moral*, but one short comment will be made here: The word *responsibility* carries a ring of reaction, of responding, of taking action after being questioned. In the words of the great C.K. Prahalad at the occasion of celebrating what would have been Peter Drucker's 100th birthday in Vienna in 2009: "responsibility is compliance, accountability is commitment" (Weber 2009). Thus, where responsibility is reactive, accountability (which is linked to ethical reasoning) is proactive.

3.1.3 Corporate social responsibility and the human centered paradigm

While the conceptualization of corporate social responsibility, as we have seen, is very broad and the domains of socially responsible behavior are many and diverse, it is evident that the main focus is on people. We turn to the KLD statistics for clarity (KLD was introduced in section 2.4.2). The KLD database reduces corporate social responsibility initiatives into six broad domains:

1 Community support (e.g., support of arts and health programs, educational and housing initiatives for the economically disadvantaged, generous/innovative giving);
2 Diversity (e.g., sex, race, family or sexual orientation, and disability-based diversity record and initiatives, or lack thereof, within and outside the firm);
3 Employee support (e.g., concern for safety, job security, profit sharing, union relations, employee involvement);

4   Environment (e.g., environment-friendly products, hazardous-waste management, use of ozone-depleting chemicals, animal testing, pollution control, recycling);
5   Foreign operations (e.g., overseas labor practices [including sweatshops], operations in countries with human rights violations);
6   Product (e.g., product safety, research and development/innovation, marketing/contracting controversies, antitrust disputes).

All affect human well-being. But can corporate social responsibility produce even more? Can socially responsible corporations trigger or at least substantially contribute to equitable conditions and social justice for members of a society where these conditions are underdeveloped?

There is, however, one other feature in the human aspect of corporate social responsibility that needs to be investigated before getting to the topic of equitability and social justice. As it is humans who care for humans, we should consider that it is the personality of business leaders (and not the commercial imperative or the quest for achieving an advantage) that drives social responsibility. Personality, here, may be reduced to a person being idealistic or altruistic, but it is in this person where the locus of responsibility is to be found. One cannot be separated from the other. This becomes apparent when looking at small business where the owner drives the activities that develop in her or his firm. The owner's leadership must be participative and interactive, through ongoing joint activities amid an easily manageable system that is marked, however, by ongoing changes or expansions of the system. Individuals' understandings and motives are much more visible in this system than in the large corporation.

A large corporation, at least in most cases, is a grouping of small entities that work like small businesses – with a leader in each entity who leads in a participatory and interactive manner, through ongoing joint activities. The author of this book, when he joined a large corporation in 1970, was often confronted with the question of who was "in charge" of the 51,000 employees who worked in the facilities of the huge headquarters. Who was in charge were the approximately 1,000 managers of the various production, engineering and research facilities and administrative units. They were held together by cohesion and consistency through a joint commitment: fulfilling a duty, acting with respect for each other and sharing a common responsibility. Each one knew what she or he contributed to the business; each one was involved, to some extent, in one or more of the six domains that the KLD statistics identify to be constitutive for social responsibility (community, diversity and employee affairs, environmental and production issues, relation to foreign business) and each one, personally, liked it. There was room for managerial discretion, and there was professional pride (e.g., being proud of maintaining standards above those required by competitive conditions). This is how social responsibility was built within the corporation: bottom-up and horizontally. The leaders at the top had to mainly set an appropriate climate. One might say there was "corporate conscience" according to the term introduced at about the same time by the US business ethicist Kenneth E. Goodpaster and on which he has reflected in many of his writings since (see, e.g., Goodpaster and Matthews 1982; Goodpaster 2004).

Equitability and social justice are also best built from below and horizontally, with leaders creating the appropriate enablers.

3.2 Equitability and social justice

The issue of social justice has been controversial since the term was used in the writings of Thomas Paine (1737–1809), an English-American political activist, philosopher, political theorist and revolutionary, and was then becoming a motive for the 1848 revolutions in Europe. What Paine had in mind, though, was to attack the legitimacy of the British monarch in America (Claeys 2014); it was the early Franco-Swiss libertarian philosopher Jean Jacques Sismondi (1773–1842) who transferred the term into the revolutionist movements of his time. His famous statement, "*chacun selon ses capacités, à chacun selon ses nécessités*" ("each one [has to give] according to his abilities and to each one [will be given] according to his needs") is the most radical expression of communism (Lutz 2015). He was reproached early on with being unable to understand the mechanisms of an economic system. But the controversy has continued.

The controversy arises from a fundamental misunderstanding: justice is about fair distribution of wealth in a society, and not about each member of the society getting an equal share. "Fair" would be somewhere in the continuum between "pure" laissez-faire and a far-reaching welfare system. Equality would relate to liberty: all are entitled to as much liberty as they can exercise without undermining the liberty of others. But there would have to be inequalities, for example, in income and possession of property, which all members of the society would accept if they were to the advantage of all, especially the least well off. Achieving one's share would have to be subject to fair competition, which would have to include competition for attaining positions of power in the society.

Thoughts on fair distribution of wealth were most elaborately articulated by the American social philosopher John Rawls (1921–2002), who arrived at a system of cooperation for mutual advantage through the concept of distributive justice – a distribution of wealth and income permitting only those social and economic inequalities that work to the advantage of the least well-off members of society (Rawls 2001; Sandel 2009). This will lead to societal cooperation in everyday life, which produces a gain for all its members; however, for this type of fruitful cooperation, certain preconditions must be present that will ensure that everyone's legitimate interests are met. What is needed are reliable conditions (the level playing field) that protect individuals from being exploited while providing incentives for cooperation. Social justice is thus equated with the notion of *equality* or *equal opportunity*.

Some authors prefer to use the term *equitability* instead of *equality*, which concurs with the philosophical notion that submitting unequal units to "equal" conditions will not to produce equality. The Irish philosopher Thomas M. Kettle gives the example of letting "a stray dog and an express train freely compete for the temporary occupation of the same tract of the railway" which will have a very foreseeable negative result for the dog (Kettle 1912 p. 149). It is, then, about conditions that enable free competition, it is about eliminating barriers and it is about *equitable* treatment.

Equitable treatment, thus, does not mean that all inequalities are eradicated. As in Rawls's clarification, social and economic inequalities will be accepted by the least well-off members of society if they work to their advantage. When inequalities are felt to be unjust, this acceptance will dissolve. This would begin with opportunities to achieve a job or a certain position in society becoming obstructed: public offices and social positions have to be "open" in the formal sense, and all should have a fair chance to attain them.

Rawls is very explicit on what might be the consequences of reserving societal positions for just a few:

> Certain requirements must be imposed on the basic structure beyond those of the system of natural liberty. A free market system must be set within a framework of political and legal institutions that adjust the long-run trend of economic forces so as to prevent excessive concentrations of property and wealth, especially those likely to lead to political domination.
>
> (Rawls 2001, p. 44)

Though he never used the term, Rawls's principles lead the way to what may be called a *just market*. But there is a caveat. The idea of a *just market* has aroused the fiercest criticism against social justice. The argument is from the distinguished economist von Hayek: "the very idea of social justice is meaningless, religious, self-contradictory, and ideological; that realizing any degree of social justice is unfeasible; and that aiming to do so must destroy all liberty" (von Hayek quoted in Lukes 1997, p. 65). Of which, with all due respect, one of his disciples, the English economist George Lennox Sharman Shackle, noted: "I think [economists] should give up giving advice, except on the most hesitant, the most broad grounds. I think they should introduce an ethical element, a more than ethical element . . . an arrangement with conscience" (Littlechild 2003, p. 115). For business people, Shackle demanded them to be persons of conscience and of a generous mind (Earl and Littleboy 2014).

3.2.1 The just market: intertwining the social perspective with the moral perspective

From an "arrangement with conscience," as per Shackle's rebuke to von Hayek's rejection of social justice, the characteristic of a just market would go beyond representation of the interests of all stakeholders (the social perspective) to a moral perspective: it would emphasize that it is particularly the interest of impoverished consumers that has to be respected. We reconnect here to the social teaching of the Catholic Church (see 2.2.1), from where five key features of a "just" market have been identified (Santos and Laczniak 2008):

1   Authentic engagement with consumers, particularly impoverished ones, with non-exploitive intent.
2   Co-creation of value with customers, particularly, those who are underserved.
3   Investment in future consumption.
4   Interest representation of all stakeholders, particularly those customers who need more voice.
5   Focus on long-term profit management rather than short-term profit maximization.

This list shows what constitutes "just market" situations, where "just" means acting with righteousness and on equitable conditions beyond laws and regulations. This is not to suggest that laws and regulations have no place in markets, but they should not overshadow the effects that flow from the social nature of people, from their personal interconnectedness with one another and to the greater community. When these relationships are governed by fairness and equity, they will promote growth, as the *World Development Report* (World Bank 2006, p. 17) points out, "greater equity can, over the long term, underpin faster growth." Not even the sternest advocate of liberalization will be able to deny this effect.

The constitution of a just market is another example of creations that develop bottom-up and horizontally. Again, there is a human aspect: whoever makes business decisions will look for some justification. Moral philosophy holds that there are certain principles that people know and follow intuitively. The Scottish ethicist Sir William D. Ross (1877–1971) calls these principles *prima facie* duties and lists six such duties: (1) duties of fidelity, (2) duties of gratitude, (3) duties of justice, (4) duties of beneficence, (5) duties of self-improvement, and (6) duties of non-maleficence. Long before the discussion on corporate social responsibility was coming to life, Ross (1930) connected these *prima facie* duties to the actions of people in business. For example, the duties of beneficence, he says, rest on the notion that providing a service to others can improve the intelligence, virtue or happiness of others. This, then, is a basic characteristic not only of building a just market, but of any marketing activity – engaging customers in an active, explicit and ongoing dialogue. But the "market" is more than merely supplier–buyer relations; it encompasses the wider relations of solidarity, associateship and citizenship.

3.2.2 Beyond mere commerciality: solidarity, associateship and citizenship

Relations in a society have various foundations. The most commonly understood relationships are found within the family, where the normal case is that
its members care for each other at all times. Each member is expected to contribute to relieving the needs of other members as far as he or she is able to do
so. The extent of this liability depends upon how close the ties of community
are between members in each case. The members will feel solidary within this
community as long as they feel that wealth is distributed fairly among them.
"Wealth" would comprise goods and jobs and positions and opportunities in
society including education, medical care, child care, care for the elderly, personal security and so forth. We are back with John Rawls's distributive justice.
But there is a refinement to his theory that was introduced by David Miller,
professor of political theory at Nuffield College in Oxford.

In denominating "wealth" as "advantage," Miller (1999) opens the stage for
disadvantages as well: whether the community is felt to be just or unjust also
depends on whether disadvantages are distributed appropriately. Disadvantages
might include military service, dangerous work, other hardships and punishment for wrongdoing. This is one of the refinements added by Miller; the other
is that Miller distinguishes between three modes by which advantages and disadvantages are distributed: need, desert (merit) or equality. If the distributive
criterion is "need," we have a solidary community such as family and kinship.
But this type of solidarity through mutual understanding and mutual trust may
be found in other groups such as work teams or collections of individuals
organized around religious or idealistic beliefs. And *Solidarność* (Solidarity) was
a name well chosen for the Polish trade union that was founded in September 1980 under the leadership of Lech Wałęsa, the first trade union in a Warsaw
Pact country that was not controlled by a communist party, using methods of
civil resistance to boost the causes of workers' rights and social change.

A distribution of goods solely by need may be felt to be insufficient in contexts where people feel they have to be rewarded on the basis of their merits,
their "just deserts." This would apply to almost all areas of business and the
economy, as they depend on each member of a group deploying his or her
skills and talents that he deploys to advance the goals of this group – these
skills and talents are instrumental for the group to survive, hence Miller's term
instrumental association (Miller 1999 p. 25). But we may find quite a few situations in the context of business where people whose merits are highly manifest renounce rewards that correspond to the performance achieved through
deployment of their skills and talents. There are quite a few companies which
report that pay differentials between jobs at the top of the hierarchy and at the
bottom are becoming smaller (Evans, Kelley, and Peoples 2010). This may be
the result, among others, of concerns raised on the issue by large asset management funds like Grosvenor on behalf of big clients such as CalPERS (California

Public Employees' Retirement System). They acknowledge that high pay disparities inside a company can hurt employee morale and productivity and have a negative impact on a company's overall performance (Mueller, Ouimet, and Simintzi 2016).

There is a third way of allocating advantages and disadvantages, and this would be the way in which governments distribute benefits and rights. When a society regards and treats its citizens as equals, benefits and rights have to be distributed equally. Equality, then, is Miller's uppermost category, and it connects to the bonds of citizenship – an "ongoing cooperation between free and equal persons committed to reciprocity" (De Bres 2012, p. 323). Depending on which mode of human relationship is being considered, need, desert or equality takes precedence. It is not possible to generalize the concept of social justice. But whichever mode of social relations, there is one principle that outweighs all others. This is the principle of inclusiveness: no one is to be left behind.

3.3 Inclusiveness

Inclusiveness has been on the social agenda at all times and at all levels. At the United Nations, the expression "No one is to be left behind" was recently applied by Secretary-General Ban Ki-moon to the implementation of the 2015 Sustainable Development Goals (United Nations 2015). While this is a program for governments of the member countries, with the outcomes expected to be in the economic, ecological, social and political spheres, the goals will not be achieved without businesses and many other institutions providing support of all kinds. This would be expertise, financial and technical resources for data management and personnel assigned to special partnership projects.

Businesses, especially when under human centered management, have the experience of including the interests of all stakeholders. Internally, and with regard to business partners such as customers and suppliers, practicing participative leadership means that all people are taken into account. From its community relations and its accountability for all consequences of business decisions, the firm will also care for a wider constituency. The creation of jobs and job opportunities is instrumental for economic growth, for promoting better standards of living and for giving voice to underprivileged people. And a business leader who comprehends the wider meaning of the social contract will also make the firm contribute to transitions towards ecological inclusiveness.

3.3.1 Economic inclusiveness – creating employment and growth

On the macro-economic level, inclusive growth is regarded as a sustained and long-term development that is shared by all strata of society, especially those in society who have historically been underserved and have not benefited from growth policies that heretofore focused on the wealthy in the society. With globalization, where even decisions made in smaller firms at the local level can have a far-reaching impact, business leaders will direct the gaze on inclusive growth to poorer countries where their products are to be sold or where they have investment projects. The impacts can be gleaned from the African Development Bank's definition of inclusive growth: "Economic growth that results in a wider access to sustainable socio-economic opportunities for a broader number of people, countries or regions, while protecting the vulnerable, all being done in an environment of fairness, equal justice, and political plurality" (Kanu, Salami, and Numasawa 2014, p. iii).

Staying with Africa, the example that best elucidates what is meant here is the agriculture sector: the African labor market is characterized by an excess supply of young and unskilled labor, a dominance of agricultural and informal employment and a small share of private industrial employment. The limited or low-quality employment opportunities in many African countries are also the source of low productivity and poor and low-income households not reaping the benefits of economic growth.

To increase and sustain per capita growth in agricultural production, businesses and governments are joining efforts to invest more in agriculture-related infrastructure (e.g., rural roads and access to electricity, water and sanitation programs), and to promote agribusiness and small/medium entrepreneurship (e.g., creating an enabling environment for private sector development and investment). A large number of international and local businesses, small and large, are involved in the endeavors, partnering with state and local government authorities, civil society organizations and farmers' associations. Responsible business leaders from all over the world have initiated or joined these partnerships. Recent contributions are listed in, among other places, a German Development Bank publication (Köhn 2014). The author of this book on an assignment in Ghana in 2016 witnessed one of these projects – Ghana Grains Partnership with Yara International ASA, a leading global chemical company. The partnership started bottom-up dialogue with local growers in 2009 and has since become one of West Africa's largest grain growing associations. This remarkable success is due to farsighted leadership and the highly active commitment of all that take part in the venture.

3.3.2 Social inclusiveness – promoting social protection and standards of living

While it is apparent that business undertakings that promote inclusive growth will also contribute to improving social inclusiveness, there is still a need for businesses to support autonomous social initiatives. One such initiative, which has a wide impact internationally, is the *Global Agenda for Social Work and Social Development* of the International Federation of Social Workers, a Geneva-based institution representing 90 professional social work associations with over 750,000 social workers. It has formal consultative status with the United Nations, and its main objective is to set and review the international standards of social work and to promote good practice outcomes (International Federation of Social Workers et al. 2012).

Social workers can significantly support the bottom-up creation of a more favorable business climate in what Prahalad (2010) has called "base of the pyramid (BOP) regions," where impoverished socio-economic groups have suffered from social exclusion. At these local levels, linkages between social workers, government authorities and entrepreneurs produce highly fruitful outcomes (Jones and Truell 2012).

Partnering with social workers for improving the propensity to learn may also be a means for firms that wish to improve the attitudes of their workforce as the employees often do not have access to other training programs. One example is the cement producer CEMEX, which partnered with social workers and masonry education projects to create a more educational environment within its Mexican facilities (Letelier, Flores, and Spinosa 2003). Leveling up the workers' capabilities contributed to both better inclusion of workers and better corporate performance.

The issue of social protection comes into the limelight when considering abusive employment practices in many regions of the world – from the status of undocumented migrant workers in Europe (see, e.g., Bell 2004) and in the US (see, e.g., Gallagher 2004) to forced labor and slavery-like conditions in Africa (e.g., Dottridge 2005) and slave labor in many of the industrial fisheries in Asia (Marschke and Vandergeest 2016), not to speak of child labor almost anywhere in Africa and Asia. It goes without saying that responsible entrepreneurs will refrain from entering into business with firms or people that practice these abuses.

With child labor, the argument is often made that their families need the income provided through the children's work. Let us look at the renowned economic analysis of the problem of child labor by Kaushik Basu, an Indian professor at Cornell University who is chief economist of the World Bank. He questions the common ethical judgment on the topic and his analysis justifies an alternative approach to this ethical problem. When parents do not earn enough and send children to work in a country that is relatively well off, a ban on child labor can be effective even though coordinate action through legal measures would be required. If the country is very poor, a total ban on child labor will not work, as companies cannot afford to entirely replace child labor with more expensive adult labor. Legal action will most likely lead to counterproductive results: if children are not allowed to work and if companies cannot afford to employ enough adults, families will be subject to hunger and starvation. Thus, for very poor countries, Basu (1999) recommends compulsory schooling combined with (light) work. Schooling will enable children to earn higher incomes later, and so help the economy avoid the child labor trap in the long run.

It is hoped that child labor will become eliminated and children will be fully protected somewhere in the future. The UN Sustainable Development Goals set this date as 2030. But we need time and careful reasoning. The worst scenario would be a specific ban in the export sector. If the international community categorically decides not to import goods manufactured with the aid of child labor, this may, Basu argues, result in child labor shifting into other, more hazardous, areas of the economy instead of attaining the original moral intention. The ethical dilemma here lies less with business leaders who will understand Basu's reasoning than with the many concerned members of quite a few civil society organizations who are not open to economic argument. The same applies to the topic of environmental protection and ecological inclusiveness.

3.3.3 Ecological inclusiveness – sharing rights, responsibilities and risks

The dilemma with environmental protection, to continue from the previous section, is that solutions for ecology issues (or the issues themselves) are not transferable, for example, from the Western world to the developing world, or from rich countries to poor countries, or from industries that are advanced to those that are have not yet achieved a high level of development. We have seen the hot discussions on the Kyoto Protocol on Global Warming and we are witnessing debates and fights about pollution and emission control almost every day and everywhere on all levels. Responsible leaders who take part in these debates will not always be able to make sure that all arguments be heard. But both globally and locally, progress will be made in sustainable development only if all stakeholders are heard and their interests respected. Interests, however, include accepting rights, responsibilities and risks. All those who are affected must agree that rights, responsibilities and risks be shared between them.

Environmental inclusiveness emerges from three different strands: (1) The poor people in poor regions depending almost solely on their local ecosystem for surviving (*subsistence economy*), (2) their extreme vulnerability through the effects of climate change and (3) the accelerating demand for limited land and water resources (Gupta and Vegelin 2016).

Living and trying to progress within the limits of a *subsistence economy* requires a different vision on prosperity and well-being. It calls for equitably allocating rights (i.e., who has the right to access resources and when can these rights be curtailed), responsibilities (i.e., who has relevant responsibilities and how can such responsibilities be monitored and implemented) and risks (i.e., who faces the risks caused by abuse of rights and responsibilities and who compensates for these risks; Gough and McGregor 2007). Engaging the relevant stakeholders in defining and implementing this inclusiveness properly will challenge human centered management in the private and public sectors everywhere.

3.3.4 Political inclusiveness – voice and accountability

There is a prerequisite for sharing rights, responsibilities and risks: universal moral respect, which is the recognition of the right of all human beings to participate in any conversation, as laid down the contemporary philosopher Seyla Benhabib (referred to in section 1.2.1). Sadly, the roots of direct and indirect drivers of inequality often lie in the ideological foundations of society and in false argumentation. This calls for the downward accountability of institutions that claim to present the underprivileged as well as for greater local accountability: where societal groups at the local level are enabled to take part in decision-making through business firms and government authorities, trust in government and businesses will rise (Rogers 2013; Narayan, Pritchett and Kapoor 2009.

The need for more participation might call for global constitutionalism and a rule of law in order to ensure that powerful actors such as governments, entities and banks are subject to common imperatives (see, e.g., Koskenniemi 2009). But the proponents for tighter regulations should not rule out the possibility that a great part of the job can also be done by close collaboration of rule setters, responsible business leaders and all stakeholders.

Giving voice to all stakeholders is the essence of true *corporate citizenship*. The factual raison d'être of corporate citizenship is that business firms take on an active role in rule-finding discourses and rule-setting processes. Through this, firms can (help to) achieve *moral desiderata* within the setting of a competitive market economy, and they can help to overcome dilemmas such as having to choose between mass dismissals or firm closure. A moral desideratum, in such a case, would be to alleviate the consequences for those that are affected and to demonstrate that those who may have caused the problem will be held accountable. Acting prudently in situations like this will contribute to easing the tension-filled relationship between profit and morality.

Whenever there are clashes between private interest and public interest and conflicts between profit-seeking by corporate actors and the legitimate concerns of other actors, an open dialogue should at least point to possible solutions. This approach to arriving at a common understanding would also neutralize the reproach that companies, when they act as corporate citizens, do not really mean it but are just displaying another skillful profit-seeking public relations strategy. If voice is given to all stakeholders, they might accept that a corporation is willing to consider moral objectives *as well as* the profit motive.

Considering moral objectives and the profit motive is not just a theoretical concept. In section 3.2.2 we referred to cases where business leaders refrained from taking advantages in favor of producing benefits for their stakeholders. We shall take a brief look here at a theoretical foundation that explains the moral objective. The point is that moral objectives and the profit motive can be conjoined through win–win design schemes. A win–win situation means that corporate actors search for arrangements that will bring their private interest in line with the interest of stakeholders. The question, then, is not whether the profit motive is too strong, and thus needs to be weakened in favor of moral objectives, or whether the profit motive is inherently good or bad. Instead, the question to be asked is whether – and, more specifically, how – a situation in which profit-seeking is detrimental to stakeholder interest can be transformed into a situation in which profit-seeking becomes supportive of stakeholder interest.

A prominent example given by Pies, Hielscher, and Beckmann (2009) is Henry Ford's public announcement of the $5-per-day program in 1914, a morally highly desirable program for which, at the time of introduction, Henry Ford was heavily criticized by stockholders and competitors. The program included a reduction in the length of the workday from nine hours to eight, a six-day workweek, and a doubling of the going rate for minimum daily pay from $2.34 to $5 for qualified workers. Ford's innovative program was designed to solve a particular problem. At the time, the industrial workforce typically consisted of migrant workers with high absenteeism and a huge turnover rate. The average employee recruited on January 1 would have already left the company by April 15. But manufacturing cars on an assembly line made workers highly dependent on each other, and high turnover rates and absenteeism created huge problems at the plants. The dramatic increase in wages and the 48-hour, six-day workweek, therefore, induced workers to bind themselves to the company. Productivity increased so much that Ford realized a high increase in net profits. The $5 workday caused a productive response by workers and thus proved to be a prudent win–win strategy. A lesson for today's entrepreneurs?

3.4 Social business and the role of social entrepreneurs

Ford's $5 minimum daily wage move might be seen as an early example of social business. Since then, the term has taken on a different connotation, with the definition by Nobel Peace Prize laureate Professor Muhammad Yunus (2007). It regards a business created to address a social problem through a non-loss, non-dividend company that is financially self-sustainable and whose profits are reinvested in the business itself (or used to start other social businesses), with the aim of increasing social impact. The spectrum is wide because the term is also used interchangeably with *social enterprise*, ranging from profit-first corporations to non-profits or charities, with social enterprises closer to non-profits and social businesses closer to for-profits. But the issue is outcomes, not delimitations.

The concept has proven to open up employment opportunities and at the same time promote responsible use of resources in developed countries, developing countries and transition economies. This holds true also for the expanded concept of *eco-social business*. Eco-social business, since the seminal publication of Bennett (1991) on the concept of *eco-preneurship*, has postulated an intersection of entrepreneurship with environmentally and socially responsible behavior (see, e.g., Cohen 2006). What has been created is a variety of entrepreneurial activities. The incorporation of sustainability also suggests an implicit commitment to a wider social dimension. Efforts in poor countries range from support to subsistence farmers in remote areas to equipping whole communities with training, access to technology, housing, education and healthcare.

There are a lot of opportunities in this area – we take the example of social entrepreneurship activities directed at balancing community and ecological concerns. Exhibit 3.1 is taken from a commentary of the United Nations Conference on Trade and Development (UNCTAD) on the impact objectives of social entrepreneurship.

Responsible leadership in this field would have to go as far as including the activities in the informal sector, since it has been estimated that well over half of the total economic activity in the developing world takes place in informal sector relationships, where relations primarily are grounded in social instead of legal contracts (de Soto 2000). What we have here has been called the "wider linkage phenomenon," linkages occurring not just between trades and industries, but spreading to new business activities in an environment that has had no business at all (or just informal business transactions). This outreach will provoke changes of thought, even of values, and of social order (Buckley 2009).

Selected examples of social entrepreneurship activities

Social dimension	Environmental dimension
– Access to clean water	Biodiversity conservation
– Access to energy	Energy and fuel efficiency
– Access to financial services	Natural resources conservation
– Access to education	Pollution prevention
– Access to affordable housing	Waste management
– Access to health services	Sustainable energy
– Disease prevention and mitigation	Sustainable land use
– Community development	Water resources management

Exhibit 3.1 Social entrepreneurship examples

Source: Impact Reporting and Investment Standards Initiative of the Global Impact Investing Network (Jackson 2013)

3.5 Impacts of culture

Both morality and leadership are considered differently in societies whose culture is different. Not only is culture a notoriously difficult term to define (in 1952 two American anthropologists compiled a list of 164 different definitions; see Kroeber and Kluckhohn 1952), but the difficulty gets worse when looking at culture in conjunction with what is moral in leadership. Let us use the wording of Dutch sociologist Geert Hofstede (1980a, p. 5): "the collective programming of the mind which distinguishes the members of one group or category of people from another," to which we should add Matsumoto's (1996, p. 16) specification: "the set of attitudes, values, beliefs, and behaviors shared by a group of people . . . communicated from one generation to the next." With the acceleration of global interdependence, even though there are values of universal purview as said in Chapter 1, the impact of culture on moral behavior is becoming more visible. So, moral issues must be grasped from what is bestowed by society at large and organizations in particular. Generally speaking, within an individualistic culture, moral liabilities of leaders are essentially meant for persons, whereas a collectivist culture wishes leaders to integrate into a group.

Individualistic and collectivist cultures are categorizations used by Hofstede in his studies on behavior in organizations, of which one specifically deals with how leadership differs and needs to be adapted in different cultures (Hofstede 1980b). He has used four main indicators of cultural differences that have been employed in a considerable number of comparative studies in economics and management: *power distance; collectivist or individualist decision-making; feminine* (= altruist) or *masculine* (= autocratic); and *uncertainty avoidance.* Anyone in a management position should be familiar with this and take account of it when preparing and executing business decisions.

Another cultural issue is that management models and leadership modes that apply in the US cannot be easily transferred to other cultures. Cross-cultural awareness is needed to help leaders avoid mistakes that may jeopardize business. Besides skills and competencies in conducting relations with a diverse work force and diverse authorities in foreign countries, certain diplomatic qualities will be required. Saner, Yiu, and Sondergaard (2000) cite the "Nicolson test," named after the British diplomat Sir Harold Nicolson (1886–1968), which determines the qualities of a diplomat as consisting of truth, accuracy, calm, patience, good temper, modesty, loyalty, intelligence, knowledge, discernment, prudence, hospitality, charm, industry, courage and tact, and the ability to make compromises and adaptations. Responsible leaders will make sure that their managers have these qualities.

Taking account of cultural differences includes the knowledge that an important goal for leaders in one country may seem less important in another. Hofstede (2007) lists the five most and five least important perceived goals (out of 15) ascribed to successful business leaders in each of four countries (Table 3.1).

When surveying Table 3.1, should we consider the moral judgment of the Danish leader as higher than that of the US leader because the first one places

Table 3.1 The five most and five least important perceived goals ascribed to successful business leaders in four countries

China	India	Denmark	USA
Most important	*Most important*	*Most important*	*Most important*
Respecting ethical norms	Family interests	Creating something new	Growth of the business
Patriotism, national pride	Continuity of the business	Profits 10 years from now	Personal wealth
Power	Personal wealth	Honor, face, reputation	This year's profits
Honor, face, reputation	Patriotism, national pride	Staying within the law	Power
Responsibility towards society	Power	Responsibility towards employees	Staying within the law
Least important	*Least important*	*Least important*	*Least important*
Creating something new	Staying within the law	Family interests	Profits 10 years from now
Game and gambling spirit	Creating something new	Power	Responsibility towards employees
This year's profits	Responsibility towards employees	Responsibility towards society	Family interests
Personal wealth	Respecting ethical norms	Personal wealth	Continuity of the business
Staying within the law	Game and gambling spirit	Continuity of the business	Creating something new

Source: Hofstede (2007), p. 415

responsibility towards employees among the important goals and the other does not? No. In the first place, both are necessarily influenced by their society's culture, which may have historical, religious or ideological roots. And second, both will have been successful in their careers with their individual prioritization of goals. That is not to say that US leaders' perception of their responsibilities towards employees is fragile. From Drucker's emphasis on businesses' responsibilities towards employees (Schwartz 2007) to the widely acknowledged recognition of putting close employee relations in small businesses at the forefront, there has been much more social resonance of the topic than negative critics would allow (Lepoutre and Heene 2006).

The American social psychologist Douglas Murray McGregor (1906–1964) said in *The Human Side of Enterprise*: "Behind every managerial decision or action are assumptions about human nature and human behavior" (McGregor 1966, p. 33). He postulated that more leaders should assume that their employees liked work, sought to develop their skills and furthered worthy organizational goals (he called these leaders "Theory Y managers") rather than believing that their employees disliked work, wished to avoid responsibility and desired security above all (the "Theory X managers").

From a cross-cultural perspective, is it possible to transfer Theory Y and the participatory leadership style that subsequently evolved in many US firms from those firms to another societal environment? And would it be a worthy case, morally speaking? There is considerable sympathy for models of management practiced in countries such as Sweden, Norway and Germany, where a type of "industrial democracy" prevails that welcomes initiatives from the bottom of the hierarchy and is codified, e.g., the German model of co-determination in corporate boards and worker-participation in shop-level decision-making (*Mitbestimmung*).

A US firm trading in Norway and Germany (and several other European countries) will have to make its expatriate leaders aware that they cannot choose their styles at will because what is feasible depends to a large extent on the cultural conditioning of their employees. But these expatriates must change their styles when they are transferred to countries where this "industrial democracy" does not fit at all. This would be the case in many African countries, especially the francophone ones with a long colonial history of autocratic governance by French rulers. France seems to be the colonial power most appreciated by its former colonies and seems to maintain the best postcolonial relationships – not the least because autocracy has produced relatively favorable conditions for their economies (Taylor, I. 2010). Employees in this cultural environment would feel very uncomfortable with leaders who tried to practice participatory management. Therefore the expatriate will have to sacrifice the well-meant intention of what he or she feels to be a moral commitment in order to prevent a culture clash that comes from a totally unexpected angle.

Preventing unnecessary culture clashes is a task for responsible leadership. Those clashes not only occur in business transactions with foreign countries, they may also arise between large firms and small firms, and between different industries (e.g., the chemical and pharmaceutical industries; see Weber and Tarba 2012). Much has been written about culture clashes, especially on mergers and acquisitions (a review of the literature is given in Shimizu et al. 2004).

One less researched issue is tourism development. But there is practical help through the Global Code for Ethics in Tourism Industry published in 1999 by the World Tourism Organization. This behavioral code for tourism has been received well by both the industry and governments (Chirilă 2009). It includes principles guiding all stakeholders in tourism: central and local administrations, local communities and suppliers of tourism services, as well as tourists at home and abroad. Considering the prediction that tourist circulation in the world will triple over the next 10–15 years (UNWTO 2016), it is thought that this initiative will help to minimize the negative impact of tourism on the environment and the cultural heritage and to maximize benefits for the populations of the countries of destination. Culture is increasingly exploited as a facility in selling a destination, and this will also encompass traditions and attitudes of people in the host countries. This requires leaders in the tourism industry as well as managers and hired hands to have high standards for moral behavior. Not only will dishonesty and cheating cause harm in business, professionals in the business who do not adopt fair play will lose their jobs sooner or later.

Chapter 4

The economic perspective

When presenting the economic perspective in the introductory chapter, two points were raised: one was whether the economic model of capitalism promotes moral behavior or not. This has been covered. The other aspect was how moral behavior impacts a leader's environment – which for a business leader is the markets. This raises the question of whether the way in which markets work generates a regime or regimes for moral behavior. This brings the essence of the market economy system to human centered management theory. The market-based approaches to business ethics will be dealt with in the following section, and from there the reverse issue will be examined, that is, the impact that moral behavior can generate in the "market." After this, section 4.2 will show impacts that go beyond the direct environment surrounding a business.

4.1 Market-based approaches to business ethics

4.1.1 Instrumental ethics

Building market-based approaches for human centered management has its first approximation through *instrumental ethics*, whereby managers choose a corporate social responsibility approach that will also lead to shareholder wealth. Quinn and Jones (1995) argue that this is the one approach to ethics that really makes sense in a world where businesses are confronted with an extant legal and regulatory environment. No big corporation, or any large institutional or small-scale investor, would endorse corporate social responsibility if did not enhance return on investment. Corporate leaders and business owners of all kinds are responsible for legal compliance and the liability of individuals, but beyond that they have to be committed to their firms' impact on society and the natural environment; they need to feel accountable. And indeed, they are accountable. But they will also expect reward?

With regard to expectations of reward, Homann (2006a) and Boatright (1999) agree that people will adhere more to ethical principles if ethical behavior is recompensed and unethical behavior is punished. Accountability, thus, ranges over compliance, as per the statement by C.K. Prahalad mentioned in section 3.1.2. In the words of Carly Fiorina, when she was chairman and CEO of Hewlett-Packard:

> I honestly believe that the winning companies of this century will be those who prove with their actions that they can be profitable and increase social value – companies that both do well and do good . . . Increasingly, share-owners, customers, partners and employees are going to vote with their feet – rewarding those companies that fuel social change through business. This is simply the new reality of business – one that we should and must embrace.
>
> (Chatterjee 2008)

4.1.2 An investment in social cooperation for mutual advantage

A second market-based approach comes from the viewpoint that corporate social responsibility, when governed by ethical leadership, is an *investment for mutual advantage* (Lin Hi 2008). This investment primarily becomes manifest in building knowledge and stakeholder relations that affect corporate performance (and advantage for the firm), for which a proof can be found in the survey exhibited in section 4.1.5. Needless to say, the firm's stakeholders gain an advantage from this investment as well, otherwise they would not do business with the firm. The wider subject of relating ethics-based stakeholder relations to corporate performance will take the issue of ethical leadership beyond the boundaries of the firm. One good example is supply chains, where trust and reciprocity are of the highest importance (Capó-Vicedo, Mula, and Capo 2011).

4.1.3 The capabilities approach

A third approach examines the interactions between individuals and between individuals and their organizations, which encompass intangible as well as tangible components. The intangible elements include the mechanisms of the SECI model developed by Nonaka and Takeuchi (1995). SECI stands for socialization, externalization, combination and internalization of knowledge. For this to become effective in the context of people-to-people relations, the notion of capabilities must be added. The nexus with human centered management lies in a perspective that derives from the approach used by Amartya Sen to denote human development. Sen (1985) enumerates five components to assess capability:

- Freedoms in the assessment of an individual's capability-advantage
- Individual differences in the ability to transform resources into valuable activities
- The multivariate nature of transformations

- A balance of materialistic and non-materialistic factors
- Concern for the distribution of opportunities.

In studying the effect of human centered management on corporate performance, we may conceive of the five components as showing the way from moral attitudes (respecting the differences in the advantages of individuals and in their ability to make use of these advantages, the multivariety and the combination of materialistic and non-materialistic rewards and the concern for widely diverse chances) to effective governance of knowledge. These attitudes per se contribute to an optimal effort (with optimal outputs) through an optimal combination of human talent.

The capabilities approach, with its focus on the drivers behind the formation, evolution and recombination of resources for generating value-creating strategies, identifies interaction between business and society. Social and ethical resources and capabilities can be a source of competitive advantage, such as the processes of moral decision-making, perception, deliberation and responsiveness to the need for adaptation and, naturally, the development of proper relationships with the primary stakeholders: employees, customers, suppliers and communities (Garriga and Melé 2004).

Transforming these resources into business activities will have the double effect of building a *moral corporation* and positioning the firm in a highly competitive state (Chiappero-Martinetti et al. 2015). There is an intermediate step, though, between identifying the resources and transforming them into strategies or activities, and this is knowledge formation. What we are concerned with here is knowledge about ethical capabilities. Leaders who manage this type of knowledge responsibly will have a lasting impact on their business and on their business environment. This impact, one would assume, is the fundamental outcome of human centered management. To verify this assumption through empirical proof, the next section presents a survey that attempts to measure this outcome.

4.1.4 Moral behavior and business processes: impacts on corporate performance and stakeholder relations

The (direct) effect of corporate social responsibility and business ethics on business performance has been researched through several approaches, one of which, the stakeholder relation approach, was presented in section 2.4.2. Apart from measuring the effect on profitability, analyses also explore the impacts on share value (e.g., Solomon 2007; Jo and Harjoto 2011) and on reputation (e.g., Siltaoja 2006). Rather than repeat exercises like those here, we will look at the results of a survey that show how businesspersons feel about integrating ethics into the processes determining firm performance. A practitioner would say: "Corporate social responsibility is smart business when fully integrated into business processes" (Kyte 2007). This also goes for business ethics. Integration into business processes would imply that principles of ethics permeate everyday decisions and that the social impact of business activities is routinely taken into consideration. The author of this book conducted a survey on this with the participants of an executive education course in Switzerland (Bardy 2015), and the main features of the survey will be reproduced in section 4.1.5. The results reflect some implications for practice, and apposite recommendations will be discussed.

The survey set out from the question of whether business ethics connect to business processes and to stakeholder relations and how intellectual capital and knowledge on ethical principles are built and managed in a firm. There should be impacts of all these on corporate performance. Both in theory and in practice, the constructs of business ethics and corporate social responsibility conjoin with the perspectives of business processes and business performance. In this reasoning, an ethical approach to business is likely to encourage open communication, problem solving, knowledge sharing and creativity among employees (the organizational capital); enhance interactions and relationships with suppliers, customers and other stakeholders (the relational capital); and retain talent (the human capital). These intangible resources are core assets a business can utilize for competitive advantage. The other resource derives from the perspective that corporate social responsibility, governed by business ethics, is an investment for mutual advantage, as said earlier. This investment primarily becomes manifest in building knowledge and stakeholder relations that affect corporate performance (advantage for the firm), as this study will show. Needless to say, the firm's stakeholders gain an advantage from this investment as well – or they would not do business with the firm.

Another input into the survey was the issue of how knowledge on ethics transcends into business behavior and business processes. The knowledge built up from business ethics can help to improve ethical decision-making by providing managers with the appropriate knowledge and tools that enable them to correctly identify, diagnose and analyze ethical problems and dilemmas. This type of knowledge will provide solutions to those problems and dilemmas, and it will also help to assess the benefits and shortcomings of corporate decision-making in any area of the firm. But any other type of knowledge, about a firm's organization and employees, its products, customers and suppliers, or its technologies, can benefit from business ethics as well. Morally enhanced attitudes in dealing with knowledge will increase both the validity of business decisions and of its consequences. An even greater effect is on creating, upgrading and disseminating knowledge, which are the intangible components of knowledge management (with storage and documentation being technological or tangible elements, i.e., the means for accessing knowledge content; see Alavi and Denford 2011, p. 107). Undocumented ("tacit") knowledge and its transfer are even more influenced by a corporate culture based on ethical attitudes such as openness, transparency and mutual consideration. A formal demonstration of this would be where a firm's knowledge management is governed by the principle of "need to withhold" rather than "need to know" (Guo 2011).

An ethical concept of how to deal with knowledge needs to depart from defining knowledge as *justified true belief* (Goldman 1979) and knowledge creation as the "dynamic human process of justifying personal beliefs as part of an aspiration for the truth" (Nonaka 1994, p. 15). This way of creating knowledge would also create a business climate that is best characterized by the term *open book management*, which will be presented in Chapter 7 where implementation issues are discussed.

The ethical concept of knowledge management transforms into a practical panorama through five fundamental effects (McElroy 2003):

1 *Overcoming tacitness and complexity within and between corporations*: individuals must be guided in their various roles to fundamentally rethink their work patterns, relationships and cognitive frameworks.
2 *Extending enterprise and networks*: be they "knowledge communities," "knowledge chains," "knowledge suppliers" or "knowledge markets" (Gilsing 2006), the foremost requirement is that their participants interact free from affectation or disguise; without this, all modern networking techniques will not produce the desired outcomes.
3 *Practicing a "learning organization"* (Senge 1994): each person dealing with others must command personal mastery, mental models, shared vision, team learning and systems thinking.
4 *Working with multifaceted and parallel approaches* ("ambidextrous learning"; Kang and Snell 2009): progress can be achieved only by simultaneously exploring new knowledge domains while exploiting current ones (Kang and Snell 2009).
5 *Maintaining continuous connectivity and communication*: beyond state-of the art technology, a methodical approach is required for updates, feedbacks, inclusion in surveys and so forth.

All five aspects delineate essentials of business ethics and will level up human capabilities in a firm and its organizational structure. It will thus alter a firm's *intellectual capital*, of which *human capital* and *structural capital* are the two major categories, with *relational capital* as a third category of its own (see, e.g., Sullivan 2000, Firer and Williams 2003). Structural capital has been divided into the two subcategories of organizational capital and customer capital (Edvinsson and Malone 1997; Bontis 1998); however, this latter composition is mainly applied to serve the purpose of attempting a valuation of intellectual capital (Ariely 2005). When using a categorization that places relational capital at the side of structural and human capital, we get closer to corporate strategizing: the role of all stakeholders is taken into account explicitly (beyond just "customer capital"), and when corporations earnestly consider stakeholder interests, we arrive at a view on stakeholder relations that has been called a *synthesis of ethics and economics* (Jones 1995). This instrumental approach, rather than a descriptive or a normative approach, is based on the connections between stakeholder management and the achievement of corporate goals, most commonly profit-ability and efficiency goals but ethical goals as well (Donaldson and Preston 1995). The argument is for stakeholder management to be both a means to an end, contingent on the value of stakeholder relationships to corporate success, and a means to deploy instrumental ethics as an addendum to the rule of creating wealth. This makes ethics a business case: managers perceive that "good ethics" is "good business" and that employing ethics in stakeholder relations increases firm value (Solomon 2007; Quinn and Jones 1995).

Making the participants aware of the issues and interrelations laid out in the preceding paragraphs was one fundamental step before conducting the survey. The other was a model that depicts the interaction between ethical/moral reasoning and outcomes of business activities.

4.1.5 The ingredients of ethics-led corporate performance: a model of interaction

The model that was presented for the participants of the survey had been solely conceived for surveying the views of high-level managers attending the executive education course. It may be valid in a European and perhaps in a North American context, but not in others. Another disclaimer would be that the proof of the model's validity may have been influenced by the setting of the survey: it was performed in a course on ethical leadership, and this certainly influenced the answers to the questionnaire.

The model endeavors to measure the effect of human centered management in a firm by gauging the impact of a code of ethics on business processes and stakeholder relations.

Before portraying the model, a few remarks must be made on ethics codes in business enterprises (a general representation of the ethics code concept will be given in section 6.2 of this book). A code of business ethics has to work in conjunction with a firm's mission statement and with more specific policy documents that govern conduct towards customers, suppliers, research partners and other parties affected by the firm's activities. Because it represents the essence of corporate culture, there are various steps to be taken when setting up a code of ethics, such as involving employees at all levels, and pointing to real ethical dilemmas that affect the business such as bribery, suppliers that use child labor and so forth. It can be valuable to consult a lawyer when drafting a code of ethics in order to determine what can be construed as legal or illegal and what can be argued in court (Ferrell and Fraedrich 2014). Writing the code should be entrusted to professionals, who can be found in the consulting business or in non-profit institutions (Webley 2003). A decision where consultants cannot really help is about who will be in charge of applying and updating the code of ethics and of monitoring compliance.

A code of ethics needs control of compliance. The size and type of business may suggest that a compliance officer should be appointed. Whoever is put in charge needs to have a strong commitment to the company's success and good people skills. Quite often the duties of this office are only or mainly directed towards detecting and preventing misuse. A recent "State of Compliance Survey" from PricewaterhouseCoopers gives an extensive list of the risks perceived in the industry and of structural/procedural features; no mention is made of the positive effects that are achieved when compliance (and ethical behavior) is observed (PwC 2014). There is only limited research and very few reports of practical experience on this positive agenda (Treviño and Nelson 2011). One outstanding exception is a report by the Conference Board of Canada (Ezekiel 2006), which demonstrates strong correlations between ethical practices and an assortment of positive outcomes, and it deplores that there is a gap between that type of disclosure and the many findings on unethical behavior. There is some proof of the effect ethical practices in a firm (and, thus, ethics codes) have on corporate performance.

With a code of ethics being one ingredient to corporate performance, the model that is shown here has four ingredients in total:

(1) A code of ethics that serves to guide employees', managers' and executives' behavior, (2) conscientious management of stakeholder relations, (3) knowledge management procedures that are enhanced by the respective statements in the code of ethics, and (4) business processes that are conducted along the same lines. The four interact with each other and with corporate performance.

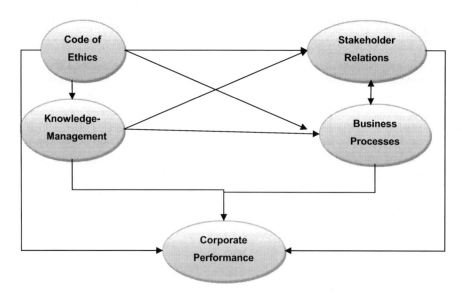

Exhibit 4.1 Direct and indirect effects of ethics principles on corporate performance

Source: Author

The term *corporate performance* is not defined in the model – it represents financial performance or market share or share-value. This ambiguity allows a flexible application, above all, when used for a qualitative investigation. For the code of ethics, the model assumes that following the statements of an ethics code improves business process performance and stakeholder relations as well as knowledge management, and also affects overall corporate performance directly.

From there, the first four questions were drawn:

Q1: *How do code of ethics statements affect business process performance?*
Q2: *How do code of ethics statements affect stakeholder relations?*
Q3: *Is there a relationship between code of ethics and knowledge management?*
Q4: *How do code of ethics statements affect overall corporate performance?*

Likewise, it is assumed that ethically enhanced knowledge management procedures improve business process performance and also have a direct effect on overall corporate performance.

This produces three more questions:

Q5: *How does (ethically enhanced) knowledge management affect business process performance?*
Q6.1: *How does (ethically enhanced) knowledge management affect overall corporate performance?*
Q6.2: *How does (ethically enhanced) knowledge management affect stakeholder relations?*

It is also assumed that conscientious stakeholder management has an effect on business processes and that, vice versa, ethically enhanced business processes affect stakeholder relations. Similarly, conscientious stakeholder management has a direct effect on corporate performance.

The corresponding questions are:

Q7: *How do (ethically enhanced) stakeholder relations affect business process performance (Q7.1)? Is there a reverse effect as well (Q7.2)?*
Q8: *How do (ethically enhanced) stakeholder relations affect overall corporate performance?*

An unmediated effect is assumed for business processes: if they are conducted in alignment with corporate ethical standards, corporate performance is affected directly:

Q9: *How do (ethically enhanced) business processes affect overall corporate performance?*

The questions were submitted to several groups of executives attending an ethical leadership course in Switzerland by way of a questionnaire they received at the end of the course. The survey followed a self-assessment approach based on a scale of 1 to 5, where respondents were asked to assess their opinion about the effects of the ethics code in their firms (all respondents' firms have a written ethics code) on their knowledge management procedures, on their stakeholder management and on their business processes.

The main result of the survey is reproduced in Tables 4.1 and 4.2. Quantitative statistics are not given here – for a detailed discussion of the results, see Bardy (2015). But the tables delineate quite distinctly where ethical leadership can lead with regard to process performance, overall performance and stakeholder relations.

In summarizing the results with regard to business processes, the survey reveals that there are effects in terms of higher transparency, of less friction at process interfaces, of increased speed of business processes, of improved output quality

Table 4.1 Code of ethics effects (I)

Description
Business Process Performance
Effects in terms of less friction at process interfaces
Effects in terms of increased speed of business processes
Effects in terms of improved output quality
Effects in terms of increased process re-engineering efforts
Effects in terms of less costly processes
Effects in terms of higher transparency of business processes
Stakeholder Relations
Effects in terms of more dialogues with stakeholders
Effects in terms of stakeholder groups reporting more issues of affectedness
Effects in terms of more social networks connecting with the corporation
Effects in terms of customer management processes becoming more transparent
Effects in terms of supplier management processes becoming more transparent
Effects in terms of industrial relationship processes becoming more flexible

Table 4.2 Code of ethics effects (II), knowledge management and corporate performance

Description
Effects in terms of
. . . having knowledge management procedures implemented that are clearly connected to what is said in the ethics code;
. . . realizing that implementing an ethics code has improved overall corporate performance directly;
. . . the ethics code statements producing an indirect effect on corporate performance through improved knowledge and business process management.

and of less costly processes and in terms of increased process re-engineering efforts. As far as stakeholder relations are concerned, the study found effects in terms of more dialogues with stakeholder groups, of stakeholder groups reporting more issues of affectedness and effects in terms of more social networks connecting with the corporation. Combining processes and stakeholder relations, there are effects in terms of customer and supplier management processes becoming more transparent and effects in terms of supplier management processes becoming more transparent as well as effects in terms of industrial relationship processes becoming more flexible. The use of this can be threefold: (1) for the theoretical discussion, (2) for the teaching of business ethics and (3) for practical consequences within corporations.

The model, as said, has limitations. The validity may hold true in a European and perhaps in a North American context only. A wider and more diverse sample should be sought for further validation. Another question is whether an ethics code for a corporation headquartered in one country can encompass the sets of values and ethical principles that prevail in other countries. Codes for multinational companies must reflect and accommodate other cultural models, for example, in markets such as Africa and Asia. But a written code of ethics should serve as an expectation and guideline for employee conduct, wherever a business is located. And for a code of ethics to mean anything anywhere, a company has to be willing to enforce it. This usually requires an example of someone being disciplined or the employment contract being terminated for a breach of ethics. However, this sharp consequence will not be upheld where cultural traditions require a softer treatment of the individual, and the same would go for the positive results that a firm expects from "conduct according to code." Will openness always be reciprocated? Will tolerance of errors always produce betterment? Will strict execution of non-bribery clauses motivate a salesperson to seek other means to acquire orders? These are the caveats that have to be included when looking at a model that seems to fit Western tradition.

4.2 Impacting the wider environment of markets and society

4.2.1 Spillover effects of responsible business leadership

Spillover effects from one business to another or from corporate activity to other sectors of society may occur in multiple ways. Introducing new technologies such as new production processes and techniques, managerial skills, ideas and new varieties of goods and services will not only impact the immediate environment of a firm but the wider social milieu as well. In order for this to occur, a certain "absorption capacity" is required, like a threshold level of human capacity. This may not always be the case within the environment of a firm, for example, when a foreign firm operates in a host country. But foreign investment per se has significant effects that might raise this threshold, and the prudent strategies of an investor collaborating with foreign stakeholders may contribute to establishing the social structures required for this threshold level. This becomes obvious when considering that one basic spillover effect is education.

Although it is commonly assumed that education is provided solely in schools, a lot of education takes place outside formal institutions and through family influence and peer group pressure within the local community. Buckley (2009) states that to benefit from formal education it may be necessary for people to "unlearn" beliefs from their informal education. Thus, unlearning beliefs is one step in changing the order of thought. One example is the economic and institutional progress in some African countries such as Rwanda and Sierra Leone (Foster and Briceño-Garmendia 2009), where improvements could mainly be achieved because people developed a positive attitude towards participation in social and business life. One source of influence was human centered management in government and business (Coulter 2015).

The combined effect of spillovers from foreign aid and investment and transfer of knowledge or technology into a host country can reach as far as moving its status to improved living standards shown in Exhibit 4.2.

The exhibit identifies Status 1 of the society where the main societal actors – business, administrative institutions and civil society – are not closely intertwined. If new business activities enter from abroad (e.g., Object 1) producing technology transfer and knowledge transfer to the investor's business partners and, by way of spillovers, to civil society as a whole, education and professionalization will improve and enlarge not only the human capital base in the

The Impacts of FDI in Developing Countries

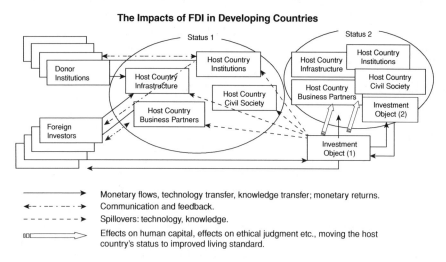

Exhibit 4.2 Spillovers from business activities to social order

Source: Bardy (2016)

host country but also the opportunities for a new kind of interaction between the recipient of the investment, the employees, and the community as a whole, with effects on living standards and on ethical judgment (Status 2). Subsequent investments (Object 2) will be better accepted and more densely integrated.

There are several real-life cases that support the optimistic interpretation of spillover effects, such as the Chad–Cameroon Oil Project, which some call a new model for oil-led poverty reduction (see Gary and Karl 2003). Here, government, investors and community leaders cooperated from the start, and the local communities gradually become stakeholders of the project, with multiple spillover effects on the social order. Social order is a comprehensive public good, and morality is one of its solid building blocks.

4.2.2 The public good of morality

From the civil societies in ancient Greece, which dwelled in well-developed urban settings, from medieval fiefdoms as described by Machiavelli and the market-driven social self-organization first described by Adam Smith in the 18th century, through Max Weber's admonitions and the teachings of Catholic Social Thought in the 1900s, human centered management has become pivotal in both public service and private ventures. It is the foremost driver of collective well-being; and it is facilitated best when the direct action of ordinary people organized into groups and associations concurs with judicious guidance of these groups and associations through (elected) government.

There will always be recurrent debate over what should be managed by governments and what by self-organization, but all critics agree that for collective well-being to thrive, a consensus between the public and the private sector is needed. The main task is for responsible leaders in government and business to stimulate and communicate a commitment not just for doing good but for rewarding good behavior and punishing evil. Morality will thus become a public good.

In business, a leader's company must "walk the talk" through conduct that earns higher levels of trust, through responsible caring, through authenticity, by eliminating negative ties and building coalitions for positive change and by aligning mutual expectations. Responsible leadership thus furthers the embeddedness of an organization as a trustworthy business in society. Society will reward honesty, fair-dealing, justice and exercising the nonobligatory virtues of benevolence and charity. Proof of this is shown in the many cases where companies that reached out far beyond their business environment not only received recognition but also gained new customers or more orders.

There are the examples of manufacturers that gave away new products free of charge to people who would never become their customers, as Burlington did in Somalia (Charter et al. 2002) or Chevron's support for reducing HIV/AIDS in Angola (Connor, Evans, and Brink 2011). But reaching out beyond the immediate business environment is not just an endeavor for big corporations.

Small and medium enterprises play a vital role in giving back to the community, setting outstanding examples for responsible leadership and thus in upholding business morality. One might say that the public good of morality is best preserved by small and medium entrepreneurs. Two issues may explain why this is the case:

1   Most small and medium enterprises (SMEs) are very active with respect to social responsibility. The *societal expectation* to them is higher, as they are closer to their stakeholders than big corporations (Whetten, Rands and Godfrey 2002). However, their involvement differs and may not be measurable in the same way and to the same extent as for large enterprises. They are visibly concerned with maintaining acceptance and feedback from the communities in which they operate – securing a *license to operate* (Russo and Perrini 2010). The instruments are personal informal communication by managers and employees, word of mouth or civic engagement by the owners in the local community who often need to respond quickly to the changing circumstances. Some research highlights that SMEs have nurtured "peculiar" corporate social responsibility (CSR) orientations revolving around intimate and personalized stakeholder while their CSR processes are almost not institutionalized (e.g., Jamali, Zanhour, and Keshishian 2008). In the developing world, where SMEs often differ from what is commonly encountered in industrialized countries and where the informal enterprises (particularly in the agricultural sector) exhibit different orientations to basic social and environmental functions (de Kok, Deijl, and Veldhuis-Van-Essen 2013; Demuijnck and Ngnodjom 2013), the individual history, values and ethics of SME owners play an important role in shaping their engagement in CSR (Jamali, Lund-Thomsen, and Jeppesen (2017).
2   SMEs are directly affected by local politics, and the effects are immediate. Therefore they need to engage in almost all community affairs (Boiral, Baron, and Gunnlaugson 2014; de Oliveira and Jabbour 2017). Hence, while their engagement is mostly motivated for moral reasons, it will also pragmatically have the expectancy that the engagement will prove beneficial, for example, better schools provide a better workforce, better county ordinances provide better working conditions. SME associations have therefore welcomed the development of a best practice standard of social responsibility by the International Organization for Standardization (ISO), which was to become ISO 26000. SME associations were well represented on a worldwide scale in the multi-stakeholder working group on this international standard (Castka and Balzarova 2008).

International standards are public goods of their own as they disseminate guidelines and best practices to a very wide community. ISO 26000, as shown in Exhibit 4.3, attains a set of goals that all are related to ethical issues: human

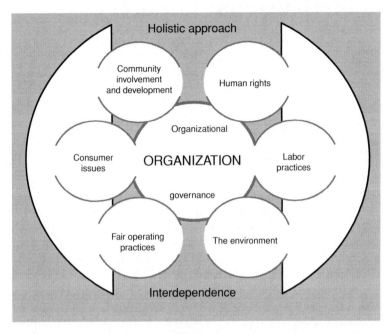

Exhibit 4.3 The seven core subjects of social responsibility in ISO 26000
Source: ISO (2010), p. 16

rights, labor practices, the natural environment, fair operating practices, good consumer relations and community involvement.

A standard like this will induce *proactive social responsibility* (Torugsa, O'Donohue, and Hecker 2013), that is, foreseeing and capitalizing on, rather than merely reacting to, emerging issues in the environment of a business. The general public and the stakeholders of the business will surely gain advantages from the various activities related to proactive social responsibility. The workplace in the firm and in its suppliers or customers will benefit from, for example, training and development opportunities within the firm and outside its boundaries; social cohesion will be created, capabilities will be built or be enhanced and best practices will be shared. This will also strengthen the institutions that encase and cooperate with the business sector – which brings us to the last of the four perspectives in conjoining morality and leadership: the institutional perspective.

Chapter 5

The institutional perspective

There is a dual correlation between human centered management and institutions: institutions influence the attitudes and behaviors of leaders, and moral leaders exert an influence on institutions. The former is seen in public and private educational institutions and also in ideological and professional associations; the latter gave birth to creeds and thought systems that became known through an outstanding leader's ideas, words and actions, such as Christianity, Islam, Buddhism or Gandhism, and are institutions of their own. Governmental institutions that play a major role in shaping the bonds within a society are not necessarily based on a thought system or an ideology – an example is the Chinese free market system (adapting a "Western" ideology) that works under a communist scheme. But any institution, governmental, educational or professional, needs a framework or frameworks for defining its policy agenda, and most have an ethical content. Managers who work there will not automatically have to abide by these policies – they should be given a chance to shape them, as will be discussed in the first part of this chapter. The second part will then take up the question of how an ethical policy agenda works in governments. This will be preceded by a brief passage on the outlines of institutional theory and how it relates to the human centered paradigm.

The relation between institutional theory and the human centered paradigm can best be inferred from a definition given by Stanford Professor William Richard Scott (see Scott 2004): "a theory on the aspects of social structure, considering the processes by which structures, including schemes, rules, norms, and routines, become established as authoritative guidelines for social behavior." Social/moral behavior is the individual aspect. There is a business aspect as well, which is marked by Nobel laureate Douglass Cecil North (1920–2015). He argued that for economic change, entrepreneurs depend on institutional changes, for example, new structures of public administration. The business sector's systematic investment in skills and their application to the economy, he wrote, must entail and cannot prevail without the (public) institutions: "The institutional framework directs the process of human learning and the development of tacit knowledge that leads the decision-making processes" (North 1990, p. 80). Institutions and business firms interfere with each other mutually.

The mutual interference is more intense in some industries and less so in others. Managers employed in construction, or in financial services, will experience intervention from public institutions in their day-to-day work; on the other hand, management in these industries must seek to be involved in shaping the rules, norms and routines that guide these interventions. Institutional intervention is needed in a society to prevent and correct failures in the market, and to prevent and correct immoral behavior. A society which does not have good working institutions will fail to provide the common good to its members. An *institutional void*, that is, ineffectiveness or inefficiency or complete absence of a public authority will also hinder all efforts to build markets in less developed countries that would provide economic and social development. Expatriates that are deployed into this type of economies need to be especially aware of these deficiencies. Property rights and autonomy, which are taken for granted as pillars of markets in modern societies and economies, often stand in conflict with existing rules of the game in societies that adhere to patriarchy, corruption and patronage in business dealings.

A complete "void" of institutions can scarcely be imagined for even the least developed country, but when it comes to remote rural communities in those countries, the rule of law that might be upheld, at least purportedly, in the capital, does not exist at all. There are examples where Nestlé started its Pure Drinking Water Supply Project and Unilever launched a social initiative to encourage women's economic empowerment in rural Bangladesh (Uddin, Tarique, and Hassan 2008). The obstacles were not just patriarchy and corruption, but also the religious concept of *purdah*, a manifestation of the belief that Allah made women weaker (Mair, Martí, and Ventresca 2012). The international managers of these companies, when training for assignments like to Bangladesh, may have learned about the cultural differences or *institutional distances* (see, e.g., Ojala 2015) between their home country and the host country. But, when their job requires displacement throughout the regions of, for example, Bangladesh, they will have come to terms with the more complicated issue of institutional distances within the host country.

The international dimension of institutionalist theory illustrates the far-reaching responsibilities of business managers who handle public institutions relations, or who have to step in when public institutions are weak. Viewed from the other way round, it is the responsibility of managers in public institutions, at home and abroad, to reach out to all members of society, and that includes business. In the first place, they have to set up a concise agenda, and then their activities and decisions must be moral to the point of being above any doubt.

5.1 Policy agendas

For any institution, the challenge is to have a clear map of the impact its activities have on society and a clear strategy to ensure that its operations and performance carry through the direction provided by its leadership. This is a question of matching the institution's purpose, strategy, principles and governance with daily management routines. What has to be prevented is decisions being made independently of social context and without regard to the attitudes and behavior of stakeholders. But it must be accepted that completely other-regarding behavior, such as altruism and altruistic or third-party punishment, cannot be fully captured in any societal or economic environment. There is a wide span between these extremes, and in order to find the proper balance an institution may opt for regulating the institution's operations through a set of compliance rules or through appealing to the accountability of its decision-makers. The first alternative would be based on the perception that the market rewards moral behavior and that there are extrinsic mechanisms in the market that guide moral decision-making. The second alternative is led by the belief that decision-makers will feel intrinsically committed to choose a morally acceptable option.

5.1.1 A moral market framework

A moral market framework is not about formal regulations by laws and ordinances that direct decision-making, but rather about (informal) mechanisms that punish immoral behavior. As we have seen from the repeated uncovering of the many corporate offenses against morality (from the Enron and WorldCom cases to Siemens and Volkswagen), there undoubtedly is such a mechanism. Using the argument in a positive way, with economic decisions, behaviors, and institutions depending on and influencing moral/ethical sentiments and behaviors, a distinct statement can be made that all economic systems are founded upon ostensible norms governing what is deemed morally acceptable in fair relations between the economic actors and with institutional actors. This would extend to norms that are deemed to produce an appropriate distribution of economic output and to questions concerning the relationship of economic activities to broader societal welfare: "Every economy is a moral economy" has been said by, among others, British political theorists and philosophers Andrew Sayer and Russell Keat (see Sayer 2007).

Sayer and Keat offer two meanings of the concept of morality (Kennedy 2012), both of which have been taken up in this book. One is what good (= moral) behavior consists of, for example, what would constitute a life worth living, what would contribute to people's well-being and what would be best for them to pursue as goals or ends. The other refers to claims about the rules that should govern people's relationships with one another, the proper limits on their pursuit of their own interests and the principles upon which income, wealth or opportunities should be distributed. At this stage of the book, we are concerned with rules governing relationships in the economic and political world and with the limits these rules should set to the pursuit of the interests of one party. An illustrative example, on the scale of global economic relationships, are the endeavors of the European Commission, representing a leading player in these relationships, to implement economic partnership with less developed countries in Africa, the Caribbean and the Pacific.

The European Union (EU) has a long history of being looked at as a benevolent development actor in its trade relationship with the African, Caribbean and Pacific (ACP) countries. Economic ties to these partners have been moralized in relation to development norms and ACP–EU trade has been envisioned as a basis for poverty elimination for vulnerable peoples (see, e.g., Brown 2002). European policy-makers have taken great care to update these moral development underpinnings.

One of the foremost issues is the EU's contribution to complementary adjustment policies destined to balance the effects of what some critics have seen as premature opening up of markets. These policies typically involve labor market reforms to enhance the mobility of the workforce both between and within industries and training programs to provide qualified employees for export-oriented companies and technological support to improve the ability of firms to compete against imports. By aligning with this policy discourse, the European Commission is defining viable strategies for creating decent jobs while respecting the ACP states' autonomy to protect an emergent domestic industrial and agricultural sector (Szépesi 2004).

While there are still concerns about labor standards in low-value and low-pay export industries such as cut-flower production (Langan 2013), the co-operative power of EU engagement is well acknowledged, as seen in the African Peace Facility 2015 Annual Report (European Union 2016).

The ACP–EU agreements demonstrate how marketplace morality induces negotiators to consider the interests of stakeholders and to pursue both their own interests and those of their business partners. Leaders in a market such as the EU when dealing with less developed countries have an obligation, based on what must be viewed at as an extended social contract, to act consistently with this marketplace morality. Their guidelines would be what Donaldson and Dunfee have called the *universal norms* or *hypernorms*, such as basic rights of freedom, movement, free speech and nondiscrimination. They suggest the use of presumptions as a means of identifying if an ethical principle is widespread. Evidence in support of a principle having hypernorm status would be, according to Donaldson and Dunfee (1999), that it is, inter alia:

- A component of well-known global industry standards;
- Supported by prominent non-governmental organizations such as the International Labor Organization or Transparency International;
- Consistently referred to as a global ethical standard by international media;
- Known to be consistent with precepts of major religions;
- Supported by global business organizations such as the International Chamber of Commerce or the Caux Round Table;
- Known to be consistent with precepts of major philosophies;

- Generally supported by a relevant international community of professionals, e.g., accountants or environmental engineers;
- Supported by the laws of many different countries.

All these qualities demonstrate that there is indeed moral capacity in the markets and in the rules that govern markets.

5.1.2 Accountability frameworks

The traditional corporate formula for accountability, where the company represents the interests of the shareholders and its performance is measured in profit and growth, has long been overruled by the demand that corporate accountability become deeper and broader. One may question whether, as is frequently claimed, this demand was brought in through pressure groups from outside. If we look at 19th-century social agendas, of which Cadbury's and Robert Owen were examples as discussed earlier, the demand was intrinsic to the firms or the firms' owners. Today, companies in general are moving beyond a single financial bottom line towards a triple bottom line that also encompasses social and environmental accountability and responsibility for wider public goods.

Like governments and their agencies that are, in the end, accountable to voters, the corporations' accountabilities extend to all stakeholders. And in both the public and the corporate sector, strong financial management and accountability is driving continual improvement in governance. So there is a beneficial consequence: accepting wider accountability will enhance best practices and thus increased performance throughout the whole organization.

With extended accountabilities in both the public and the private sectors, the issue is not whether one should emulate the other. Rather, it is about evaluating the practices of other organizations, whether they are private or public, and then implementing the best of these practices. This also relates to information disclosure. Social accounting and reporting has become a practice of businesses of any size – from the small firm describing how it trains apprentices and has been certified by environmental auditors to the large corporation with expertise in dealing with labor relations worldwide and specialists for all sorts of ecological concerns. What this type of accounting basically reveals is that firms and their leadership not only feel that they are accountable for their decisions' moral impact (i.e., the impact on society) but also make public the scale of this accountability.

The organization with the most notable policy agenda affecting all sectors of society and with a clear-cut accountability scheme is the United Nations Human Rights Council (UNHRC). The UNHRC is an intergovernmental body whose 47 member states are responsible for promoting and protecting human rights around the world. It was established in 2006, replacing the UN Commission on Human Rights, which had been set up in 1946 to determine a drafting committee for the Universal Declaration of Human Rights, adopted by the United Nations on December 10, 1948.

After its establishment, the Human Rights Council issued a regime of periodic reviews of all 193 UN member states, with information based on reports coming from three different sources: the government of the state under review, authorities of the UN and local stakeholders including national human rights institutions, and civic associations and other civil society actors. Each review is facilitated by a group of three rapporteurs, which are states outside the review area. They have to prepare an outcome document on the review, which includes a summary of the review proceedings, recommendations, conclusions and voluntary commitments presented by the state under review. With the local stakeholders being entitled to report on any observation they make on human rights abuse in a business or a government authority, both the corporate and the public sector may come under tight scrutiny. This is what the mechanism intends, enforcing the accountability of non-state actors and enforcing respect for, for example, codes of conduct, trade union laws and rights of association.

A forerunner of the Human Rights Council, at least in fighting abuse of fundamental rights of workers and engaging all relevant actors in its operations from the beginning, is the International Labour Organization (ILO), created in 1919 as an agency of the League of Nations following World War I. Using a tripartite structure of representation, the ILO ensured the participation of business, labor and governments in developing worker rights and minimum labor standards for member states. It was in the interest of business that universal standards contributed to minimize competitive distortions. The ILO and the UNHRC work closely together, with the former providing concepts, training and programs on emerging issues such as the situation of migrants, and the latter exercising control through the reporting scheme.

There is another group of institutions in society apart from government and business whose importance and involvement is growing, and this is the *third sector* – voluntary and community organizations, lobbyists, charities, charitable trusts, civic associations, self-help groups, social enterprises, mutual societies and co-operatives and other non-profit organizations (civil society organizations, or CSOs). They focus on social services, the environment, education and other issues that are deemed to be unmet needs in a society.

Peter Drucker suggested that the non-profit sector provides an excellent outlet for a variety of society's labor and skills (Drucker 1995), and in the US, approximately 10% of gross domestic product (GDP) is attributable to the third sector (Salamon and Sokolowski 2004). With this magnitude, it sounds logical that non-profit organizations not only have a financial accountability towards the communities by which they are sponsored, but that there is also a strong imperative for holding them accountable for their activities. However, with many CSOs, several important questions are left unanswered (Onyx 2008):

- To whom is the organization accountable, and for what?
- How is this accountability to be demonstrated, and what compliance mechanisms are available and necessary to ensure that the organization remains within its accepted zone of conduct?

- Put another way, who has (or should have) the power to enforce compliance, and if this is the state, does such power potentially curtail the capacity of the organization to operate autonomously?

With the wide array of activities that CSOs pursue – sometimes overlapping, even contradictory, including the exertion of pressure and other questionable means, the need for holding them accountable has become even more important. In most cases, CSOs present a serious concern of a group of people or they take up the concerns of less powerful people. Many of the larger ones such as Greenpeace, the World Wildlife Federation (WWF) and Oxfam have offices all over the world, but there are myriad smaller ones (e.g., it is estimated that the number of CSOs in the UK was more than 900,000 in 2011–2012, with an estimated 2.3 million people employed as paid staff; see NCVO 2014). From their omnipresence, it becomes obvious that they can exert a substantial influence on the moral behavior of corporate officers and leaders.

The stake that CSOs hold in a corporation is very different from that held by other stakeholder groups, all of which have a direct, mostly contractual, relation to the firm. By contrast, CSOs are bundling the interests of people or groups who are not in a position to voice their concerns clearly enough. As an example, local residents in the vicinity of an airport would be unlikely to be heard one by one by the airport authority when another runway is being planned. But when residents join a local association they are much more likely to get their views across. From this very local stage the spectrum of CSO intervention goes up to where WWF or Greenpeace represent the interests not of people but of the natural environment. There is nothing new in this, with the exception perhaps of the scale of the issues, if we look at the long history of, for example, the Royal Society for the Prevention of Cruelty to Animals (RSPCA), which was founded in 1824 and is the oldest organization that represents "nature" – or beings that cannot speak for themselves.

The topic of CSO accountability has been revitalized with the recognition of the role they play in contributing to the implementation of the UN post-2015 Sustainable Development Goals (SDGs) together with the corporate sector. As the UN is using the term "non-governmental" for all that is not an official representation of the member states, the way in which UN agencies treat CSOs and businesses is deemed to be the same.

The involvement in the SDGs has a clear moral background, but the rules of the game have yet to be defined between CSOs, business firms and the UN agencies. Similarly, in the relations of non-governmental organizations (NGOs) with business firms, the backgrounds and the rules are very often undefined. One question is how a firm recognizes whether or not a group is worthy of entering into a dialogue with; another question is about the means that CSOs might use to gain attention. How to discern if a CSO is genuinely representing its intended beneficiaries and to what degree it is accountable has become a tricky question for business leaders and politicians (Slim 2002). How to deal with CSOs will be taken up in Chapter 7, which discusses stakeholder relations (section 7.5).

5.2 Ethics in government and public office

People who lead in the public sector need to achieve multiple and complex objectives. This multiplicity and complexity makes leading in the public domain very demanding and often fraught with ethical issues. Another field of concern is the relationship between business (i.e., business leaders) and the public domain (i.e., politicians), and raises questions of whether powerful corporations shape public policy, whether lobbying is a moral exercise, how far businesses must take part in developing regulatory frameworks, and similar questions. All of these questions look at the moral content of business activity with government and government authorities.

Despite decades of compliance efforts, the abuse of public office for private gain continues to flourish in local and state governments all over the world. But there are also outstanding examples of authorities that are successfully accomplishing moral conduct. This is not so much achieved by compliance rules, strict oversight and severe punishment for offenders but by exemplary leadership. Human centered management is essential for assuring that public officials behave morally; apart from setting examples, they need to influence the organization's culture by defining the core principles that underlie how agency decisions are made at all levels of any government agency.

The core principles for morality in the public domain do not differ from those in the private domain: integrity, accountability, and trust and trustworthiness are ethical requirements for each officer in any institution. But trust is even more meaningful in the public domain, since public service is a public trust, and if there is anything unique about public service, it derives from this proposition. For a public administrator, upholding the public trust means faithfully executing one's duties in support of the public interest and the collective good. From there, the first provision in the US *Principles of Ethical Conduct for Government Officers and Employees* (Office of Government Ethics 1992, p. 1) reads "Public service is a public trust, requiring employees to place loyalty to the Constitution, the laws and ethical principles above private gain." As public officers spend public money, and they wield the power of the state in carrying out their role, they should be held to a higher standard than others, but public opinion often holds that government officials do not necessarily meet that higher standard (Lewis and Catron 1996; Leiserowitz et al. 2013). There is a lack of trust, a deficit in confidence.

The confidence deficit was also an issue in the context of the public-sector reforms that started in Europe at the end of the 20th century. They have all striven to overcome the confidence deficit, and ethical standards in public life have become a foremost political issue. Direct interest in this has been taken by the Organisation for Economic Co-operation and Development (OECD), whose Public Management (PUMA) department emphasized that a fourth "E" (for *ethics*) should be added to the reform triumvirate of *economy, efficiency* and *effectiveness* (OECD 1996). Research into the phenomenon by, among others, Bishop and Preston (2000) has revealed that the moral failures in government often derive not from willful misconduct (if we exclude blunt corruption) but from ignorance and the lack of capacity to cope with the complexity of government tasks. The source just quoted comes from Australia, where there may have been an overburdening of public officials with several new legislations coming forward at the same time, such as the Financial Management Standard of 1997, the Government Owned Corporations Act of 1993 and the Public-Sector Ethics Act of 1994 (Mackenroth 2004). Bishop and Preston show that requiring high standards of moral conduct by all public officials to be included in all decision-making processes does not come without a price, as it may raise complexity and slow down the procedures. There is, however, a compensating effect that comes with the advent of e-government, where Australia has become one of the leaders internationally (Guo and Lu 2004).[1]

The confidence deficit may partly be due to moral dilemmas created for public servants, because the complexity of their duties may sometimes dictate contradictory actions. Moral imperatives for public service are very wide: "Not doing harm, easing or reducing injury, accounting for stakes and stakeholders, and taking care of the dependent and vulnerable" (Office of Government Ethics 1992, p. 5). As harm and injury claimed by one party to a dispute that a public authority has to settle may be completely the contrary from another stakeholder's perspective, the public officer's decision will necessarily disappoint one of them. This is just one type of quandary; public service encounters quite a few of them. It has been said that this is the fate of public servants since they have to deal with a society with unresolved value conflicts and moral ambivalence and they are "pulled this way and that in a 'dilemmatic space' of its own" (Hoggett 2005, p. 183).

The quandaries encountered by public service officials in fulfilling their wide-cast moral imperatives – their ethical dilemmas – may not be visible to a citizen or a business firm. What they notice are outcomes; they cannot see that the public official has to weigh care versus justice, individual claims versus the greater good, or consistency versus responsiveness. As with many issues in public administration, improvements in the dialogue with their counterparts would help the officials to acquire a better reputation. On the other hand, there is no way out of the twofold nature of public administration: it needs to restrict businesses (and citizens) through regulation that follows societal needs – for example, preventing practices that threaten health and asking for contribution to the maintenance of infrastructure. But, at the same time, the role of public administration is to enable business (and private) activities: markets can only function if they follow basic rules established by public authorities. It is from both aspects that ethical issues arise in the relationship between the public sector and businesses.

When government acts as a trustee of society (as in its role of defining rules and regulations), the relation to business, in many democracies, includes the process of hearings and consultations in the pre-legislative phase. This ensures that constituencies that are affected by a regulation get a voice and are respected before the regulation is passed – and it should also ensure that those who are affected will abide by the rule. But government also has a relationship with the business sector where both partners are mutually dependent on each other beyond the regulatory. Businesses expect governments to provide a profitable and stable economic environment, and governments expect businesses to provide taxes, jobs and investment. Behavior of one party that contradicts the other party's expectation will produce damage; examples can be found in today's political dilemma of managing the proper procedure towards renewable energy, where the German chancellor lost some of her acceptance by corporate leaders, or in the never-ending debate about US health insurance reform. From the ethical point of view, this context raises two questions: (1) Is it legitimate that business influences politicians (e.g., the broad-ranging lobbyism in the US)? (2) As the public sector is accountable to all members of society, to what extent must a government base its decision-making on both the common good and the long-term prospects for an industry, when both are impacted by rapid changes of policies (e.g., the brisk turn to heavily subsidized wind and solar energy in Germany)?

The main concern raised by the non-business sector in all countries of the world is the way in which business influences government through lobbying, as it is mostly private (no transparent public discussion) and uses direct access (no intermediation through corporative associations). Despite lobbying's historical identification with the corruption of governmental processes, even the fiercest critics admit that it would be almost impossible to conduct public affairs without lobbyists (Fernandes 2009). From the practical side, lobbyists provide information to officials that they could not otherwise obtain; they bring and explain argumentation and they assist in identifying the consequences of proposed government action. Not only is it practical, in avoiding a bureaucratic apparatus to get that same information, but argumentation and advice also save taxpayers money. But lobbyists and lobbying are difficult to control.

From an ethical perspective, one would have to distinguish "good lobbying" from "bad lobbying." The Woodstock Theological Center's report on *The Ethics of Lobbying* has issued several principles, of which the first one is that " the pursuit of lobbying must take into account the common good, not merely a particular client's interest narrowly considered" (Woodstock Theological Center 2002, p. 84). But anyone who has ever acted as a lobbyist or has dealt with a lobbyist will agree that it is the common good (however defined) on which parties to a negotiation on a business or a public project would come to terms. While well intended, this principle will not deter the malevolent nor will it be able to monitor lobbying processes. There are approaches that serve the case a little better – morality, here, would need to be supported by laws.

A first legal device to control lobbyism at the federal level in the US was the Lobbying Disclosure Act of 1995, afterwards amended by the Honest Leadership and Open Government Act of 2007. And on January 21, 2009, President Barack Obama issued an Executive Order denying lobbyists employment in his administration. At the state level, there are laws and regulations covering everything from disclosure and reporting requirements to activities and conduct, and several jurisdictions have specific ethical guidelines and prohibitions on certain interactions between lobbyists and government employees (Rosenthal 2001). In the European Union there is no uniform regulation because every member nation has long-standing regulations for the relations between state and society. The original attempt by the European Commission was the issuance of a voluntary and self-regulatory code of conduct in 1992. The code set minimum standards only, as the Commission invited lobbyists to adopt their own codes on this basis. Only a few responded, with the most prominent being the code adopted by the Society of European Affairs Professionals (SEPA), of which the basic principles are as follows (Society of European Affairs Professionals 2007):

In their dealings with the EU Institutions, European Affairs Professionals shall:

- State their identity (name and organization);
- Declare the interest represented;
- Neither intentionally misrepresent their status for the nature of their inquiries to officials of the EU Institutions nor create any false impression in relation thereto;
- Honor confidential information and embargoes;
- Not disseminate false or misleading information knowingly or recklessly and exercise proper care to avoid doing so inadvertently;
- Not sell for profit to third parties copies of documents obtained from EU Institutions;
- Not obtain any information from European Institutions by illicit or dishonest means;
- Avoid any professional conflicts of interests;
- Neither directly nor indirectly offer nor give any financial inducement to any EU official, nor any member of the European Parliament, nor their staff;
- Not exert any improper influence on public servants;
- Only employ EU personnel subject to the rules, and registration and confidentiality requirements of the EU Institutions.

Even though the SEPA code is drafted in general terms, the strict self-discipline which it demands and its internal sanction mechanisms fulfill the major purpose of providing transparency (Coen and Richardson 2009).

The Commission, dissatisfied with the low response to the call for voluntary obligation, launched a Green Paper on a European Transparency Initiative in 2006, with the process of delivering a pertinent EU Directive still going on. For their part, a coalition of CSOs grouped under the ALTER-EU alliance (Alliance for Lobby Transparency and Ethics Regulation) has signaled its readiness to apply a code of ethics applicable to all lobbyists across the board, including its members; it also calls for mandatory registration. Registration is already in force in the European Parliament, which has an accreditation system for all persons needing frequent access to this institution. The system regulates physical access to the Parliament. The quaestors issue special passes that are valid for one year, stating the holder's name, the name of the firm that employs the holder and the organization the holder represents. A register of accredited lobbyists is published on the Parliament's website.

Ethical considerations of lobbyism must have in mind that effective lobbyists are experts who are well versed in the legislative process and have political acumen that enables them to identify opposition coalitions and sources of support. They will apply these skills to achieve favorable results for their clients. This capability and competency must be met by the counterparts in the legislature and the public administration, and it is there where efforts also have to be made to educate office holders.

To end this section on ethical issues in public institutions, a quick look will be taken at a study carried out on Regulating Conflicts of Interest for Holders of Public Office in the European Union (Demmke et al. 2007), concurring with the subject just discussed. The study shows that reform processes are under way internationally that lead to new perceptions and procedural innovations in conflict of interest situations for public office holders. The trend is moving towards more disclosure requirements in registers and the setting up of new independent ethics committees and other monitoring bodies. However, the authors are afraid that there may still be an ethical deficit. As one single violation by only one public office holder may be sufficient to cast public doubt on the integrity of the whole class of office holders and the whole institution, public office holders must constantly be reminded of their specific public responsibility. And the authors continue:

> The adoption of more rules and standards require that more concentration should be given to implementation issues. The more rules exist, the more management capacity is required to implement these rules and standards. Here, new paradoxes are about to emerge. Whereas individual requirements in fulfilling new obligations (mainly in the field of disclosure policies) are increasing, in many cases control and monitoring bodies (e.g., ethics committees) are still weak and lack resources.
>
> (Demmke et al. 2007, p. 8)

They also state that uniformity throughout the whole of the EU is not a means to achieve the goal, and they recommend that ethics regimes be carefully designed to fit the relevant institutional system, its structures, processes, resources, culture and tradition.

As per Demmke et al.'s report, it is implementation and taking account of cultural differences that will fulfill the requirements for and the expectations on human centered management. This also applies to the business sector, as will be set out in the next chapter.

Note

1 Discussing the ethical challenge of electronic procedures in government and business lies beyond the scope of this book. It is covered in a wide array of publications on information ethics. See, e.g., Quinn, M.J. (2014). *Ethics for the information age*. Upper Saddle River, NJ: Pearson.

Chapter 6

Implementing human centered management

The ethical, social, economic and institutional perspectives presented in Chapters 2–5 are the essential dimensions of both a conceptual framework for business ethics and the practice of human centered management. And so is the holistic interrelatedness of the perspectives. These perspectives and their interrelationship are a concept that is likely to appeal to practitioners. But the real test is the implementation of a concept. Even if a concept is understood and accepted, there are often difficulties in implementing it properly, in a sustained manner and for a wide scope of activities and geographical distribution. The effort to implement the concept of human centered management may get caught up in *situational ethics* – a propensity to take the particular context of an act into account when evaluating it ethically, rather than judging it according to absolute moral standards. And even though a leader might know what is right in a given situation, he or she might not know how to do what is right. The following three major problems of implementation will mostly be found, irrespective of the context, be it a small business, a large corporation, a civil society organization (CSO) or a government entity:

One problem is the limitation of knowledge: which approach would be valid for which situation? Whichever the context, situations are almost always complex and do not permit facile answers.

Another problem is the inability to produce the desired results, and results that are easily visible. The outcome of an act cannot be predicted at all times; people's expectations of a given act are not all the same, and people have different skills in making things happen. As the U.S. politician and economist Jack N. Behrman said: "To *do* good is different from *trying* to do good and from *expecting* or hoping to do good. Remember Don Quixote!" (Behrman 1981, p. 64).

Third is the problem of timeliness. There is no opportunity to experiment – in most situations a leader has one chance only. It very rarely happens that one will face exactly the same situation twice.

Contextualism (assessing situations from the context in which an act occurs, hence it is also called situationism) may lead to wrong judgments. This comes to the fore when implementing ethical concepts. This chapter will deal with the dilemmas that arise from placing too much emphasis on context. Also, situational ethics is sometimes considered to be the belief that "what is wrong in most situations might be considered right or acceptable if the end is defined as appropriate" (LaBeff et al. 1990, p. 191). But, rather, it is about accepting norms that are contextually grounded and for which the common view among a specific reference group has to be discovered. This would apply to the context of political culture referred to in the previous chapter with regard to diverse nature of public office in different countries or to specific business contexts such as an investment project in a foreign market.

A good example of conflicting views on what is right or wrong in a specific situation is given by Puffer and McCarthy (1995), who portray the dilemma faced by the senior American involved in Ben & Jerry's Homemade, Inc.'s ice cream operations in the Karelia region of western Russia. When the senior Russian partner began to "borrow" company materials and equipment for use in his other businesses, the American was dismayed and viewed such behavior as unethical. The Russian manager, however, felt that this was a very reasonable way to utilize the equipment since he was a co-owner of the company.

One way out of the dilemma would be for the two partners to define what moral values they share.

In this chapter of the book, the issue of common values will be discussed first, leading to the topic of ethics codes, then to the topic of corruption. This will be followed by recommendations on how to conduct stakeholder relations responsibly. Then, another chapter will look at the relations between a moral person, a moral leader and a moral organization.

Common values are what makes a society stick together. But with growing ethnic diversity, one may come to think that social cohesion may be threatened. However, as shown by the example of the US, an effective set of social relationships can successfully deal with diversity, rather than a situation necessarily characterized by homogeneity (Harell and Stolle 2010). The next section will exhibit how that can shape a consensus on values, and American values will serve as illustration. But there is also criticism: the United Nations Millennium Declaration, signed in September 2010, listed an expansive array of common universal values, including freedom, equality, solidarity, tolerance, respect for nature and shared responsibility, of which critics say that they were never held in common by all societies at any time in history (Bok 2002). Skepticism is surely needed. But even as hatred and violence are still flourishing in many parts of the world, there are also powerful movements that have arisen in response to these threats, both through governmental and non-governmental institutions and private individuals. Aid to developing countries, caring for refugees and the needy, humanitarian or philanthropic relief, protecting the environment, empowering the underserved — all of them have a human centered foundation. And the human centered paradigm is undoubtedly based on values and beliefs.

6.1 Arriving at a consensus on values

Defining what a business leader (or a leader in any institution) understands by ethical values will always be the beginning of his or her human centered management. One simple approach is to use ethical value synonymously with goodness or virtuous behavior. Another, more operational, approach would be the one used by the Global Ethics University (https://globalethicsuniversity. com), which lists and explains the properties required for moral conduct, such as Trustworthiness, Respect, Integrity, Fairness, Caring, Teamwork and Citizenship. "Value" and "virtue" are extremely broad terms, whatever the setting – business organizations, government authorities, non-profit institutions or the military. But there are common imperatives: any organization's core values would have to encompass all of the properties listed previously, and there are more that could be added, such as professionalism and stewardship.

The US National Defense University, in its briefing on "The Ethical Dimensions of National Security," lists four organizational values (loyalty, duty, selfless service and integrity) and four individual values (commitment, competence, candor and courage; Johns 1998). And in a book on ethical leadership for police officers, an ethical leader is defined as being one

> who possesses a philosophical moral foundation upon which decisions and behavior are based. An ethical leader is trustworthy and possesses good character, competence, and commitment. The ethical leader challenges the process, inspires shared vision, encourages and enables others, provides a model of appropriate behavior, and maintains accountability, personal perspective, and balance.
>
> (Meese and Ortmeier 2010, p. 22)

These types of catalogues can be found in relevant mission statements and guides to codes. As with institutions like the military or the police, businesses also have codified statements on their ethical values. We will turn to these ethics codes, as the first ingredient of human centered management in organizations, in the next section. First, we will inquire into the nature of values.

So what are values? Values define what is desirable or not and how one should behave in a given situation according to the rules of one's society. As stable basic traits close to an individual's personality, values play a part in the building of motives that result in behavior. Once more, we are at a nexus between societal and individual reasoning. Consequently, values have been called the "central integrative concept that could bring all social sciences together" (Mahrt 2010, p. 25; see also Schwartz 1992, p. 68; Hitlin and Piliavin 2004), that is, psychology with its approaches to personalities and individual differences, studies of social learning and socialization, comparative studies of cultures, political disciplines and theories of human development.

In addition to the comprehensive review of the sociological literature on individual behavior by Hitlin and Piliavin (2004), Kluckhohn also provided a seminal work (1951) and gave the following definition: a value is "a conception, explicit or implicit, distinctive of an individual or characteristic of a group, of the desirable which influences the selection from available modes, means, and ends of action" (p. 395). The reference to "a group" highlights that individual values are constituted through the imitation of and respect for rules of behavior and goods valued within a given society, and they are thus a product of culture. This has already been dealt with in section 3.5. With regard to the "culture" of capitalism, Porter and Kramer introduced "shared value" as a new conception of capitalism, claiming it as a powerful driver of economic growth and reconciliation between business and society (Kramer 2011).

If values are to be a guide to moral behavior for both an individual and a group, they need to be clearly defined and holistic. There has been a critical view on this since the negative view of Thomas Hobbes in the mid-17th century, when he theorized in *Leviathan* that "the same man, in diverse times, differs from himself, and at one time praises, that is, calls good, what another time he dispraises, and calls evil" (Narveson 2007, p. 10). Since then, however, societies have become more coherent, and while education was a privilege of the upper class in Hobbes's time, people of today have a different scope of knowledge.

Modern philosophers, of whom Jürgen Habermas is one of the better-known representatives, believe that (common) values can be defined through a rational debate and from deductive reasoning. While this *ethics of discourse* may differ from the instrumental rationality applied in the business world, there is *cognitive adequacy* in Habermas's reasoning (Fisher and Lovell 2003, p. 18), and it clearly emphasizes that the outcome intended with sincere discourse is consensus (Friberg-Fernros and Schaffer 2014). Shaping the internal culture of an organization needs discourse, and this is consistent with managerial purpose.

But is there such an archetype as "common values" throughout a modern society? If we take the heterogeneous pattern of beliefs and attitudes in the US, and if we take into account that people living in the US would consider that every individual is unique, one might think that the same list of values could never be applied to all, or even most, US citizens. But this looks very different from the outside, and Kohls (1984), in his seminal work for which he used studies over more than 30 years, devised a list of 13 commonly shared American values, discussed in the following section.

6.1.1 Values of a society: the case of American values

The maxim followed by Kohls was that actions performed by Americans that might otherwise appear strange, confusing, or unbelievable when evaluated from the perspective of a foreigner would become much more understandable to him or her if judged from their beliefs – the beliefs by which they live their daily lives. The list enumerates 13 of them (Kohls 1984):

1   *Personal control over the environment* – Individuals in the US believe that first and foremost, each individual should look out for his or her self-interests by controlling nature and one's environment.
2   *Change* – In the US, change is associated with personal progress, improvement and growth.
3   *Time and its control* – Time is one of the most valued resources in the US; time is to be used wisely on productive tasks to improve one's personal achievement, status and esteem.
4   *Equality/egalitarianism* – Americans believe that "all people are created equally," and tend to disregard hierarchies in class and power.
5   *Individualism and privacy* – Individuality and uniqueness are valued above group cohesion. Moreover, privacy is desirable and not associated with isolation and loneliness.
6   *Self-help concept* – Sacrifice and hard work are highly valued in the US to attain personal success, as exemplified in the "self-made man/woman" ideal.
7   *Competition and free enterprise* – Americans are driven by competition rather than cooperation to achieve one's personal best.
8   *Future orientation* – Americans believe that they are in control of their future and work hard to better it.
9   *Action/work orientation* – Americans view action as superior to inaction, and value hard work over leisure because it produces greater personal success, material wealth and status.
10 *Informality* – Americans are comparatively casual in dress and speech.
11 *Directness, openness, and honesty* – One's personal opinions and feelings are more valued than others, and should be expressed with confidence and assertiveness in order to gain the respect of others.
12 *Practicality and efficiency* – Americans are philosophically pragmatic and industrious.
13 *Materialism/acquisitiveness* – Material possessions are valued as outward products of hard work and success.

All of these values are seen by Americans as very positive ones. This may be different in other parts of the world. Change (value 2) may be seen as negative, destructive and threatening (an example is Germany, where atomic energy is seen as evil; the German word *Angst* represents a feeling of powerlessness towards a phenomenon that is unknown). The problem with the values of a society, even in the globalized world of today, is that they are often considered with the negative or derogatory connotation that they might have for members of another society, based on their own experience and cultural identity. Leaders in a society must be aware not only of the values shared by their peers but also of the outside view on these values.

The values by which a society lives are the primary source of the attitudes its members display in the workplace. It is the workplace where people gain life experience – and, unfortunately, they also gain negative experiences. This is the reason researchers give for high levels of cynicism found in the workforce.

A study on the US by Mirvis and Kanter (1991) reviewing the results of national surveys about people's attitudes about life and their jobs bluntly concludes: "Loyalty and *esprit de corps* have given way to mistrust and looking out for oneself" (Mirvis and Kanter 1991, p. 45). Their list of answers respondents gave to questions about trust, fairness, fellow-feeling, community and time perspective is given in Exhibit 6.1.

We have seen many positive evolvements in the 25 years since the survey was undertaken, the internet being the foremost one, but there has also been an increase in mutual understanding between generations and across cultures. With the retirement of many Baby Boomers (born 1946–1964), the workplace is changing. Organizations are experiencing an influx of younger workers, many born after 1982 (and called, variously, Generation [or Gen] X, Y, or Z, Millennials, nGen, or GenMe; see Twenge 2006). Leaders who accept the challenge of these younger generations' expectations will be successful in recruiting retaining and motivating the members of this multi-generational workplace.

Several cross-sectional studies have been made, e.g., on US information technology workers, which found that GenX scored higher in job involvement and normative commitment to the organization than Boomers, and GenX and especially GenMe scored higher than Boomers in perceiving themselves as "ambitious and career-oriented and the degree to which they prefer to work to demanding goals and targets" (Twenge 2010, p. 201). So there is hope that the cynicism of the 1990s has been overcome. But there is still a major difference between enterprises and industries; in the opinion of the public, bankers are the least trusted and Silicon Valley technicians are the most trusted (Vranka and Houdek 2015). But we have to look inside the businesses.

6.1.2 Values of business and business enterprises

For a business context, we posit that values, as they are factors that guide action, must necessarily refer to (long-term) goals. And these would be economic goals in the end. Connecting values to goals might imply that values, like goals, can be measured quantitatively. If we take the example of "trust," an analysis carried out in 2011 by McEvily and Tortoriello shows that 129 different measures of trust have been attempted in theoretical and practical research, of which only 11 have been carefully developed and thoroughly validated. But there is no common platform, and this would apply to similar attempts for other value constituents. Nevertheless, the connecting of values to goals is highly rewarding as it signals an assessment of values according to their impact. Quantitative

	% agreeing/4 pt. scale		% agreeing/5 pt. scale
TRUST			
Most people will tell a lie if they can gain by it.	66%	I often doubt the truth of what management tells me.	41%
If you aren't careful, people will take advantage of you.	81%	Management will take advantage of you if you give them a chance.	49%
FAIRNESS			
A lot of people seem to get ahead even though they don't deserve it.	54%	Getting ahead in my company depends on who your friends are, not on how good a job you do.	27%
The best way to handle people is to tell them what they want to hear.	39%	Management of my company never lets employees know the real reason behind decisions that affect them.	39%
FELLOW-FEELING			
People pretend to care about one another more than they really do.	58%	Management in my company isn't interested in what the average employee thinks or feels.	47%
These days a person doesn't know whom he or she can count on.	59%	A lot of people in my company do just enough to get by.	56%
COMMUNITY			
An unselfish person is taken advantage of in today's world.	55%	In my experience, it doesn't pay to work extra hard for my company	26%
What I do or think doesn't really count for much.	26%	My job is not considered to be important by my employer.	18%
TIME PERSPECTIVE			
Nowadays, a person live for today and let tomorrow take care of itself.	46%	Management in my company is more interested in profits than in people.	36%

Exhibit 6.1 Americans' attitudes about life and work from a 1991 survey

Source: Adapted from Mirvis and Kanter (1991), p. 51

measures would rather serve to determine the outcome of means, through weighing their effectiveness and efficiency, and not of ends. Friendship, respect, reverence and diligence are not measurable numerically, but their impact on business relations, on performance and on fulfilling contracts can certainly be weighed. And that can also be said for any item in a list of values. We will use a list similar to that given by Global Ethics University, as laid out in section 6.1 (see Behrman 1981, p. 55), which embarks on

- What would be good to pursue in society: Justice, Charity, Stewardship, Equity, Status;
- What we should live by: Honesty, Reverence, Loyalty, Mercy, Truth, Trust, Prudence;
- What we should we employ in work: Efficiency, Diligence, Progress, Cleanliness, Orderliness.

The list shows that those values are not unidirectional, and they may conflict. Can one have mercy with justice? If justice is done, and society accepts this to be a goal, then mercy is not necessary, but it tempers justice. The example of "justice" shows that there is a sliding transition between a goal and a value: values are being exercised in achieving a goal. They are used as one moves towards a goal. Thus "ethics is values in action," as stated by Drucker in his book *Management* (1974, p. 456): "Morality does not mean preachments. Morality, to have any meaning at all, must be a principle of *action* . . . . It must be *practices*" (emphasis added).

A practice-orientation of business values can be found in the Baldrige Award criteria. The award, which has arguably become one of the most influential vehicles for creating quality awareness and a widely accepted model of performance excellence, was built upon a set of interrelated core values and concepts that exemplify beliefs and behaviors found in high-performing organizations (Criteria for Performance Excellence 2004). Based on these general criteria, a firm needs to choose the values that are appropriate for the practices and activities in its business environment and to build a guideline or code on that basis by which all managers and all employees have to abide. One firm might choose to confine this code of ethics, as it has come to be called, to basic values by, for example, just enumerating the principles of Covey's conception mentioned in section 2.1: security, guidance, wisdom and power (Covey 1989, p. 20).

Other value systems that organizations might have a source in faith, for example, the Ledesma-Kolvenbach model, a humanistic management framework proposed by Jesuit business schools that commits to four main dimensions: utility, justice, humanism and dignity (Aguado and Albareda 2016). Peter-Hans Kolvenbach (1928–2016), who was Superior General of the Society of Jesus (SJ) between 1983 and 2008, referred to Diego de Ledesma, the 16th-century rector of what is now the *Pontificia Universitas Gregoriana* in Rome. Ledesma's four dimensions may be taken from faith, but they are valid in any secular environment as well. Another example for the secular contextualization of spiritual values is the writings of Raymond Charles Baumhart, SJ, who served as the president of Loyola University, Chicago, from 1970 to 1993 and who was one of the first to publish on ethics in business (Baumhart 1962). Baumhart was ordained a priest in 1957 after many years of studies in theology and philosophy, and then earned a doctorate in business administration at Harvard. He indicated that top management in order to set the tone for ethical behavior must have value systems, of which the foremost feature is the appreciation of human dignity (McMahon 2004).

A reference to human dignity can be found in many nations' constitutional groundwork, like, e.g., the German *Grundgesetz* (Basic Law for the Federal Republic of Germany) where Article 1.1 states: "Human dignity shall be inviolable. To respect and protect it shall be the duty of all state authority." But a primordial source of what human dignity concerns has been and will always be Christian faith. When Pope John Paul II issued his encyclical *Centesimus Annus* in 1991 (which bears this name for the hundredth anniversary of his predecessor Pope Leo XII's encyclical *Rerum Novarum*), while acknowledging the legitimate role of profit because profit "means that productive factors have been properly employed and corresponding human needs have been duly satisfied," he spelled out the warning that it is possible for the financial accounts to be in order, and yet for the people – who make up the firm's most valuable asset – to be humiliated and their dignity offended. Besides being morally inadmissible, this will eventually have negative repercussions on the firm's economic efficiency . . . and human and moral factors are at least equally important for the life of a business.

(Pope John Paul II 1991, para. 35)

Last but not least, the adoption of a set of commonly shared values needs to appeal to sentiment as well as to reason. Leaders must understand human nature and attitudes towards values. There are always attitudes that are explained by drivers other than, or in addition to, economic rationality, and leaders should be able to recognize them. The issues to explore in this context cover the role of emotions, instincts and human bonds in personal and collective behavior. As quality of life depends on emotional as well as material rewards, the pursuit of emotional rewards also boosts material rewards – as in highly motivated teams.

It is a characteristic of moral leaders that they arouse an emotional response in their followers. The followers are enthused, and by assessing their own emotional response to the vision they can assess the magnitude of the emotional rewards that they will obtain. And it works the other way as well: in a high-trust society, there are significant emotional penalties for breaking commitments – disloyalty and lack of perseverance bring guilt and shame (Casson 2006).

The reference to aspects other than intellectual reasoning for value propositions is not new. In his *Pensées*, the French mathematician, physicist and philosopher Blaise Pascal (1623–62) says: "*Le coeur a ses raisons que la raison ne connaît point*" ("The heart has its reasons of which reason knows not"; Pascal 1670/1966. This line draws a wise distinction between intellectual inquiry and cognition that has its roots somewhere else. We do not know for sure why we become ethical – the motivations may be rational, they may be based on faith, and they may be grounded in emotion. With regard to business ethics, there is a growing insight that both rationality and emotion are of relevance for moral reasoning, and combining reason and emotion in business ethics is considered a basic necessity, for example, by Buchholz and Rosenthal (2005) and Homann (2015, 2016).

It is not that emotion has been ignored in business ethics when it comes to value systems, but it routinely is subordinating emotion to reason. However, the role of emotions for societal and institutional relations has been well acknowledged in contemporary business literature. For example, Voronov and Weber (2016, p. 456) postulate that emotions "are the way through which people experience institutions as real and personally meaningful and a way by which they can connect institutions to their sense of self." But while this is a very useful sociological concept, it does not really connect to business ethics. There are two attempts to bridge this gap: a philosophical one and a physiological one. Both prove that emotion is no less important for decision-making and thus for (moral) performance than reason.

One philosophical approach is ascribed to Bauman, who challenges the reduction of business ethics to an element of a formally rational discipline. Bauman's *Postmodern Ethics* (1993) can be seen as a severe critique of the assumption that the formulation of rules, codes and so forth is all that is needed to ensure moral behavior. His notion of the *moral impulse* or *moral drive* claims that this (emotional) impulse or drive may induce unpredictable behavior because it is not regulated by social convention. From there, Bauman concludes that even if society cannot override this emotional impulse, it can silence it, but it can and must harness and exploit it rather than merely suppress or outlaw it (ten Bos and Willmott 2001). It is nothing out of the ordinary that emotions need to be contained (children learn this in kindergarten), but this containment should never be used to eradicate all empathy in societal life and in business life, as Bauman suggests, to rule out business morality through "calculation" (Bauman 1993, p. 57) and to use "organization" as an impediment to morality (1993, p. 55).

Followers of Bauman have mitigated the argument by bridging the opposition between emotional receptivity or lived experience, on the one hand, and ethics as active reason or universalizable duty, on the other, through a conception of (business) ethics as a process of struggle in which emotions that reflect upon conduct can facilitate a process of moral learning (Holian 2006). But it seems that this construction of an opposition between emotions and intellectual reasoning does not lead any further. There is no opposition, not even dualism, but holism, as demonstrated by the physiological approach.

The physiological approach is based on the results of neuroscientific and brain research. Each individual, it states, is a holistic entity, including his or her spiritual and moral skills. There are always several regions of the brain that are simultaneously active. One is the mesolimbic level, which is the center of subconscious emotional conditioning. This is the seat of emotions such as fear, anxiety, pleasure and joy. The mesolimbic system has been implicated in incentive reward motivation, remaining selfish and self-centered throughout life. Its subconscious question is "What do I get?" (Davidson and Irwin 1999, using this question as a book title). By contrast, the upper limbic levels develop cognition, with the inner part in control of social behavior, empathy, cooperation, social and moral standards and assessment of the consequences of one's own actions, that is, the conscious emotional life, and the outer part controlling memory, intellect, rational reasoning, and language and communication skills.

Brain sections interact all the time, and therefore subconscious emotional motives and conscious objectives will always determine decisions (including decisions about which value system to adopt). What counts is how the brain (in total) assesses the benefits of the decision, and one important ingredient is if reward experience (from a value system) justifies expectation of future rewards. Therefore, any leaders who want their personal value system to be shared by their followers at least partly will connect it to reward (Homann (2015). One good example is the value of efficiency, which will be contrasted with the values of integrity in the next section. Efficiency can be coupled easily with rewards, but can integrity?

6.1.3 Two prominent values exemplified: integrity and efficiency

Integrity is one of the values that is fundamental in organizational life and in executive decision-making. The definition of integrity is broad: Adler and Bird (1988) link integrity with emphasis on congruence, consistency, morality, universality and concern for others. Covey (1992) describes integrity as honesty, matching words and feelings with thoughts and actions for the good of others. Srivastva and Cooperrider (1988) highlight a way forward that is very wide-ranging: "Executive integrity is dialogical. Executive integrity is more than the presence of morality or the appropriation of values: integrity involves the process of seeing or creating values . . . [it] represents the 'insightful assent' to the construction of human values" (p. 7).

Integrity, in the comprehensive meaning that encompasses dialogue and reflection, will transform the mere interaction between leaders and followers into participation, communication and mutual empathy. A leader who displays moral integrity and performs accordingly will motivate the organization to achieve its objectives. When a leader's integrity is in doubt, then all attempts by the leader to influence followers – however noble, well crafted and articulate – will fail.

Discourse about integrity involves two fundamental intuitions: first, integrity is equal to acting morally, and second, integrity is a formal relation one has to oneself or between parts or aspects of one's self (Cox, La Caze, and Levine 2005). So for leaders to gain legitimacy and credibility from their followers they must not only tell the truth, keep promises, distribute to each follower what is due and employ valid incentives and sanctions, they must also integrate various parts of their personality into a harmonious, intact whole. Integrity, then, is a matter of keeping one's self intact and uncorrupted. This is a very human aspect; therefore, for a good explanation we can turn to moral philosophy, in particular, Henry Frankfurt.

According to Frankfurt, as every individual is subject to many conflicting desires, if one simply acts at each moment out of the strongest current desire, with no deliberation or discrimination between more or less worthwhile desires, then one clearly acts without integrity. Integrity, thus, is bringing the various levels of desire into harmony and fully identifying with them. Having integrity, then, is equal to being and acting without ambivalence (that is, based on unresolved desires for a thing and against it) or inconsistency (that is, unresolved desire for incompatible things). Frankfurt calls this "wholeheartedness" (Frankfurt 1987).

And how about rewards for integrity? Leviton and Bass (2004, pp. 10–11) present a case from the academic world that speaks for itself:

> In the 1980s, a large foundation created a national initiative that, over time, proved to be fatally flawed. A university-based evaluation team was hired at the outset of the program. Their report concluded that the program had no discernible effects and pointed to some very cogent and constructive reasons for the lack of effect. The foundation had sought a highly placed, politically powerful advisory committee for the initiative. According to several parties, the chair of the committee threatened the evaluation team with political consequences if they released their conclusions. One member of the evaluation team was coming up for tenure. The evaluation team defied the national advisory committee, presented the foundation with their original conclusions, and subsequently published their findings. There is some reason to believe, however, that the evaluation team may have lost a book contract due to political pressure on reviewers.
>
> From the foundation's perspective, however, the committee's threat boomeranged. Far from having its intended effect, the threat against the evaluation team enhanced the team's credit in the foundation's eyes. The

foundation officers, already unhappy with the way the program was going, knew they could trust these evaluators to tell the truth, courageously. Over the next decade, the foundation entrusted several other major evaluations to this team. The untenured evaluator received tenure, became a trusted foundation consultant, and eventually directed a prestigious fellowship program funded by the foundation.

Integrity, as the example shows, pays off!

With regard to efficiency, what first comes up is the question of why this is a moral value. It is not helpful to simply define efficiency as the least costly input for arriving at a given output (which output is sometimes described, mistakenly, to be the maximum possible: you can only have either minimum input for a given output or maximum output with a given input). But from the outset, what makes a person or an organization efficient includes thoughtfulness and productivity; avoiding mistakes or, if they occur, recognizing and learning from them; and watching for signs of stress and taking timely measures to right the balance. In essence, it is about reaching one's full potential.

There are authors who closely link ethics and efficiency, either from the viewpoint of new institutional economics, emphasizing social arrangements that improve efficiency (van de Klundert 1999); or from the discussion on shareholder primacy, the view that managers' fiduciary duties require them to maximize the shareholders' wealth and preclude them from giving independent consideration to the interests of other constituencies (Lee 2006); or from public service accountabilities (Wolf 2000); or from the general standpoint that fair dealing of firms with their constituencies is the essence of business efficiency (Chorafas 2015). The overarching idea is that doing good requires the full effort of a person and that taking on accountability always rests on producing the best possible outcome.

Efficiency encompasses a creative attitude towards failure. Failure is intrinsic to being human, and leaders must think about failure the right way. They must accept that people commit errors, and they should take advantage of experiences with errors. But they should not believe that learning from failure is simple and straightforward. It does not suffice to ask people to reflect on what they did wrong and exhort them to avoid similar mistakes in the future or to assign a team to review and write a report on what happened and then make it public. Effectively detecting and analyzing failure requires specific attitudes and activities. Harvard professor Amy E. Edmondson states, "The wisdom of learning from failure is incontrovertible. Yet organizations that do it well are extraordinarily rare" (Edmondson 2011). She provides a practical categorization of failures and good guidance on how to make it safe to speak up, which she calls "blameless reporting," and how leaders can set boundaries that make good use of the evidence, and also determine where the limits are.

Sometimes, a failure detection and analysis strategy works indeed. Procter & Gamble, when holding performance review meetings, encourages the participants to talk about their failures and how they were overcome; Eli Lilly has "failure parties"; and Tata awards an annual prize for the best failed idea (see Cannon and Edmondson 2005).

The opposite of efficiency, from a moral standpoint, is deliberate indifference. It is well known that doing nothing impacts performance, and it is a leader's reaction that changes lack of action. "Doing nothing does something" (von Bergen and Bressler 2014), and if leaders do not respond to undesirable employee performance, future behavior will change for the worse. Just as some managers seem incapable of expressing their appreciation to employees who perform well, some hesitate to challenge employees needing corrective counseling. Both practices can substantially hurt a firm or any other organization; they provoke heavy moral damage. It may lead employees to believe their performance is acceptable, and if a leader neglects deliberate indifference he or she will lose credibility with followers. Deliberate indifference is often ignored in procedural manuals or in ethics codes. In this area, businesses can learn from law enforcement practice or clinical treatment practice, where the term is explicitly used in codes and regulations.

6.2 Ethics codes

There are strong advantages to having a formal ethics code and many organizations have had them for decades. The counterargument is that the promulgation of a code seems a trivial approach because one should expect people to be responsible for themselves. But as we have seen when discussing the "moral manager–moral market" juxtaposition, it is the lack of personal responsibility, for oneself and for one's relationship to others, that constitutes the need for codes. "Human centered" must encompass not just the bright side of human character and human relations; there is, unfortunately, a dark side, too. There is always, to say the least, a willingness to deceive or lie if this provides a personal benefit; in the business world, this would be reinforced by deception in advertising and misrepresentation of product qualities, of which the Volkswagen emissions scandal is the most recent and probably the most far-reaching example (EPA 2015).

Volkswagen not only has an ethics code, but the company is also a signatory of various voluntary commitments such as the Forum for Sustainable Development of German Business (http://econsense.de/en), the German Code of Corporate Governance (www.dcgk.de/en/home.html) and the Wittenberg Center Code of Responsible Conduct for Business (http://wcge.org/html/en/529.htm). So is Volkswagen's ethics code just a piece of paper? And how about the ethics of the company's engineering and manufacturing professionals?

While the ethics of a profession are best understood not by examining the worst conduct of its members but by attending to the conduct that is commonly expected and generally found, the opposite approach shall be used here, because the Volkswagen scandal provides a striking example of what happens if the human centered paradigm is inexcusably neglected in a business. There was certainly a "human factor": in any engineering team, there are members who uphold moral standards, and there will have been such people in the engineering teams that developed a device that cheated emissions tests to be installed in Volkswagen's diesel cars. But their voice was obviously suppressed.

It will never become public which was a specific "command line" at Volkswagen that motivated the installation of a cheating device, but at least some revelations may come out, as various executives have been and are going to be charged in the US and elsewhere for giving false statements (see, e.g., Reitze 2016). One general motive can certainly be found in the corporatist approach to governance in Germany with its far-reaching co-determination. It is only from the outside that one is led to believe that co-determination places an emphasis on the interests of individual employees and gives them a voice; in fact, the co-determination approach to a large extent serves the interest of employee representatives. With decision-making tightly ruled by far-reaching agreements between these representatives and the employer, the individual and his or her argumentation are likely to be overlooked (Elson, Ferrere, and Goossen 2015). A brief discussion on the pros and cons of co-determination will be held in section 7.1. Here we first look at professional ethics codes and then at those of enterprises and institutions.

6.2.1 Professional ethics codes

Any profession, from the tradespeople on building sites to high-tech surgery and sophisticated legal advice, provides a service to people. In providing services to others, the foremost question is "What are my responsibilities to others?" The internalization of responsibility to others also extends to observing the professional conduct of other professionals, and it will encourage conduct that both reflects the ideals and core principles of the profession and truthfully reports misconduct.

Professional ethics, as opposed to personal, sets the standards for practice, and it should be an essential part of professional education because it helps to deal with issues that practitioners will face in professional practice.

There are numerous calls for ethical conduct in the financial profession, for which the reader is referred to John R. Boatright's seminal publication *Ethics in Finance* (Boatright 2013). It would be redundant to repeat all this here, and because there has so much been written about misconduct in the financial sector, we would rather choose examples in other professions. They are engineering and public relations. The engineering profession's emphasis on ethics dates back to the 19th century when large-scale production raised awareness of increased responsibility to the general public. In 1946, the US National Society of Professional Engineers (NSPE) released its Canons of Ethics for Engineers and Rules of Professional Conduct, which evolved to the current Code of Ethics, adopted in 1964 (www.nspe.org/resources/ethics/code-ethics). The code's

"Fundamental Canons" read as follows (National Society of Professional Engineers 1993, p. 14):

> Engineers, in the fulfillment of their professional duties, shall:
>
> 1   Hold paramount the safety, health, and welfare of the public.
> 2   Perform services only in areas of their competence.
> 3   Issue public statements only in an objective and truthful manner.
> 4   Act for each employer or client as faithful agents or trustees.
> 5   Avoid deceptive acts.
> 6   Conduct themselves honorably, responsibly, ethically, and lawfully so as to enhance the honor, reputation, and usefulness of the profession.

This introductory statement is followed by a set of rules for practical application, then the code spells out the obligations of an engineer, with explicit encouragement to adhere to the principles of sustainable development; it ends with a note on the human perspective:

> In regard to the question of application of the Code to corporations *vis-à-vis* real persons, business form or type should not negate nor influence conformance of individuals to the Code. The Code deals with professional services, which services must be performed by real persons. Real persons in turn establish and implement policies within business structures.
>
> (National Society of Professional Engineers 1993, p. 15)

The NSPE has established a Board of Ethical Review that serves as the profession's guide through ethical dilemmas. Its purpose is to render impartial opinions pertaining to the interpretation of the NSPE Code of Ethics, develop materials and conduct studies relating to ethics of the engineering profession.

The other example is the Professional Charter of the UK Public Relations Consultants Association, which sets honesty, safeguarding of confidences of clients and prohibition of conflicts of interest of competing clients at the forefront. While the charter points out that the professional should act in the interests of a client by any means, it also points to the risk of resorting to financial inducements and prohibits the offer of these inducements to persons holding public office. It sets rules about conduct towards the public, the media and colleagues in the profession. Like the engineering profession, public relations consultants also have an Arbitration and Disciplinary Procedure and a Professional Practices Committee (see www.prca.org.uk/about-us/pr-standards/professional-chartr-and-codes-conduct).

6.2.2 Corporate ethics codes

Voluntarily adopted corporate codes of ethics have existed for decades in the US, in Europe and in most countries which adhere to the OECD Guidelines for Multinational Enterprises (www.oecd.org/corporate/mne), which may also be deemed an ethics code. Historically, a new wave of code writing developed in response to highly publicized scandals and major legal developments in the US such as the Sarbanes-Oxley Act 2002 (see section 6.3). This is from where the major criticism comes, which sometimes says they only ask for cosmetic compliance and are just a reaction to public pressure (Krawiec 2003).

Madsen and Shafritz (1990, pp. 219–220) have categorized the subject content of corporate ethics codes in clusters. They are:

Cluster I: 'Be a dependable organization citizen.'

#1– Demonstrate courtesy, respect, honesty, and fairness in relationships with customers, suppliers, competitors, and other employees.

#2– Comply with safety, health, and security regulations.

#3– Do not use abusive language or actions.

#4– Dress in business-like attire.

#5– Possession of firearms on company premises is prohibited.

#6– Use of illegal drugs or alcohol on company premises is prohibited.

#7– Follow directives from supervisors.

#8– Be reliable in attendance and punctuality.

#9– Manage personal finances in a manner consistent with employment by a fiduciary institution.

Cluster II: 'Don't do anything unlawful or improper that will harm the organization.'

#1– Maintain utmost scrutiny with regard to records and information.

#2– Avoid outside activities which conflict with or impair the performance of duties.

#3– Make decisions objectively without regard to friendship or personal gain.

#4– The acceptance of any form of bribe is prohibited.

#5– Payment to any person, business, political organization, or public official for unlawful or unauthorized purposes is prohibited.

#6– Conduct personal and business dealings in compliance with all relevant laws, regulations, and policies.

#7– Comply fully with antitrust laws and trade regulations.

#8– Comply fully with accepted accounting rules and controls.

#9– Do not provide false or misleading information to the corporation, its auditors, or a government agency.

#10– Do not use company property or resources for personal benefit or any other improper purpose.

#11– Each employee is personally accountable for company funds over which he or she has control.

#12– Staff members should not have any interest in any competitor or supplier of the company unless such interest has been fully disclosed to the company.

Cluster III: 'Be good to our customers.'

#1– Strive to provide products and services of the highest quality.
#2– Perform assigned duties to the best of your ability and in the best interest of the corporation, its shareholders, and its customers.
#3– Convey true claims for products.

Un-clustered Items:

#1– Exhibit standards of personal integrity and professional conduct.
#2– Racial, ethnic, religious, or sexual harassment is prohibited.
#3– Report questionable, unethical, or illegal activities to your manager.
#4– Seek opportunities to participate in community services and political activities.
#5– Conserve resources and protect the quality of the environment in areas where the company operates.
#6– Members of the corporation are not to recommend attorneys, accountants, insurance agents, stockbrokers, real estate agents, or similar individuals to customers.

Madsen and Shafritz, like many others, are critical of the impact of ethics codes on important business decisions. And from the example of the Volkswagen emissions scandal, it might look as if they are right. But as said before, it is not the bad examples that should guide judgment. The business community worldwide has made great efforts since the 1990s not only to introduce codes but also to monitor and enforce compliance. Kaptein and Schwartz (2008) investigated the impact of codes on behavior, and they indicate that only 33% of the studies they surveyed yielded significant impact. While one study even finds that a code has a negative impact on behavior, the result, carefully worded, is that business professionals employed at firms with ethical codes of conduct are significantly less accepting of ethically questionable behavior (McKinney, Emerson, and Neubert 2010).

There is much more involved with ethics codes. One critical success factor is the process for launching a code. Compliance not only depends on the contents of the code, but it is also heavily influenced by the interaction of various stakeholders in its formulation and implementation: clear commitment by corporate leaders and managers at all levels, participation by employee representatives and advice by legal professionals. Beyond the content of the code, corporate leaders need to specify the purpose, objectives and procedures as well. If the processes of setting up, disseminating and administering such a code are carefully conducted, the result is a "Living Code" (Kaptein 2008).

Making an ethics code work often also depends on a good compliance officer. Organizations often locate this function within the legal department, although the core activities of the officer are separate from legal compliance. The officer's responsibility is certainly related to legislation, but the main duties revolve around devising and implementing voluntary codes, policies and a workplace culture that inform employees of the law and their organization's position in relation to the legislation. In the US, an Ethics & Compliance Officer Association (ECOA) was founded in 1992 to represent the interests of this profession. It is estimated 85% of the Fortune 500 companies had officers who joined ECOA by 2010 (Chandler 2011).

In addition to US-based organizations, members of ECOA are based in Belgium, Canada, Germany, Greece, Hong Kong, India, Japan, the Netherlands, Switzerland and the UK. ECOA publishes a National Business Ethics Survey each second year, which contains a measurement of program effectiveness of ethics codes based on the following indicators, which are taken from employee surveys (Lawney and Brooks 2015):

- Supervisor provides positive feedback
- Can approach management without fear of retaliation
- Prepared to handle moral dilemmas
- Company gives recognition for following ethics standards
- Company does not reward questionable practices.

One interesting result shown in the 2013 survey is given in Table 6.1.

The four outcome improvements that are listed in Table 6.1 are attributed, according to the survey, to the effectiveness of the ethics program established in an institution through a code and a compliance officer on the one hand, and through the cultural coherence within the institution on the other. The column

Table 6.1 Ethics program outcomes

Ethics outcomes	Percentage point (ppt) improvement when . . .	
	. . . program is effective	. . . culture is strong
Felt pressure to compromise standards	−20 ppts	−36 ppts
Observed misconduct in previous 12 months	−29 ppts	−47 ppts
Reported misconduct when observed	+55 ppts	+18 ppts
Reporters who experienced retaliation	−55 ppts	−50 ppts

Source: Adapted from Lawney and Brooks (2015)

at the far right indicates the effects attributed to cultural coherence, such as good working climate and transparency; the other column lists effects attributed to an effective compliance and ethics program. The percentage points specify the extent of improvements over the last survey; for example, the number of respondents from firms where corporate culture is strong and who said they felt pressure to compromise ethical standards went down by 36%; likewise, there were 20% fewer responses from firms with an effective ethics program on this issue.

Similar research is conducted by the British counterpart of the ECOA, the Institute of Business Ethics, with triennial surveys into employees' views of ethics at work in the UK. Its latest report indicates that employee awareness of corporate ethics programs raises moral consciousness and perceptions of morality in a firm's culture (Johnson 2015). But we also find the contrary: auditors Ernst & Young surveyed nearly 400 chief financial officers between November 2011 and February 2012 (Stucke 2013) with findings of which three are very disturbing (see Stucke 2013, p. 791):

- When presented with a list of possibly questionable actions that may help the business survive, 47% of CFOs felt one or more could be justified in an economic downturn.
- Worryingly, 15% of CFOs surveyed would be willing to make cash payments to win or retain business, and 4% view misstating a company's financial performance as justifiable to help a business survive.
- While 46% of total respondents agree that company management is likely to cut corners to meet targets, CFOs have an even more pessimistic view (52%).

One reason for the disparity between the employees' opinions on moral attitudes and the executives' statements on dubious activities may be that the view of employees is somehow biased from positive experiences, while, on the upper levels, as deplored by an article in the *Journal of Corporate Law* (Stucke 2013), many business executives take a "check the box" approach to their programs, rather than satisfying the full intent of the ethics code. But one cannot deny that there is much left to be done. Peter Drucker (1974, p. 325) once said that "the axe needs to fall quickly" when misconduct occurs in order to warn off other offenders. There is some hope, after the economic crisis, that leaders' ethical insight on their obligations and strict law enforcement will induce companies to boost moral behavior.

Apart from the public opinion on ethics codes, one critical view comes from agency theory: as even top managers serve as agents for the stockholders of a business, the ethics codes they design and to which all members of the firm need to adhere must be regarded as a duty of loyalty. And this is generally a negative duty, that is, the duty is defined by proscriptions on the agent's behavior which are designed to protect the principal's interests (Kurland 1995). A positive duty approach would be to commit to a higher level of moral reasoning. A common example of higher moral reasoning which transcends a corporate ethics code is that of Johnson & Johnson, which ranks responsibility to the community (of customers, the medical profession and patients) on equal terms with the responsibility to stockholders. During its handling of the criminal contamination of its highly profitable Tylenol capsules, instead of just seeking to prosecute the criminals and contain the actual damage, Johnson & Johnson placed public interest above self-interest and replaced all Tylenol capsules worldwide with caplets (Husted 2005; Shaw and Barry 1998).

Codes are, at any rate, voluntary agreements. They cannot substitute code law which is enforceable – even though moral appeal, voluntary commitment and ethical obligation may at times force execution of an inter-industry agreement as well. From the outside, this would be achieved by peer pressure; from the inside it is ethical obligation.

6.3 Ethical obligations and the law

Much of what needs to be said about ethical obligations and the law corresponds to the rationale of Plato, as quoted in Parsons (2004, p. 67): "Good people do not need laws to tell them to act responsibly, while bad people will find a way around the laws." Common values and a written agreement on which values to pursue and in what manner may suffice within a societal group that is self-sufficient and not connected to others. Historically, this is how prescriptive systems developed that addressed a tightly knit and closed society, such as the Ten Commandments for the biblical society of the Jews. Using another biblical theme, when the Jews came under the reign of the Roman Empire with its sophisticated legal system, adherence to the Ten Commandments and subsequent scriptures was no longer sufficient; Jewish society in interacting with all the other societies needed to abide by the Roman legal system, even though the biblical code required more of them than any reasonable body of laws. Legality and illegality came to be defined by criminal and civil law – as within the modern societies of today.

But ethics calls on us to do more than simply observe criminal or civil law and also to do more than just respect others' rights. Good and evil, legal and illegal are four categories that are both different from each other and overlapping. Four combinations can be formed:

1   Actions that are good and legal but not a legal obligation.

   An action, although it is good and legal, may still cause ethical concern because as it is not a legal requirement people do not take the action. An example is the widespread resistance against installing surveillance cameras in public areas.

2   Actions that are evil and illegal.

Often, an action that is both evil and illegal may not be placed by some people in this category. An example would be traffic offenses by cyclists being tolerated because "they are the weaker ones."

3   Actions that are legal but evil.

Many of the moral and ethical issues that affect business leaders fall into this category, from marketing methods that disguise product properties to accounting techniques that conceal losses that should be disclosed in a financial statement.

4   Actions that are good but illegal.

People, and leaders, are often placed in situations where they need to defy a legal rule. A recurring example in Europe is where asylum seekers who have been denied immigration status are hidden in churches or locations of charitable organizations.

But if moral appeal, voluntary commitment and promulgation of good practice do not achieve the objective, legal commitment must step in. Most pertinent is the US Sarbanes-Oxley Act (SOX) (2002), which aimed at cleaning up corporate corruption and improving corporate accountability and ethics. SOX grew from a collective frustration on the part of shareholders and the public in general on the lack of accountability and ethicality on the part of corporate leaders. At the heart of SOX are three main issues. First, the question of independent internal auditor functions. Second, punitive accountability for key executives, including financial and criminal consequences based on accuracy and moral behavior. Third, its extraordinarily detailed requirements on internal financial controls and demands that the controls be tested and validated with little tolerance.

SOX requires a public company to disclose whether it has adopted a code of ethics for the company's principal executive officer and senior financial officers. The act encourages – indeed, it mandates – that management power when it is inclined to bad behavior be challenged by the other professions, such as auditors and public relations officers, and by professional agencies. This may be perceived as public "whistle-blowing," but it is indeed a moral motivation; stories abound of Enron managers who recognized the ethical implications of Enron's financial practices but did not act to stop them. Recorded conversations revealed that some of Enron's employees and executives knew they were performing illegal and immoral acts, but they valued power, control or job security over ethics (Schminke, Arnaud, and Kuenzi 2007).

Placing job security above other values, in order to keep providing for one's family, to maintain one's livelihood and to support an acquired standard of living may be viewed as excusable when a person gets into a moral dilemma. The attitude is not outright immoral. But, hard as it may sound, a leader's obligation is to be fair to all sides – to all stakeholders of the organization. And it may often be that, from the outset, a first step is needed to free oneself from the dilemma. This may also be the case in the much worse temptation of corruption and free riding.

6.4 Fighting corruption and free riding

Corruption is utter disregard for morality. From whichever angle we look at corruption ("the misuse of public office for private gain" or "inducing a responsible office holder by monetary or other rewards to take actions which favor whoever provides the reward"), we end up with a person "perverting the judgment of another person who holds a position of trust to perverter" (Nye 2002, p. 966). This is at the individual level. At the societal level, corruption is an outcome of a country's legal, economic, cultural and political institutions. Corruption can be a response to non-existent, too benevolent or harmful rules (e.g., paying bribes to avoid penalties) or to inefficient institutions (e.g., paying bribes to get around a ruling). The majority of studies related to corruption cover this societal level. There is one level in between this macro-level and the business level, which is the meso-level of trade and industry associations with influence markets, cartels and business clans.

This book gives only a brief glance at the huge topic of corruption as an outcome of a country's legal, economic, cultural and political institutions. The best source to look at the topic is the annual Corruption Perceptions Index (CPI) produced by Transparency International (www.transparency.org). The survey obtains opinions from expert groups in 168 countries on how they perceive the status of the country they observe. Surveys of businesspeople and assessments by country analysts from independent institutions enter the CPI. All sources employ a homogeneous definition of "extent of corruption." The assessments are gathered from experienced respondents and give an understanding of real levels of corruption (Saisana and Saltelli 2012). The scores have been relatively stable throughout the years, with Scandinavia at the top with the least perceived corruption; Germany, Luxembourg and the UK sharing rank 10; and the US at rank 16. The lowest ranks are Sudan, North Korea and Somalia. Changes in the rankings are mostly due to improvements in the effectiveness of institutions in a given country.

Apart from publishing the annual Corruption Perceptions Index, Transparency International co-authors the Business Principles for Countering Bribery, for which it joined forces with Social Accountability International in 2003. Social Accountability International is a non-governmental organization that was set up in 1997 and whose mission is to advance the human rights of workers around the world. The Business Principles were developed with the cooperation of specialists from business, academia, trade unions and other non-governmental bodies. The Business Principles have influenced a wide range of anti-bribery standards and initiatives of governments and corporations (see www.transparency.org/whatwedo/publication/business_principles_for_countering_bribery).

Businesses have to tackle the issue of corrupt institutions whenever they approach countries with low moral standards, as mirrored in the Corruption Perceptions Index. Transparency International has earned its name here. Much less transparency is to be found at the meso-level: the terms "influence markets," "elite cartels," "oligarchs" and "clans," and "official moguls" may sound exotic, but we can find the influence of pressure groups and cartels in the US (associations of big industry), Japan (*keiretsu*), and Germany (together with corporatist structures where trade associations join forces with employers) and elite clusters of manufacturers in Italy and South Korea. This is a long way from blunt corruption, but there is a give-and-take mentality in all these. We find oligarchs and clans in Russia, the Philippines and Mexico, with attitudes often close to the immoral, and there are powerful moguls in Indonesia dominated by intensive integrated production combines, and close ties between makers and marketers, all fostered by a benevolent state policy (Gitlow 2005; Johnston 2014).

At the business level, firms in the US have often accused European tax authorities of not prosecuting bribery when it occurred outside their jurisdiction. Germany was the last country in Europe to remove this regulatory gap when it changed its tax code in 1996. The criticism was that this practice had favored some industries in corrupting a client's executives to become instrumental in selling a product or service. The US Foreign Corrupt Practices Act (FCPA), the UK Anti-Bribery Statute and the OECD Anti-Bribery Recommendation have all helped to prevent misconduct, but while until 1998 there were few prosecutions under the FCPA, prosecutions have increased many times over with a peak number of cases filed in 2007. There were 27 cases (16 against individuals) with many prominent firms in the roster, including Walmart, Halliburton, IBM, Johnson & Johnson, Daimler, Monsanto, BAE Systems, Avon, Alcatel-Lucent, General Electric, Chevron and Lockheed. The economic crisis of 2011 produced a growth in the list, and as of March 2012, 81 companies were under investigation. Generally, the offending companies tend to settle their cases by paying fines and implementing strong anti-bribery controls. The largest penalty was paid by Siemens for violating anti-bribery rules in the US and in its home country of Germany (Choudhary 2013). In 2016, the number of enforcement actions on the FCPA filed by the US Securities and Exchange Commission and the US Department of Justice was 54 (Stanford Law School 2017).

There is a problematic collateral effect of international anti-bribery legislation: in countries where bribery is perceived to be relatively common, the enforcement of this legislation ultimately deters investment and functions as de facto economic sanctions. This is contrary to the legislation's purpose, which is to build economic and political alliances by promoting ethical overseas investment. There are two formal responses that might possibly complement international anti-bribery norms without impeding economic development:

- One response is to extend the existing regulation that is focused on the supply side (seeking to punish the briber) to the demand side, which is the solicitation or receipt of bribes. Some accords in this direction have been ratified by the Organization of American States and the African Union (Spalding 2010).
- There is another avenue to avoid disproportionate punishment of bribery destroying growth opportunities in developing countries. This would mean repealing or at least mitigating the common law doctrine of *respondeat superior* ("May the supervisor answer"), by which employers are held liable for the conduct of their employees. US or European corporations with ventures in countries where bribery has long been regarded as a customary and even necessary way of doing business with a government will be penalized if a lower-level employee in such a country closes a deal by paying a bribe. This creates a risk that large international companies feel they cannot afford to take, and they withdraw from higher-risk markets where their investment would otherwise be beneficial to the underserved population (Cassin 2009). There is an imperative human perspective in this – again, a moral dilemma!

Corruption is the worst scenario of immorality in business. But it is only a small step to corruption from another immoral activity, and this is free riding (to which the term "free loading" is applied as well). Free riders accept the advantages of the cooperative behavior of others but fail to cooperate themselves. The immorality in this may be elucidated by a statement from moral philosopher John Rawls (see Bowie 1999, p. 18). Rawls sets out from considering that an individual who voluntary participates in a social institution would thereby accept its rules. Presumably, these rules work to the benefit of all participants – otherwise they would not voluntarily participate in this institution. Now, those who accept those benefits from others following the rules but do not play by the rules themselves are unfair. They do not make a contribution to the institution that relies on the contributions of those who participate.

The individual who makes profits by means that the community does not agree are acceptable destroys the business system – once more we see how the perspectives of morality, the social and economic spheres and the societal institutions are closely intertwined. The "agreement of the community" will not tolerate profit being made just for the sake of profit and free riders are profit seekers on their own, abusing the free market. But an agreement in the society is easily reached when profit is defined as the result, not the goal of economic activity. The goal is to provide value, and destroying the business system is destroying value.

Destroying a business system may start, on a person-to-person level, with the sharing of MP3 files. Are people who share music files on the internet acting like free riders? A defense might be that some downloaders do not have the means to buy some of the music they download, for example, students or people living in poor regions. They would never be able to buy CDs, and thus they cannot be considered as unfair free riders – there is, some argue, a "public good" aspect of information goods (Demuijnck 2008). But one cannot say that there are some cases of piracy that are not morally condemnable and are others that are. The counter-argument must be that fairness and refraining from theft are also public goods, and they definitely rank higher.

The MP3 files example leads to the general question of how networks can be protected against free riding – if they wish to be protected. If a business association found that divulging its services to non-members had positive externalities on the achievement of the goals of the association, it would not feel betrayed if a non-member made use of those services. But networks that wish to be protected may find ways to secure access. However, there are many other areas where a good that is provided by some businesses is widely open for free riding, such as scientific research and development results presented to a specific knowledge community, roads maintained by a private firm, programs to eliminate waste.

A very high potential for free riding by manufacturing firms and energy producers is in the carbon dioxide emission reduction program. The program, which is basically emissions trading, is motivated by the idea that pollution reductions may be achieved at lower cost (both to firms and society) through a market mechanism than through governmental regulation. Given that participation is voluntary, and industry members cannot be forced to participate, there will be firms that elect not to participate, enjoying the fruits of the labor of self-regulatory participants while avoiding the costs. Low enrollment in the program might make it fall apart, and the fear of such failure might cause firms to participate (Lenox 2008). In the end, it pays to be a stakeholder and fulfill obligations to other stakeholders rather than being a free rider. Conducting stakeholder relations responsibly is at the center of human centered management, and the next chapter will delineate this extensively.

Chapter 7

Conducting stakeholder relations responsibly

As with most of the perspectives presented in this book, where we have reciprocities, stakeholder relations are also not unilateral. Exhibit 7.1 depicts the inputs from and the effects on stakeholders in these relations.

Stakeholders, mostly, are not anonymous institutions but human beings – be they shareholders, employees, clients or citizens of a firm's constituency. They all have moral rights not to be harmed, and this includes the shareholders' ownership rights. Do these also go so far as to determine the moral responsibilities of the management that works for the owners? From the other way, how far do obligations of the management go to serve the interest of the

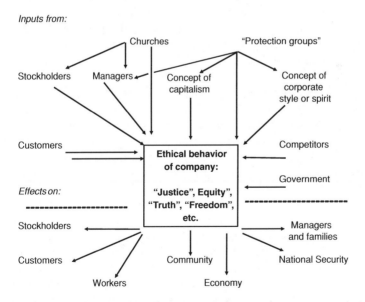

Exhibit 7.1 Inputs from and effects on stakeholders

Source: Adapted from Behrman (1981), p. 70

owners? Managers are agents for the shareholders; they are not "owned." This very special relationship will be covered within this section, which will first deal with employees, as the human centered paradigm applies here above all, and then with the other main group of constituents, such as clients, suppliers and the investment community. The section ends with the more complex relations towards (local) communities and the biosphere.

In any business stakeholder relations are conducted at many levels, from the chief executive to the people who lead functional areas within a corporation. Their moral responsibilities play a decisive role in the corporation's performance, reputation and sustained success. And they face moral dilemmas almost everywhere, from the market manager who needs to choose between a profitable decision and a socially responsible one, to the research and development (R&D) engineer whose technical judgments and risk assessments conflict with time-to-market deadlines, to the human resources manager who needs to straddle the fine line between the individual rights of employees and corporate interest. More often than not, and even though there are ethics codes and procedures manuals at hand, clear directions for resolving these types of dilemmas are not available through the corporate system.

An ethically guided manager could find answers from a general recommendation provided by a decades-old *Harvard Business Review* article by Laura L. Nash (1981), which has maintained its validity from when it was written during the not very turbulent 1980s through the financial and economic crises in the first decades of the 21st century (but seems not to have been followed very often, unfortunately). Nash, one of the presidents of the Society for Business Ethics, recommends a clear-cut procedure to test pragmatically the ethical content and human fallout of everyday decisions in business and other organizational settings (see Nash 1981, p. 80):

> First you have to define the problem as you see it, then (insofar as possible) examine it as outsiders might see it. You explore where your loyalties lie and consider both your intentions in making the decision and whom your action might affect. You proceed to the consequences of disclosing your action to those you report to or respect, and then analyze the symbolic meaning to all affected.

This would result in 12 questions (as per Exhibit 7.2) that were set up by Nash.

All stakeholder relations are complex and often have multi-level cause–effect chains. This requires systemic thinking. Executives often deal with issues where merely solving one relational problem does not improve the situation, so they need to learn to see behind the problem, why it evolved and how it is connected to other issues (Heracleous and Rao 2008). Systems thinking expedites the management of complex issues. With complexity defined as "many parts that interact with each other in multiple ways" (Principia Cybernetica Web 1996), a systemic approach helps to solve interconnected issues one by one

---

Twelve Questions for Examining the Ethics of a Business Decision

1	Have you defined the problem accurately?
2	How would you define the problem if you stood on the other side of the fence?
3	How did this situation occur in the first place?
4	To whom and to what do you give your loyalty as a person and a member of the corporation?
5	What is your intention in making this decision?
6	How does this intention compare with the probable results?
7	Whom could your decision or action injure?
8	Can you discuss the problem with the affected parties before you make your decision?
9	Are you confident that your position will be as valid over a long period of time as it seems now?
10	Could you disclose without qualm your decision or action to your boss, your CEO, the board of directors, your family, society as a whole?
11	What is the symbolic potential of your action if understood? if misunderstood?
12	Under what conditions would you allow exceptions to your stand?

Exhibit 7.2 Twelve questions for examining the ethics of a business decision

Source: Adapted from Nash (1981), pp. 79, 81

in isolation. For instance, executives become aware that customer satisfaction, employee capacity and competitive technologies are entwined with each other. But from the logic of division of work, solutions for each of these different issues may not be closely intertwined. In systems thinking, the three issues would be viewed as complements that complete the system of a business operation. Similar interconnections exist in personnel management.

7.1 The employer–employee relationship

The focal point of a human centered perspective on ethics in labor relations is Kant's second formulation of his categorical imperative: "Act in such a way that you treat humanity, whether in your own person or in the person of any other, never merely as a means to an end, but always at the same time as an end" (Kant 1785/1993, p. 36). Kant's argument was not just that humans are entitled to respect – they have to be respected because they have dignity. An object that has dignity is beyond price; even though labor may have a price and a cost and be an input for production, and is interchangeable with other resources such as machinery and financial capital, violating respect for people in this context is off limits.

The dignity of humans in the workplace comes with their ability to be autonomous and self-governing. Autonomy and self-governance are the conditions for responsibility; acting responsibly and being held responsible in the work-place are self-explanatory. Employee dignity also requires that an employment contract should neither be coercive nor deceptive:

> Coercion and deception are the most fundamental forms of wrongdoing to others ... [they] violate the conditions of possible assent and all actions which depend for their nature and efficacy and their coercive and decep-tive character are the ones that others cannot assent to.
>
> (Korsgaard 1996, p. 113 f.)

From Kant's argument, we can conclude that since work is necessary for the development of selfhood, treating humans as an end and not a means would indicate that the firm needs to provide meaningful work. Norman E. Bowie, one of the important voices in ongoing debates over business ethics, in his Kantian approach to business ethics (Bowie 1999, p. 70 f.) derives six principles regarding the moral value of work from Kantian thought that go beyond the prospect that work just gives independence and self-respect. The six principles are:

1   Meaningful work is work that is freely chosen and provides opportunities for the worker to exercise autonomy on the job.
2   The work relationship must support the autonomy and rationality of human beings.
3   Meaningful work is work that provides a salary sufficient for the worker to exercise his or her independence and provides for his or her physical well-being.
4   Meaningful work is work that enables a person to develop his or her rational capacities.
5   Meaningful work is work does not interfere with a person's moral development.
6   Meaningful work is work that is not paternalistic in the sense of interfering with the worker's conception of how he or she wishes to obtain satisfaction from work.

Bowie connects these principles to 16 management practices that have been found to manage people successfully by Stanford professor Jeffrey Pfeffer in *Competitive Advantage Through People* (1994). The practices list is far-reaching, and it would seem that corporations did not employ all of them at the time when the book was written:

1   Employment security
2   Selectivity in recruiting
3   High wages
4   Incentive pay
5   Employee ownership

6   Information sharing
7   Participation and empowerment
8   Teams and job re-design
9   Training and skill development
10 Cross-utilization and cross-training
11 Symbolic egalitarianism
12 Wage compression
13 Promotion from within
14 A long-term perspective
15 The measurement of practices
16 An overarching philosophy.

Pfeffer was avant-garde and advocated the deployment of these practices in many other writings (e.g., Pfeffer 1998, 1995). In the two decades that have passed since then, the practices have become commonplace tools for personnel management in most companies, with the advent of the internet adding some features that extend autonomy from high-ranking white-collar workers to blue-collar employees. Information technology (IT) has dramatically improved the ability to collaborate, access data, and make decisions on one's own. However, this empowerment also carries the risk of potential drains on productivity posed by employees surfing the Web, chatting over email or instant messages and accessing peer-to-peer networks for music or games. The loss of employee time and resources due to such activities has been estimated at approximately $50 billion annually in the US (Tafti, Mithas, and Krishnan 2007). But when firms exert too heavy managerial control through time tracking and monitoring IT use, this may undermine practices that are intended to empower employees, to give them a greater sense of autonomy, and to encourage information sharing. Another moral dilemma. To cope with it, careful management of the control–autonomy duality is required.

The control–autonomy duality, or so it may seem, becomes visible when looking at employees as stakeholders of the firm. Crane and Matten (2004, p. 228) give a list (Exhibit 7.3) from where it may look that the rights are outweighing the duties by far.

The argument supporting the obvious imbalance between employees' rights and duties often is that employees are the less powerful partners in employment contracts. On the collective level, however, employees are often on a par with employers. The collective level will be discussed in the following subsection before investigating the individual level. Since collective relations will be studied mainly from the situation in Europe and in the US, a short note is inserted here on the situation that firms encounter outside their homeland.

Employees of a firm, in a globalized world, are scattered throughout all the locations of the firm on all continents. Corporations that operate in many countries will not only have to abide by labor laws and labor culture of those countries, they must also be aware that their behavior in this respect will be

Employee rights	Issues involved
Right to freedom from discrimination	• Equal opportunities • Affirmative action • Reverse discrimination • Sexual and racial harassment
Right to privacy	• Health and drug testing • Work-life balance • Presenteeism • Electronic privacy and data protection
Right to due process	• Promotion • Firing • Disciplinary proceedings
Right to participation and association	• Organization of workers in works councils and trade unions • Participation in the company's decisions
Right to healthy and safe working conditions	• Working conditions • Occupational health and safety
Right to fair wages	• Pay • Industrial action • New forms of work
Right to freedom of conscience and speech	• Whistleblowing
Right to work	• Fair treatment in the interview • Non-discriminatory rules for recruitment

Employee duties	Issues involved
Duty to comply with labor contract	• Acceptable level of performance • Work quality • Loyalty to the firm
Duty to comply with the law	• Bribery
Duty to respect the employer's property	• Working time • Unauthorized use of company resources for private purposes • Fraud, theft, embezzlement

Exhibit 7.3 Employee rights and duties

Source: Adapted from Crane and Matten (2004), p. 228

under scrutiny in their homelands as well – from civil society organizations (CSOs) and "watchdogs" and organizations such as Social Accountability International referred to in section 6.4 in connection with the Business Principles for Countering Bribery.

There are many CSOs that critically observe how multinational firms treat the rights of workers around the world. Critics have argued that firms choose countries that have weak labor laws, as it leads to low costs, abusing the lack of worker protection. This has been called a "race to the bottom" – but the other way to look at the issue of economic globalization on workers' rights is "climb to the top," meaning that foreign direct investment inflows are positively and significantly related to improvements of workers' rights.

Generally speaking, the effects of economic globalization are contingent on the particular ways in which a developing country is integrated into the global economy. Inflows of direct investment are associated with better collective labor rights. In countries that are roughly disconnected from world trade or have only limited trade openness, workers' rights will be on the low end of the spectrum (Mosley and Uno 2007). As adherence to the OECD Guidelines for Multinational Enterprises is mandatory for firms headquartered in an OECD country, those firms will quite likely transplant their home standards to a host country. Further, they may urge governments directly to improve the rule of law, protect the vulnerable, and invest in social services and infrastructure (Richards, Gelleny, and Sacko 2001). This would be another demonstration of true human centered management.

7.1.1 The collective level

Employee rights are far reaching in most EU countries, where legislation resulting from the Social Chapter of the Maastricht Treaty, apart from regulating individual workers' rights and protection, also asks for extensive worker representation. The agenda was expected to be very far-reaching, from the outset, and to produce constitutional and practical difficulties (Fitzpatrick 1992). This was the reason why the UK negotiated an opt-out from the Social Chapter. The agenda may seem overly bureaucratic, but there is an escape clause in Article 2 that asks for avoidance of administrative, financial and legal constraints that would hold back the creation and development of small and medium-sized undertakings. There may well be cases where the costs triggered by these constraints outweigh the benefits to employees even though there might be moral arguments for these benefits. With the enlargement of the European Union, several of the new member states have chosen not to adopt quite a few policies of the framework.

Business leaders who adhere to moral principles will not require compulsory regulation like the Maastricht Treaty Social Chapter for handling workplace issues that affect rights and duties of employees. To take just two cases of employee treatments that reach much further: one is the participative management at all levels of the Cadbury conglomerate in the UK (Saee 2005). The other is Levi Strauss' (US) extensive workplace democracy, of which a good example is the involvement of forklift drivers in the decision on which new forklifts to purchase (Mirvis 2012). A firm that provides work conditions along the lines laid out before may be viewed as a "moral community" (Bowie 1999, p. 74; Pursey et al. 2008). The term has been developed to encompass the ability to mediate organizational conflicts that are inevitable in any firm – between functional departments, between different divisions, between managers and the board, and between employees and managers – and to create a strong relationship of employees with the firm based on shared values.

At first glance, the arguments for moral community, meaningful work and dignity may seem to be sufficient to regulate all employer–employee relationships. But there is also an argument that an employment contract is an action into which the employee enters voluntarily. If both parties to the contract are fully informed, one could argue like this: workers need to accept that the price of using a machine may become cheaper than the cost of labor, and when entering an employment contract they have unspokenly agreed that this development would have consequences for their employment status. Therefore, wages include a premium for the risk of layoffs (Williamson 1989, p. 145). This is acceptable if the "worker" is a high-paid executive who risks being fired if a new owner wants to replace his job by, for example, the capital that the new owner brings into the firm. But a layoff on the shop floor is not for the workers an ordinary event like receiving orders from the supervisor or being held accountable for the outcome of operations.

Even though there are legal provisions almost everywhere that protect workers from the negative consequences of layoffs, there are cases – all over the world – where business owners try to evade them. This has various features of immorality – negating responsibility, tricking legal institutions and often creditors as well and, above all, leaving employees without resources.

A striking case of business owner immorality towards employees occurred in Germany in 2012–2013. Schlecker AG, a German family-owned drugstore chain with roughly 7,000 stores and led by the second generation of the family, was led into insolvency on purpose, and assets were removed by the family and secured outside Europe. The structure of the enterprise, where each store was a firm of its own, had been built in this manner to stay out of the obligation to have employee representatives, and even the very powerful trade union of sales employees did not have a chance to intervene (Hiebl 2015).

A controversial aspect of the Maastricht Treaty's Social Chapter is employer–employee consultations, which are required to be held whenever a management decision affects the employees. This has corroborated the long-standing German practice of co-determination through works councils. In other European countries, this EU suggestion has been met with criticism, and it was one of the reasons why the UK immediately opted out of the Social Chapter. The UK criticism was certainly based on the intervention of industrialists who had no interest in measures that would increase labor costs, above all in view of Britain's productivity being lower than that of, for example, Germany (Falkner 2002). In the long run, though, it has become questionable that the British negotiating success really delivered an advantage. Researching the effects of Brexit, UK economists deplore that there has been virtually no increase in UK productivity since 2007 (Gudgin et al. 2016). There was cost increase from the effect of works council consultations, and consequently there was no pressure to compensate. One might say, however, that those consultations could as well have produced cost savings. The argumentation on productivity, in hindsight, was not a helpful criticism. There is, however, a moral argumentation.

The moral argumentation is about the moral justification for employer–employee consultations. The argument goes that if an employer–employee dialogue is directed at preventing conflict or confrontation, then clearly the aim of consultations has moral content. The same applies when there is a recognizable economic advance arising from consultation, e.g., from dialogues about increasing productivity (even though this might also be achieved through quality circles). But there are many other situations, such as planning a new production line or downsizing a business, where dialogue might even produce confrontation. With regard to the negative effects that this compulsory consultation has on the creation and development of small and medium-sized undertakings, a utilitarian argument against workers' councils is that they will discourage the formation and growth of businesses.

In the US, one major focus of workers' rights is on equal treatment. With this in mind, the Equal Employment Opportunity Act was passed in 1972. The measure is connected to the overall Affirmative Action Initiative against discrimination of workers on which formal legislation was launched in 1961 through an executive order issued by President Kennedy. While this order referred only to projects financed with federal funds and demanded that employment practices for these projects be free of racial bias, subsequent orders issued by Presidents Nixon and Carter established federal support for minority business enterprises. After this, additional legislation and court rulings drew the field wider to include all private and public organizations. Affirmative action is a subject of controversy in American politics. Opponents claim that some policies, such as racial quotas or gender quotas, are a form of reverse discrimination.

During the economic and financial crises, a more important topic in the US was job security. This is not a new topic, but it has received higher priority. Job security has always been an issue in the labor market, as reported over a long time span in research on employment conditions by, for example, the US consulting firm Willis Towers Watson (see www.willistowerswatson.com/en/insights). Their latest report shows that there are two more concerns that worry the public: retirement security and workplace safety, health and work-related risks (Willis Towers Watson 2016).

Job insecurity takes a toll on employee engagement, as does lack of transparency about the employer's business strategies and about the firm's financial performance. It affects each and every one, but it does so in different ways. Leaders should access this issue at the individual level.

7.1.2 The individual level

Human centered management exerts a positive influence on employee performance through intrinsic motivation and truthful job response. Leaders who head their employees responsibly encourage employees to report problems and suggest solutions. The recipes are all well known: increasing engagement of employees by involving them in decision-making, which is *workplace democracy*, accepting that workers have a say over their jobs and hold leaders accountable, self-managed teams and making workers think like executives. There is also a wide range of business practices that can remove the feeling of employees that they are somehow forced into a job procedure and that they are not fully informed. This refers back to what has been said previously about the need to avoid coercion and deception in the employment contract. One good practice is open book management. Open book management goes towards correcting the asymmetric information that supervisors possess. Another device is profit sharing, which Starbucks introduced right at its beginning, entitling employees to buy shares in their company in the future at the price in effect at the time this option is granted. It has been reported that with this option, employees with 10 years' service at Starbucks will secure stock options worth three times their salary (Bollier 1996 p. 218).

So, if all the recipes are well known, why do we still hear of abusive supervisors, disinformation and managers who withhold not only information but also benefits to which employees are entitled? One answer may come from what was said in the previous section about the desire to remain in a secure job. This often suppresses criticism and complaints even though compliance officers and ombudspersons would be available to listen. And just why are abusive supervisors abusive? One answer conceptualizes abusive supervision as a function of the mistreatment that supervisors experience at the hands of their own superiors – the trickle-down effect (Mawritz et al. 2012); or as reciprocity for actions of subordinates who provoke mistreatment – the victimization effect (Lian et al. 2014).

If the effects of abusive supervision are known, remedies can be sought in trying to influence both sides – persuading the parties to contain hostility and to translate whichever mindfulness they have into changes of behavior (Liang et al. 2015). This would be the psychological approach. For an approach that is managerial, we can turn to open book management again, because as said earlier, it can override abusive behavior of supervisors. The adoption of practices such as open book management, by correcting the asymmetric information that managers possess, would contribute to eliminating abuse of power and deception. Seizing the tool of information power from abusive managers will probably educate them for the better.

Under open book management, all employees are given all the economic information about the company on a regular, frequent basis. Experience shows that, with complete information and the proper incentive, employees behave responsibly without the necessity of layers of supervision (Kavaliauskas 2011). And how does open book management work? The simplest answer is:

> People get a chance to act, to take responsibility, rather than just doing their job. Open book management gets people on the job doing things right.

And it teaches them to make smart decisions because they can see the impact of their decisions on the relevant numbers. There is a cost effect as well: No supervisor or department head can anticipate or handle information for all situations, and a company that hired enough managers to do so would go broke from the overhead.

(Case 1995, pp. 45–46)

There is also another side apart from the rational: human centered management must also address the needs of employees for social belonging. There are always three major human needs that must be satisfied in a workplace. Employment must provide:

- The basic economic resources and security for a worker to lead a good life
- Meaningful work and the opportunity to grow and develop as a person
- Supportive relationships.

Supportive relationships need to go across all areas and all levels of a firm. This may often be established by new leadership, as in an example reported by French sociologist Philippe d'Iribarne who has researched intensively on the influence of national cultures on the way organizations work. His book *The Logic of Honor* is essential for anyone who wishes to understand why corporations are managed differently in different parts of the world (D'Iribarne 2003). An example in a more recent publication (D'Iribarne with A. Henry 2007) is the endeavor of French food products multinational Danone to transfer a culture of social belonging to its establishments in, among others, Mexico. The idealistic objective was to create a "community of equals, in which mutual assistance can change individual weakness into collective strength," where "helping one another to grow" would generate "a strong and proud whole made up of weaker elements . . . a family of brothers . . . a community of equals" (D'Iribarne with A. Henry 2007, pp. 46–58).

The Danone experiment in Mexico was successful. The firm implemented a mode of collective operations in its subsidiary that makes very effective use of the meaning that the Mexican context gives to a tight-knit and egalitarian community life, characterized by intense relationships founded on mutual aid. One feature was to connect the activity inside the company with an outside project aimed at helping disadvantaged children. The Let's Build Their Dreams project (*Construyamos sus sueños*) was seen as embodying the company's dual commitment towards employees and society. There is, in every society, not just in Mexico, the desire to help – sometimes latent, sometimes clearly manifest. Knowing how to activate this desire and employing it prudently is one of the wisdoms of human centered management.

Leaders who address social needs of employees in the internet society must take account of today's "disclosure culture," that is, what is documented in the blogs and other outlets of the internet. People are recording their daily lives, emotions and observations on Twitter, YouTube and Facebook. Much of this self-expression spills over into people's experiences as workers. Firms can make use of this interactivity: at the least, they should pay attention to how employees (together with consumers, investors and others) are talking about them online; but they can also engage in these online conversations. Handling all this can be delicate; it relates to the issue of privacy in the workplace, which is the last topic to be dealt in this section on employees as stakeholders.

7.1.3 Privacy in the workplace

The handling of employee affairs lends itself easily to immoral treatment and not only on the large scale in actions such as laying off employees without fair notice or compensation. There are other subtler types of mismanagement that also go (intentionally) against fairness, justice and equity.

Protection of privacy has four areas: the physical area, that is, an employee being entitled to his or her "own space" (e.g., placing surveillance cameras in bathrooms and rest areas compromises physical privacy); the social area (freedom to interact with whichever persons and in whichever way one might choose); the informational area (determining how and to what extent private data is released to others); and the psychological area (not being compelled to share private thoughts and feelings). The fundamental aspect of privacy is that it serves to secure personal autonomy. Hence, a very conflictive theme is workspace surveillance. There will only be a common understanding on this if the issue is openly discussed. Voluntariness, choice and consent are essential ingredients for meaningful implementation. Whereas open-plan offices facilitate direct observation, computer-based performance monitoring, for example, key-logger systems and telephone call accounting, is not only more sophisticated, but it also provides an instrument for measuring employee capacity or productivity, which in some countries may collide with statutory law.

Informational privacy concerns the extent to which employees can decide matters that concern them personally, control who has access to information about them and establish and develop different types of relations (Palm 2009). This not only includes obviously sensitive data such as sexual orientation or genetic makeup, but also information that can become privacy sensitive in the context of work, for example, as a result of combinations of different types of data about the content of an employee's computer screen and so forth. Electronic privacy in the workplace has come to the forefront in many disputes within firms and in labor courts. There are dissenting approaches when comparing Europe and the US.

No statutory or common law in the US guarantees a right to electronic privacy in the workplace unlike in Europe. Issues of privacy are dealt with by case law, which makes some critics believe that "we will see a legally guaranteed zone of privacy in the American workplace" (Kesan 2002, p. 289). But it seems that the issue has been satisfactorily addressed through a market-based, contractarian framework. US firms typically develop principles on employer–employee e-policies regarding access to email and the internet. The dilemma arises when a firm's aspiration to fully capitalize on the enhanced efficiencies of the internet may result in an overall loss in the employer's power and weakens the ability to take effective, unilateral action against misuse. In Europe, where national legislation was required through the EU Data Protection Directive, the experience has been that industry and government organizations in most countries, following the law, have issued binding guidance on electronic workplace monitoring practices (Bamberger and Mulligan 2013).

No monitoring practice will be able to eliminate what has been called "cyberdeviance," referring to inappropriate or criminal behavior in a digital context. There is an alarming trend in individuals behaving inappropriately with information technology in the workplace. In many cases employees repeatedly break security protocols leading to the compromise of sensitive customer and important organizational data resources. Even with detailed guidelines, employees continue to cause breaches in security (Oakley and Salam 2012). We are talking about average PC users in organizations and their interactions, not cybercrime by felons. Workplace-related cyber-deviance causes significant damage in both human and financial terms. Firms need to act firmly on this, at least with disciplinary actions, otherwise the cost would be termination of contracts, loss of employees, breaches of corporate confidentiality and loss of reputation, court cases for personal and organizational liability and the associated legal expenses, as well as billions of dollars in lost productivity (Weatherbee 2010).

There are studies, though, which cast some doubt on the effectiveness of disciplinary actions with regard to specific types of deviant behavior in computer and internet usage (Holt and Bossler 2015). Even though whistle-blowing barriers have decreased online, the community of malevolent internet users obviously is very tightly knit and comes into the open only very reluctantly (Fichman and Sanfilippo 2016).

Whistle-blowing is a prominent example of a moral dilemma. It verges on the topics of workplace privacy, loyalty to co-workers and loyalty to the organization, and the question is where the limits of loyalty lie. When an employee finds out that the behavior experienced in his or her firm is at odds with what is morally acceptable in society at large, what is he or she supposed to do? This might begin with a supervisor asking an employee to invade the privacy of another, or asking an employee to tell lies or conceal the truth about pollution or safety standards. The decision to report another person's unethical behavior to a third party – to engage in whistle-blowing – may place a person in an impasse. Some whistleblowers receive acclaim; others, especially in the cyber world, are blamed for fraying the social fabric. They face revenge from their community (Dyck, Adair, and Zingales 2010) and they risk reassignment, dismissal and diminishing job chances.

What, then, drives a whistle-blower? The ethical motivation is differences in people's valuation of moral norms, and the decision to place fairness over loyalty. Fairness demands that all persons and groups be treated equally. By contrast,

146 Conducting stakeholder relations

loyalty dictates preferential treatment, a responsibility to favor one's own group over other groups. In the US, the Dodd–Frank Act, which was signed into law in July 2010 spurred in part by the Bernard Madoff Ponzi scheme, contains whistleblower provisions meant to both encourage reporting and expand protection from retaliation for informants. Dodd–Frank was not in force when an informant reported the fakes in Enron's accounts, and when a Boeing employee reported seeing a fellow engineer with proprietary documents marked "Lockheed Martin." But when Boeing fired the engineer, he sued the company for wrongful termination, claiming that Boeing fired him to cover up a company policy to seek out sensitive Lockheed information. Boeing denied those charges and won the lawsuit on a summary judgment. The legal problems did not end there. After an investigation by the Defense Criminal Investigative Service, the engineer was indicted in 2003 on federal charges of conspiracy, theft of trade secrets, and violating the Procurement Integrity Act (Oliver 2009).

In the UK, the Public Interest Disclosure Act 1998 protects both internal and external disclosures from retaliation. In order to encourage companies to institutionalize whistle-blowing, the UK Financial Services Authority introduced the Combined Code on Corporate Governance in July 2003 (now the Corporate Governance Code, as per the update of 2010, where clause C.3.5 states that the audit committee of a corporation "should review arrangements by which staff of the company may, in confidence, raise concerns about possible improprieties in matters of financial reporting or other matters"). There is no whistle-blowing provision in the German Corporate Governance Code, and German courts seem to be ambiguous on whistle-blowing. The Employment Court of Wuppertal made a decision against Walmart in 2005 regarding its new Code of Business Conduct and Ethics, which contained a specific whistle-blowing procedure that included a hotline. Walmart had failed to consult the works council before implementation, and while the court stated that works council consent was required, it did not take a position on whether or not the hotline was legal according to German law (Hassink, De Vries and Bollen 2007).

The cases presented here give evidence of differences not only in the legal situation but also in the cultural awareness of the issue. And they show that leaders face multifold dilemmas. Was the German Walmart executive well advised to install procedures in Germany that he should have known were not compatible with German attitudes and regulations? Or did he think it was a moral compulsion for him to bring "Walmart culture" to the German subsidiary? Should a leader or a compliance officer/ombudsperson encourage a whistle-blower who might severely damage the firm's business, or should he or she search for solutions that protect both?

Whistle-blowing, to lead into what the next section will discuss on a firm's relation to its customers, points to a conflict between the ethos of the organization and public criticism of organizations' separation from society's ethics. This was the motive in the early 1970s of Ralph Nader, noted for his work in consumer protection, to campaign for legal protection for whistle-blowers.

When the question is asked whether a firm's whistle-blowing policies make "employees responsible or liable" (Tsahuridu and Vandekerckhove 2008), the answer should be that there is a contradiction in the question. Implementing whistle-blower policies turns responsibility into liability, making employees responsible not only for reporting organizational wrongdoing but for organizational wrongdoing. But this is what the business community owes to society. Interestingly, in that context, the Japanese government's regulation on whistle-blowing is an integral part of the Quality-of-Life Policy and part of the Cabinet Office's Ideal Consumer Policy for the 21st Century package (Mizutani 2007). This relation to consumer policy dates back to when the Quality-of-Life Policy Council was established in the Japanese Economic Planning Agency in 1965, which then redefined consumers as being autonomous rather than needing protection. Availability of information is a basic consumer right, and in line with this, all information sources that serve the purpose are protected by law (Yamagami 2004).

7.2 Relations with customers and consumers

Within this relationship, business leaders must look at five dimensions: the marketer, the offer of goods or services, the nature of the prospective buyer, the payment to be collected and the promotional representation. These elements roughly encompass the five "Ps" of marketing – product, price, place, promotion and people. The human perspective is twofold: while "people" refers to the persons involved in the marketing process ("the marketer"), the "nature of the prospective buyer" also includes attitudes and behavior.

7.2.1 The product

The moral way to bring a product into the consumer market would avoid harm, not deceive, and create value for the customer where profit for the seller is a result and not an objective. It is about marketing only "good" products or services. Philosophy offers two aspects for "good": an object is intrinsically good when its value does not depend on the fact that it is desired; by contrast, an object is extrinsically good when its value depends entirely on the fact that it is desired (Hill 2011; Reginster 2007). But there is also a distinction between two types of desire. Object-based desires are desires motivated by one's recognition of the object's intrinsic desirability: it is because one judges the object "good" that one comes to desire it. Need-based desires are motivated, instead, by a pre-existing need. Without this need, the object loses its desirability and therefore its appeal or interest. One example is the desire for a good night's rest: it is need-based; the desire for a particular sleeping pill would be object-based.

This brings us to the ethics of creating desire. Whether need-based or not, desires met by marketing divide into two kinds: those existing antecedently to marketing and those created by it. Is it moral for business to create desire? Or is doing so unjustifiably manipulative? It would be a mistake to claim this right away. Many things that make life enjoyable are not needed either biologically or for moral reasons. However, if a firm advertises cigarettes for minors, it would violate the moral obligation of not doing harm.

A firm should also not create desires that have disproportionate strength – disproportionate in that though not need-based themselves, like the consumption of hard drugs, they come to outweigh need-based desires. For example, the drug addict fails to value housing and eating. Hard drugs are the extreme of addiction; but there may be other addictions, such as online gambling or even smartphones. It is the marketers' moral obligation to explore how their products or services affect the promotion of human good. Marketers should primarily aim at persuading potential customers with arguments based on their needs, and if their business is about goods that are not need-based, they should refrain from evoking excessive desires by manipulating with images and information that produce intemperate addiction (Audi 2012, pp. 65–66).

7.2.2 Pricing and the place of product/service delivery

Competition over price is the core element of a free market economy, but misuse of this freedom occurs repeatedly. There are several notions of pricing that connect to immoral behavior: price collusion, price-fixing, deceptive price advertising, predatory pricing, resale price maintenance, price confusion, and price discrimination, to name just the most commonly known. This not only erodes the markets and damages public well-being, but it also distorts the objectives to be achieved with proper pricing, such as meeting revenue, communicating a certain level of quality, suggesting savings or a deal, encouraging customers to "trade up" to a higher-priced product in the line or increasing market share. Consumers are harmed when the sacrifice they make, in the form of the price they pay, is excessive; eventually the economic system will break down and the natural forces of competition will fail. Similar effects arise when firms misuse their power to determine the place of product/service delivery to the disadvantage of the customer.

Abuse of a dominant position is an explicitly moral dimension because the causing of injury is intentional. This not only relates to unfair selling prices (if too high, to the detriment of consumers; if too low, to the detriment of weaker competitors) but also to granting high rebates in order to hold on to discriminatory prices (charging one customer more than another, thereby placing the first customer at a competitive disadvantage). These abusive practices were a major concern when the European Economic Community (EEC, later to become the European Union) was formed in 1957. Article 86 of the EEC treaty is a clear description of what regulators need to look at when the free market is endangered. The article states:

> Any abuse by one or more undertakings of a dominant position within the common market or in a substantial part of it shall be prohibited as

incompatible with the common market in so far as it may affect trade between member states. Such abuse may, in particular, consist in:

(a) directly or indirectly imposing unfair purchase or selling prices or other unfair trading conditions;
(b) limiting production, markets or technical development to the prejudice of consumers;
(c) applying dissimilar conditions to equivalent transactions with other trading parties, thereby placing them at a competitive disadvantage;
(d) making the conclusion of contracts subject to acceptance by other parties of supplementary obligations which, by their nature of according to commercial usage, have no connection with the subject of such contracts.

The pertinent regulatory body in the US is the Federal Trade Commission (FTC), established in 1914 at a time when trusts/price cartels and trust-busting were significant political concerns. The FTC (and its counterpart in Europe, the European Commission's Directorate General for Competition) also supervises mergers and acquisitions – where abuse of a dominant position may also occur. Corporate leaders on both sides of the Atlantic have had to appear before the FTC or its European equivalent in numerous cases.

The longest-running case on the abuse of a dominant position is that of Google, which both the FTC and the European Union have formally charged over its alleged monopoly abuse that has, it is claimed, hit businesses of all shapes and sizes across the world. There is not much doubt about Google's superiority in market share in search and search advertising, but there is room for more than cursory debate about its significance and persistent or possibly transitory nature. If competition, as Google often says, is "just a click away," then market shares may not signify very much. A more severe accusation is that the search market exhibits major barriers to entry, in which case a persistently dominant or super-dominant position would carry special responsibilities, which may well include refraining from at least some of the practices alleged against Google.

The huge case of the European Union vs. Google is in the limelight of free market critics – but they often do not really analyze how the public authorities work. The critics are mostly absent when there is proof that both the authorities and the market achieve consumer protection. Fortunately, cases become widely transparent nowadays. Consumers modify their purchase and consumption behaviors when they experience price abuse; they change their attitude towards a firm if they become aware that it is facing allegations, and usually there are repercussions on the firm and its marketing strategies. Firms will not reap the benefits from price-fixing and monopolistic behavior for long. But they are, in any case, in the minority.

On the positive side, there are numerous enterprises with transparent pricing schemes and full product/service descriptions. They will "help the consumers to know themselves." Product disclosure regulation, which is increasingly asked for by consumer activists, may look socially desirable (and may be effective in, e.g., the food industry). But it is the market that will regulate the issues: the buyers who understand that they need to become informed or generate demand for information, and the sellers who understand that they need to provide the information (Bar-Gill and Ferrari 2010).

7.2.3 Promotion

The main instrument of promotion, advertising, has been a controversial topic for many years. Thirty years ago, a scholarly paper could still argue that advertising "does not require of merchants they tell all" (Machan 1987, p. 59). Not only has consumer awareness changed since that time, legal provisions have changed as well, with EU Advertising Directives for a wide spectrum of goods, the UK government's advertising regulations and the US Federal Trade Commission, which opens about 50 advertising investigations a year and publishes rules that have the force of law (Petty 2015).

These legal provisions are in close linkage with rules against unfair competition and they pronounce regulatory frameworks where consumers' interests are at stake. The moral justification for this type of legislation seems relatively straightforward. Any secret collusion amounts to dishonesty or at least a violation of the free market philosophy that businesses conduct their marketing in open competition to the benefit of consumers. Most businesses will operate openly and fair for this reason alone. On the other hand, even the regulators, such as the UK Competition and Markets Authority (CMA) have pronounced at times that the consumers also have a responsibility: "Rational self-interest of consumers, properly pursued, removes unfairness and inefficiency to a great extent" (CMA 2016, Appendix 1). Still, for the sake of balancing powers, as the CMA says, the operation of self-interest needs to be supported by regulatory, educational and policy initiatives. This assistance would help the consumers and the businesses to "exercise a duty of care on their own behalf" (Sorell and Hendry 1994, p. 76).

The responsibility laid on the consumers does not withstand the fact that there is no point any more to the "buyer beware" principle (caveat emptor), which advocates of individualism and laissez-faire have upheld until the 20th century as best serving the promotion of free trade. Caveat emptor ceased to be a ruling norm with the introduction of consumer protection laws in most developed countries. From an ethics perspective, it is the broader moral responsibility of business in society that connects disseminating advertisement content with being responsible for not only what consumers believe they will purchase but also for how that product or service may be used.

For legal reasons, and so as not to set precedent, businesses will generally disclaim responsibility for protecting consumers from wrong usage of a product, but many cases have shown that the general public will hold them accountable. Corporations have learned this since the disastrous error of Nestlé in promoting the sale of processed milk formula in many developing countries. In India, Nestlé gave gifts to health workers and used saleswomen dressed as "nurses" to provide donations of formula and advice to mothers. Poverty, illiteracy and poor sanitation often led to improper formula preparation. Mortality in very young infants from malnutrition, diarrhea and pneumonia, virtually unknown previously, increased dramatically (Post 1985).

So morally, in advertising, a duty of care needs to be exercised intensively. Exercising a duty of care is at the core of moral behavior. Caring on one's own behalf or "rational self-interest," as per the denomination of the UK Competition and Markets Authority (CMA 2016, Appendix 1), must, however, find its limits on behalf of others; self-interest must be constrained by employing morality in the systemic way that is the concept of this book – an interconnected respect for ethics, society, stakeholders and economic interest. Morality of this multifaceted type is needed over and above self-interest to determine the scope of and the limits of a firm's responsibility towards consumers.

As said before, a producer needs to make aware the harm which can be caused by its products. The warnings which have to be exhibited in, for example, tobacco advertising, are a clear example of this. However, where the risk carried by a product is identifiable but remote (such as a butcher's knife that might conceivably be used for murder), the moral reasons for protecting the customer would have to carefully weighed. This does not mean that consumer protection is always overdone, but while consumerism, that is, the belief that consumers' interests are always weightier than those of producers or sellers, is second nature in a consumer society, there needs to be some counterbalance. For instance, in the issue of consumer credit and consumer indebtedness, both the businesses and the customers/consumers have responsibility for things going right.

7.3 Relations with suppliers and competitors

Much like relations with customers and consumers, it is not just businesses that conduct supplier- and competitor relations: it is businesspersons, and there is always a human side. The ethical issues are about fairness and honesty, honoring promises and positive bargaining attitudes. The negative side might be procurement staff offering or being offered bribes, exploiting the seller with unfair clauses in the vendor contract or shortchanging consumers by collusive agreements with competitors over pricing. Ethics in negotiation will be included in this section.

Suppliers have close ties with a firm – but why are competitors considered to be stakeholders? The assessment of competitors as secondary stakeholders is derived from the corporate accountability of all firms that belong to an industry sector. It is in the interest of all members of the industry that each of them acts responsibly. Irresponsible behavior can damage a whole industry. Another angle is the legal rights that protect a firm from its competitors, such as the protection of brand names and intellectual property, but also the right to freely enter a market, to set prices free from coercion and the right to provide information on services and products. From there, we get to the moral rights and duties, that is, what should be expected morally from an organization that competes with others in a free market. There is no carte blanche, no free rein, for a firm, that is, its leaders and employees, to act in whatever way seems necessary to beat a competitor. Lying, deceiving or spreading false information about competitors or poaching their staff are not only immoral but punishable by law as well.

7.3.1 A case of outright immorality

The immoral treatment of suppliers has become infamous through the practices applied by José Ignacio López de Arriortúa at General Motors and Volkswagen in the 1980s and 1990s. Since then, the view that suppliers need to be "squeezed" has been replaced, not only in these companies, by collaborative practice. Still, the López case serves very well to explain how far the immoral can go in supplier relations. López continually reopened negotiations with suppliers and provided proprietary information of one supplier to other suppliers so that they could provide a product more cheaply. This might be termed as lying and stealing, respectively. That such a person would leave his employer General Motors to join its German competitor Volkswagen should be no surprise, then. Nor that he took with him some of his associates and General Motors' proprietary purchasing data. One might ask why the new employer even considered hiring a person of whom suppliers would report that he lied to and stole from them. Sadly, similar questions as to why things happened have to be asked in the recent Volkswagen emissions scandal (see section 6.2). With López, in the end, General Motors took Volkswagen to court for up to USD 4 billion in damages, and López was charged by German prosecutors with the theft of trade secrets (Wernz 2014). But the damage to the supply market lasted for a long time.

Since the López era, collaborative practices have been adopted in buyer–supplier relations (developed at Toyota; see Langfield-Smith and Greenwood 1998), which prevent unethical practice at the organizational level. These partnership-based approaches involve personnel at all levels on the buyers' and vendor's sides, from technicians and engineers in R&D departments to procurement and sales officials up to the leadership level of the firms. At the level of the individuals who conduct these agreements, temptation always lingers – of giving and accepting gifts, bribes, hospitality and other inducements that lead to terms that are not in the interest of the firm. Another topic is the use of questionable tactics on negotiation (of which the López case gave an illustration and which will be dealt with as follows).

Before leaving the organizational level, we need to briefly cover the misuse of market power (which is also an issue in competitor relations, as will be set out as follows). To take one example: in Germany, France and the UK, a handful of very powerful supermarket chains dominate the food market, and farmers are often forced to accept disadvantageous sales terms. None of their suppliers would take any action if products were withdrawn from the market. The criticism against this abuse of power does not stop with condemning the immoral behavior of the supermarkets (and their leaders) in squeezing their suppliers; what needs to be condemned as well is their indifference to the wider consequences, such as forcing the market to provide reduced quality, job losses from suppliers going out of business, lack of investment and overall industry decline. The opposite of power abuse is assisting the less powerful partners in the market with knowledge, financial support and management resources where needed. These are signs of loyalty to suppliers.

7.3.2 Loyalty to suppliers, and ethics in negotiation

Loyalty to suppliers can be warranted both at the organizational and the individual levels. If suppliers are going through difficult times, at least payment terms should be honored. Payment delays are not morally excusable in general as it is morally wrong to break an agreement (on paying at the stipulated time). But it may seem to be morally right to withhold payment of a debt to a cash-rich firm to the benefit of a cash-poor creditor. Other organizational means would be providing state-of-the-art techniques, prepayments and managerial support. They would all have to be accompanied by empathy and some kind of altruism. The opposite would be greed and selfishness at the buyer's end, which brings us to the topic of ethics in negotiation. Do purchase agents really need a directive on how to negotiate properly? There are ethics codes in the procurement profession on principles and guidance (see the example in Exhibit 7.4).

Again, as in other areas, the appeal to act morally is often not taken up voluntarily and participants in negotiation do not feel an automatic obligation to behave as laid out, for example, in guidelines like the one shown previously. In the US, rules for responsible procurement were codified in the Procurement Integrity Act at 41 U.S.C. § 423. It prohibits disclosing or obtaining procurement-sensitive information, including contractor bid or proposal information and source selection information for public tenders. Court rulings in the US have extended the jurisdiction of the act from government contracting to contracting between private business firms.

But what are the temptations and the pitfalls in negotiation? Is it "tricky tactics" or even "dirty tricks"? Reitz, Wall, and Love (1998, p. 5) list 10 popular negotiating tactics. They are:

1   Lies – about something material to the negotiation.
2   Puffery – exaggerating the value of something.
3   Deception – including misleading promises or threats and misstatements of facts.

Principles	Guidance
Members shall always seek to uphold and enhance the standing of the Purchasing and Supply profession and will always act professionally and selflessly by: – maintaining the highest possible standard of integrity in all their business relationships both inside and outside the organisations where they work; – rejecting any business practice which might reasonably be deemed improper and never using their authority for personal gain; – enhancing the proficiency and stature of the profession by acquiring and maintaining current technical knowledge and the highest standards of ethical behaviour; – fostering the highest possible standards of professional competence amongst those for whom they are responsible; – optimising the use of resources which they influence and for which they are responsible to provide the maximum benefit to their employing organisation; – complying both with the letter and the spirit of: i) the law of the country in which they practise; ii) institute guidance on professional practice; iii) contractual obligations.	In applying these principles, members should follow the guidance set out below: – Declaration of interest: Any personal interest which may affect or be seen by others to affect a member's impartiality in any matter relevant to his or her duties should be declared. – Confidentiality and accuracy of information: The confidentiality of information received in the course of duty should be respected and never be used for personal gain. Information given in the course of duty should be honest and clear. – Competition: The nature and length of contracts and business relationships with suppliers should always be constructed to ensure deliverables and benefits. Arrangements which might in the long term prevent the effective operation of fair competition should be avoided. – Business gifts: Business gifts, other than items of very small intrinsic value such as business diaries or calendars, should not be accepted. – Hospitality: The recipient should not allow him or herself to be influenced · or be perceived by others to have been influenced in making a business decision as a consequence of accepting hospitality. The frequency and scale of hospitality accepted should be managed openly and with care and should not be greater than the member's employer is able to reciprocate.

Exhibit 7.4 Chartered Institute of Purchasing and Supply (CIPS) Code of Ethics

Source: CIPS Corporate Code of Ethics

4   Weakening the opponent – by directly undermining the strengths or alliances of the opponent.

5   Strengthening one's own position – for example, by means not available to the opponent.

6 Non-disclosure – deliberately withholding pertinent information that would be of benefit to the opponent.
7 Information exploitation – misusing information provided by the opponent in ways not intended by them.
8 Change of mind – engaging in behaviors contrary to previous statements or positions.
9 Distraction – deliberately attempting to lure an opponent into ignoring information or alternatives that might benefit them.
10 Maximization – exploiting a situation to one's own fullest possible benefit without concern for the effects on the other.

All these tricks and tactics come with losses. In the long run, suppliers (or buyers) will discontinue procurement relations, which will probably result in not only cost of change (in production, design and engineering), but also damage to reputation, cost for hiring replacement personnel and legal expenses. "Dirty tricks'" like this are also found when firms try to outmaneuver competitors. Another activity to the detriment of suppliers is "phoenixing," which is bringing a business into doubtful solvency or insolvency, depleting the assets of the failed company shortly before the cessation of business, and setting up a new one to trade in the same or similar trading activities as the former. The new firm does not honor the debts of the old one, creditors' claims are on hold; and it may also happen that preferential payments are made to key creditors of the old company to assure supply to the successor company. Fraudulent phoenixing activity is of increasing concern in some industries, especially in the construction industry. It is intentional fraud that is immune to any attempt at deterrence or moral persuasion.

Deterrence or moral persuasion might work in another context, which is the prevention of bribery. The activities of Transparency International (mentioned in section 6.4) have not only turned the global spotlight on corruption with tools such as the Corruption Perception Index and the Bribe Payers Index, which targets supply-side corruption. They have even achieved some improvements in a few countries. However, the reports also show that there has been a gradual escalation in the bribe amounts (Logue 2005). Translational bribery is bad enough, but bribery at home? The UK legislature, in passing a modern Bribery Act in 2010, explicitly mentioned it should serve to combat "bribery at home and abroad." Although the UK has a good rating on the Transparency International Index of Perceived Corruption, the legislature obviously felt there was a need to provide for strict criminal liability for an organization failing to prevent bribery by that organization. Criminalizing private bribery wherever it occurs underscores the need for totally transparent business transactions. The act is meant to close the loophole of facilitating "courtesy payments" – payments that used to be given to government officials on a small scale (Osajda 2011).

7.3.3 Second, third and fourth tier suppliers and fair trade

A corporation's responsibility reaches beyond its relations with its immediate suppliers. Businesses have faced serious consequences for not monitoring working conditions among their suppliers' suppliers (Locke, Qin, and Brause 2007). For example, Nike and other apparel distributors such as Levi Strauss, Benetton, Adidas and C&A, which were under scrutiny for questionable procurement and production practices occurring at their suppliers, have learned their lessons (Preuss 2001; Locke et al. 2007). They take employ institutions that audit their second, third and fourth tier suppliers along internationally established and accepted standards such as SA 8000 or AA 1000.

SA 8000 was founded in 1997 and is now under the control of Social Accountability International (SAI), a partner of Transparency International. The standard is designed to manage, audit and certify compliance with workplace practices.

AA 1000 was created by the Institute for Social and Ethical AccountAbility as a standard for assessing and strengthening the credibility and quality of an organization's social, economic and environmental reporting. Stakeholder engagement is central and enables AA 1000 to build confidence and give legitimacy for a good reputation.

Reaching beyond the first tier supplier is also associated with the concept of fair trade. Consumers in developed countries are familiar with the term from grocery products such as chocolate or coffee labeled with, for example, the logo of FLO (Fairtrade Labelling Organizations International), which works to secure a better deal for farmers and workers in developing countries. And one might find this in a responsible organization's cafeteria. But the concept extends beyond farming to other small-scale enterprises, for example, independent garment workers in Bangladesh or small enterprise development in non-traditional exports in Mozambique (Carr 2004).

According to Fair Trade Labelling International (www.fairtrade.net), fair trade is about development and trading standards that stipulate that buyers must

- Buy from registered groups that are democratically organized
- Pay a price to producers that covers the costs of sustainable production and living ("living wage")
- Pay a premium that producers can invest in development
- Make partial advance payments when requested by producers
- Sign contracts that allow for long-term planning and sustainable production practices.

Fair Trade Labelling International monitors and inspects producers and exporters to ensure confidence in the guarantees being offered behind the claim of "fair trade." The effort will extend the benefits from trade and market liberalization to those segments of the population in developing countries who are at the bottom of the supply chain. There is growing trust in the replicability and sustainability of fair trade achievements, which has led to new ventures. Support comes from responsible purchase agents of morally led organizations and from policymakers throughout the world that establish programs to enable a shift of access, power and returns in favor of low-income producers and workers within global value chains.

7.3.4 Moral issues and competitors

Abusing the openness of a free market, unfair advantage seekers repeatedly employ tactics that restrict competition. The intention is to put rival firms out of business. Anti-competitive practices usually contravene competition law, as said earlier. However, charges that would stand up in court can be extremely difficult to prove, and many smaller competitors may well be forced out of business before authorities intervene. Even though it could be claimed that they are not necessarily motivated by deliberate intention, the aggressive market expansion strategy of high street brands such as McDonald's, Starbucks and Gap squeeze out smaller competitors such as independent cafés, coffee shops and boutiques. By increasingly saturating an area with more and more stores, overall company sales increase, and the big chains accept that returns from individual stores may be reduced through this "cannibalization."

Overly aggressive competition may resort to illegal tactics for securing information about competitors that go as far as manipulative intelligence gathering (as we have seen from the López case) and industrial espionage. Less blatant questionable activities would take advantage of the fact that corporations consist of, and deal with, multiple individuals, making control of information difficult. Much corporate activity takes place in public and quasi-public spaces such as shops, hospitals and colleges, and via shared infrastructure such as buses and railway cars. Conversations can be overheard; documents can be furtively copied. The more sophisticated attempts attack telephone lines, fiber optic cables and so forth, which are open to being easily observed and usually quite legitimately. With improvements in information and communication technologies, the ease of replication of digital information, as well as the refinement of reverse engineering techniques (where competitors' products are stripped down, analyzed and copied), unauthorized access to and exploitation of protected intellectual property has been on the rise (Parr and Smith 2013).

Beyond illegally stealing secrets and spying on competitors, there are some tactics that fall under the category of being immoral but not illegal (see Jones and Pollitt 1998):

- Negative advertising: where the firm deliberately sets out to publicly criticize its competitors or their products, or any product or performance claims a competitor may have made.

- Stealing customers: where a rival's customers are specifically approached in order to encourage them to switch suppliers, often using underhanded methods such as misrepresentation, providing false information, bribery or impersonating the competitors' staff.
- Predatory pricing: as we saw in the previous chapter, this involves the deliberate setting of prices below cost in order to initiate a price war and force weaker competitors out of the market.

Also in the spectrum are collusion and cartels, where select groups of competitors are banding together in price-fixing or other trading arrangements for their own mutual benefit. Again, this was discussed earlier in this book. This is not just a threat to consumer interests; insufficient competition harms the chances of job creation and innovation for newcomers in a market. This is a cause for ethical concern beyond the affected industry because all members of the society would be disadvantaged as a result.

7.4 Relations with investors

Shareholders are owners of a firm, and respect for their rights as owners, as set out in Chapter 2, is one of the cornerstones of the free market system. Shareholding is a morally desirable form of public ownership of business, because shareholders are less justified in taking a return on investment at significant expense to the business than other investors, such as loan holders who mostly are secured against the assets of the firm. Shareholders have obligations from their ownership, such as keeping in touch with the management in order to convey and receive information, ensuring the presence of independent directors on the board, exercising and enlarging voting rights, to name the most important ones. Reciprocally, management that is acting as the agent of the shareholder ("the principal") must conduct a continuous thorough and transparent dialogue with the owner in spite of any conflicts of interest inherent in this relation.

Agent and principal share risks: both wish to maintain and enlarge the firm's capital, and both have to uphold the reputation of the firm. But they may have different views on how to accomplish these goals, which investments to choose, which key personnel to hire and so forth. It is often said that as the principal–agent relationship involves a transfer of trust and duty to the agent, this should exclude opportunism and the pursuit of personal interests. A widely held belief is that this can be solved by structuring executive incentives, for example, stock options, in such ways that they align executive behavior with stockholder goals (e.g., Davis, Schoorman, and Donaldson 1997). Is there another solution?

The principal–agent issue is a topic that has been studied in practice and examined by economists (see, e.g., Rogerson 1985), sociologists (Shapiro 2005), and management theorists (see, e.g., Laffont and Martimort 2009). Much of the discussion revolves around incentives. If managers were paid on a long-term performance basis, the argument goes, short-term opportunism would recede as managers strove to fulfill long-term performance goals (De Ruiter and Souër 2005). However, finding and agreeing on adequate targets that meet the ultimate goal of long-term profit maximization will not be without difficulty. Nobel laureate Jean Tirole contends that the stakeholder society is best served by flat remuneration structures, meaning fixed salaries without performance-oriented incentive structures (Tirole 2001). So we are left with ambiguity.

Let us try another solution. From a moral standpoint, business leaders who act as agents for shareholders face conflicts between "self-interest and altruism, ethics and interests, ethical demands and economic realities, moral and financial costs, profit motives and ethical imperatives, and even consumer's interests versus the obligation to provide shareholders with the healthiest dividend possible" (Stark 1992). Business leaders need to make choices – but it is not that their motivation would be either altruistic or self-interested; it is always both, as we have seen in the explanation of advantage-based business ethics in Chapter 2.

In order to address the multiple moral dilemmas that managers face daily, leadership not only needs to understand the underlying motivations but also has to employ novel concepts such as moderation, pragmatism and minimalism. This also applies to handling the complex connection to shareholders. Managers have genuine moral responsibility to shareholders, and this responsibility is derived from what may be called Adam Smith's fundamental theory of welfare, where the "invisible hand" should make it possible to improve any one person's condition without worsening someone else's: the manager's obligation to help the shareholder get a reasonable return on its capital is a derivative of the latter's entitlement to do so. There are no normative conclusions in this ("it is the duty of . . ."), but a predetermined reasoning (Heath 2004; Maak and Pless 2006). This reasoning would also serve as guidance for disentangling the conflicts enumerated by Stark (1992). Like conjoining the profit motive and an ethical imperative, self-interest and altruism can also be bound together and will cease to be conflictive, ethical demands do not get in the way of economic realities, and consumers' interests do not oppose shareholders' expectation of dividends.

The too close connection between of majority shareholders and corporate executives is broken when all the shareholders get equal access to information. This has become easier through the transparency provided by online corporate reporting. From there, one area that is becoming more and more visible in shareholder relations is activist investors: the term "activist business ethics" was first applied to defending the rights of minority shareholders by the Israeli businessman and academic lecturer Jacques Cory (see Cory 2002).

In Cory's opinion, the greatest danger for minority shareholders and other stakeholders who are not represented on company boards lies with the immorality of an impenetrable alliance between top executives and majority shareholders. The alliance is immoral in the sense that it leads irresponsible business leaders to withhold information, to reap risk-free rewards from preferential warrants by the companies they lead and even to manipulate share prices. The recent history of the stock markets in the US and in Europe is filled with negative developments that corroborate Cory's opinion (Hannes 2013; Wray 2011); what is worse though, is that those who commit wrongdoings have not been clearly ostracized by society. But there were also those activist shareholders who succeeded in changing the initiatives of very large companies (see, e.g., Prado-Lorenzo, García-Sánchez, and Gallego-Álvarez 2012).

The investor community lives on information about an investment object – and this is mainly information from corporate accounting. Business leaders ought to be held accountable for all information given out by their firms. With trust and reliability being two of the moral values per se, proper representation of a firm's financial position becomes an ethical issue. There is a wide body of literature on this subject, from basic books and articles on "financial shenanigans" (e.g., Schilit 2010) to extremely sophisticated papers on forensic accounting (e.g., Bierstaker, Brody and Pacini 2006).

The underlying challenge in financial reporting is that there always exists a space for judgment because all accounting standards and rules, even though highly specific in some instances, need to be generally applicable, and they cannot prescribe which particular figure has to be assigned to a specific book entry. Inventories and real estate property can be understated or overstated in the accounts; contracting a loan can be performed through channels that remain outside the statutory accounts such as the "special purpose entities" used by Enron; and depreciation and write-offs are another field that is open to judgmental discretion.

Enron's "special purpose entities," where debt was incurred without burdening the statutory accounts of the firm, is an example of a legal instrument whose deployment is immoral when its only purpose is to avoid disclosure. In disclosure, generally, the borderline between legal and immoral is thin. Deceiving may start with obscuring the financial statements through technical terms that are only understandable for a few readers, or by using ambiguous language, or by presenting graphs with scales that blur the record. External auditors who are hired by the firm have a dilemma when their professional standards are challenged by reporting modes that are not against the law but might prevent less knowledgeable investors having proper insight. And they will also find themselves in conflict-of-interest situations at times when a powerful client pronounces the intention to hire another auditor.

Conflicts between an accountant and an auditor may be brought to the table of the audit committee that publicly listed companies are required to have in most countries. As audit committees are staffed with independent (external) directors, a discussion with this body could solve the problem. But the moral issue may persist. Auditors' independence from their clients is often compromised by any relationship that builds a common identity between the two – which may very well be explained by common professional backgrounds. As auditor independence and the quality of auditing decisions necessarily deteriorate when the auditor–client relationship lengthens, morally responsible leaders in both the corporation and the audit firm should accept the need for auditor rotation. Switching to another auditor would thus be a moral demand. Again, moral appeal not being sufficient, legal provision comes into place. Corporate governance codes all over the world request auditor rotation (Du Plessis, Hargovan, and Bagaric 2010).

7.5 Community relations

Business involvement in communities or, generally speaking, in civil society, usually begins with charitable giving and other forms of corporate philanthropy and voluntary participation in community affairs – educational institutions, libraries, the arts, sports and so forth. This is based on the notion of "giving back." Some corporations have made enormous contributions to civic life through such activities. Corporate giving is significantly larger in the US than in Europe, with US corporations giving, for example, something like five times more to charity than UK companies (Campbell, Moore, and Metzger 2002). US corporations usually enjoy more generous tax breaks on charitable donations than European corporations; in Europe the state and the church have traditionally been expected to take responsibility for public welfare, although in the US much of this is also taken care of by organized religion and church groups.

But the constituency of an enterprise, or the "community" in which it operates, is much wider than the local citizens. It stretches even wider than to customers of the firm's customers' customers, or to the third and fourth tier suppliers. Those suppliers are a part of the firm's community, too, and businesses need to monitor working conditions among their suppliers' suppliers as was mentioned previously. They must also be aware that they can be held accountable for their predecessors' wrongdoings, which may result, for example, in the obligations to indemnify all victims of environmental damages caused a long time before by firms they acquired, like Chevron in the Ecuador/Texaco dispute (see Giorgetti 2013).

Attending to issues that relate to the area of environmental damages and of harms to humans from environmental wrongdoing requires careful diligence. Business will seek collaboration with local expertise and with expertise on international human rights and on the relevant standards and resolutions, such as global and national human rights networks and organizations, both official and private. The United Nations Human Rights Council and its offices in the UN member states cooperate with a large number of private associations that can be joined or consulted. Three will be presented here briefly as they are exemplary:

- The International Service for Human Rights (ISHR) is an independent, non-profit organization with offices in Geneva and New York (www.ishr. ch). Its mission is to strengthen international and regional human rights systems by supporting human rights defenders at international and regional levels through advocacy, training and information services. Financial support comes from donors including governments, trusts and foundations, law firms and private persons.

- The Extractive Industries Transparency Initiative (EITI) is an international organization that maintains a standard for assessing the levels of transparency regarding exploitation of oil, gas and mineral resources worldwide (https://eiti.org). The EITI International Secretariat is located in Oslo, Norway, and as of 2016 the EITI Standard is implemented in 48 countries. Funding is twofold. There are membership fees provided through the industry, and governments can ask for financial assistance from a trust fund managed by the World Bank for the costs associated with implementing the EITI Standard in their country.
- The Ethical Trading Initiative (ETI) is a London-based alliance of companies, trade unions and CSOs (www.ethicaltrade.org) that promotes respect for workers' rights around the globe. Companies that join adopt a code of labor practice that they expect all their suppliers to work towards. Codes address issues such as wages, hours of work, health and safety, and the right to join free trade unions. Funding derives from a combination of members' fees, a grant from the UK Department for International Development, individual project finance and trading income.

These three organizations will provide support to an industry and to the communities affected by its business, and they will arbitrate and monitor. They will also be helpful for corporations that wish to assess the extent and limits of collaboration with CSOs from the viewpoint of power imbalance and mutual benefits. One would expect business partners to be considerably more powerful than CSOs in terms of size, capital, political influence and other key power resources. However, such a perspective tends to overlook the important power that CSOs wield in terms of specific knowledge, communications expertise and public credibility (Dahan et al. 2010).

With regard to the benefits of partnerships between businesses and CSOs, a caveat is often raised. The benefits of many CSO–business partnerships may be garnered more by the CSO partners than they are by the constituencies that are supposed to be aided (Ashman 2001). Globalization has spurred this evolvement. In particular, sometimes anti-corporate sentiment has been mobilized across the world, with international protests and boycotts, the use of sophisticated technology to transmit images into the media, and a circus of protesters travelling around the globe (with zero benefits for those whom the protesters pretend to "defend"). This reached its peak in the late 1900s and then started to diminish (St. John 2008), but corporations need to take account of this.

While many firms would rather focus on engaging with multiple local civil societies they are faced with something more akin to a global network of campaigners with giant CSOs such as Greenpeace and Friends of the Earth International (FoEI) as the frontrunners. Some of their objectives may be reasonable, but some are absolutely questionable, such as FoEI's campaign report *Fuelling the Fire: New Coal Technologies Spell Disaster for Climate* (Walker 2016). The study admits that there is only one supposedly commercial underground coal gasification (UCG) plant in the world (in Uzbekistan; p. 5) – but the campaign makes the layman believe that the world is coming to its end because of this technology. However, responsible business leadership has to maintain a dialogue on a global level with these campaigners (and devote considerable resources to building argumentation, proofs and technical documentation).

At the other end of the spectrum, issues originating at the local level require no lesser attention. There are issues with local government, tax authorities, neighboring municipalities and so forth. They may have an effect that requires the attention not only of the company professional who deals with this specific relation but of top management as well. Following the well-known saying that "all business is local," most of the issues that emerge at a local level will spread up to the corporate level and throughout, like the Nestlé baby formula case that was referred to earlier. One case that started on a local level in Myanmar and developed to an unprecedented lawsuit in US federal court was the Moattama Gas Project.

> The Moattama Gas Project in Myanmar started as a joint venture in 1992 between TotalFinaElf Petroleum of France, Unocal Corporation of California, the Burmese Myanmar Oil and Gas Enterprises and PTT Exploration and Production of Thailand. The venture was formed to develop the Yadana natural gas field located in the Andaman Sea, off the southern coast of Myanmar, and to erect a pipeline from there to the border of Thailand. The history of the project is fraught with controversy because one of the stakeholders had to be the military regime in Myanmar. Even though the project comprised a series of corporate social responsibility projects, including housing, schools, health care and hospitals for the Burmese communities that were affected by the project, these were severely tarnished by reports on human rights abuses, such as forced labor, forced resettlement and killings. In response, the international CSO EarthRights International together with two California-based law firms, brought a lawsuit against, among others, Unocal, two top Unocal executives, Total, and PTT. The plaintiffs were able to file their unprecedented lawsuit in the U.S. federal court because of the federal Alien Tort Claims Act. The Alien Tort Act allowed victims of egregious human rights abuses committed abroad to sue those responsible in U.S. federal courts. The scope of the Alien Tort Act was eventually restricted to a great extent by the US Supreme Court in April 2013 because it found that it violates the presumption against extraterritoriality. But in the late 1990s, the Act was fully endorsed, and subject matter jurisdiction was granted over the plaintiffs' claims against Unocal

in favor of the plaintiffs. In the aftermath, Unocal's vice chairman resigned from his position.

(Carey 1999)

TotalFinaElf, as a consequence, and to set the record straight, consented to an engagement with EarthRights International and to execute the project under its supervision. The extraction and transport of gas is now up and running, and according to the regular updates published by the company EarthRights International is no longer advocating for Total to withdraw from the country. There is now a close communication between Total and the villagers in the area according to representatives of the International Labor Organization (ILO).

(www.total.com/en/dossiers/total-myanmar-
commitment-and-responsability)

Wider constituencies, overcoming economic, technological, political and ideological divides, and workers' rights are all human-related. Nature is a concern of humans as well, and so it is to be treated as another stakeholder of responsible business.

7.6 The natural environment: a multifaceted stakeholder relationship

Business has been a partner of nature since the beginnings of organized agriculture millennia ago. Agriculture and its output was a main topic of economists of the 18th century, with Thomas Robert Malthus (1766–1834) coming to prominence for his 1798 essay on population growth. In it, he argued that population multiplies geometrically and food arithmetically; therefore, the population eventually outstrips the food supply. Malthus anticipated terrible disasters resulting from population growth and consequent imbalance in the proportion between the natural increase of population and food. However, since then the world population has grown nearly six times larger, while food output and consumption per person are considerably higher now, and there has been an unprecedented increase both in life expectancies and in general living standards, even in the poorest regions of the world.

The fact that Malthus was mistaken in his diagnosis as well as his prognosis 200 years ago does not, however, indicate that contemporary fears about population growth must be similarly erroneous. The increase in the world population has vastly accelerated over the last century. And there is certainly reason for concern. But the world community is acting, and the UN accord of September 2015 on the Sustainable Development Goals sets challenging but nevertheless achievable objectives for nutrition, access to water, minimization of waste and other essentials for human well-being. Civil society will have to contribute a big effort to reach these goals, and so must business. One contribution is ever-improving technology and better means for exploitation of natural resources.

There has undoubtedly been overexploitation of natural resources in many places, which needs to be stopped and its effects need to be repaired. The effects go far beyond the depletion of nature: we still see what is called the "natural resource trap," the paradoxical situation that the discovery of valuable resources such as minerals and fuel is not a catalyst for prosperity but a curse, because it causes malfunctioning of social order when governments and enterprises fail to provide inclusive governance (Collier 2007). Technology is just one part of the contribution this story tells: business – responsible business – when bringing the technical means to improve agriculture and mining in developing countries must also comprehend that the people who live in these areas have a relationship to nature that is much closer than in the Western world.

In their relations with nature, businesses always encounter the dilemma between leaving it intact for future generations or changing its landscape for improving the living conditions of the present generation. This dilemma is what produced the definition of sustainable development by the Brundtland Commission: "Development that meets the needs of the present without compromising the ability of future generations to meet their own needs" (WCED 1987). But to meet both these needs man must change the landscape of nature. We live off nature – it is our capital ("natural capital" – like investors living off their financial capital). Implicit in this proposition is that we must, to the best of our ability, live off the "interest" on this capital stock and not draw it down. One well-intentioned notion of the proposition that the current generation must leave to its descendants a stock of capital no less than is currently available has been coined in the term "transient caretakers" by Mervyn King and Teodorina Lessidrenska (2011).

The only way to ensure that our descendants get the same amount of fruit as ourselves depends on natural capital bearing the same amount of fruit at all times. By making better use of the capital we are still responsible caretakers. Thus, if a part of this capital is consumed, it must be replaced by substitute capital. Therefore, we can consume some of our natural capital (in the form of environmental degradation, for example) as long as we offset this loss by increasing our stock of man-made capital, by making use of the technological advances mankind is continuously adopting. This way of dealing with resources has been called "weak sustainability" as opposed to "strong sustainability," which requires that the resource structure must remain unchanged (Pearce and Atkinson 1993).

Advocates of the "strong sustainability" criterion see nature as an indivisible heritage and reject what they call "commodification" of the environment. In their view, the market functions as a collective action against preservation as extraction/production of resources subjugates nature to human technology and methods, when it should rather be the other way around (Scherhorn 2004). There may be reasonable arguments on how much substitution of man-made and natural capital is moral. However, it is commonly agreed that natural and man-made capital should be managed at optimal levels and these should be maintained over a very long period.

One example of the relationship between natural resources and technology is that the productivity of bigger fishing nets (man-made capital) will decline with the decline in stock of fish, and their relation is complementary (Daly 1990). This may be transferred into improvements in mining and the stock of phosphate or copper ore. Maintaining the stock of natural capital is not an issue of the size of fishing nets or mining devices. If the stock is limited, economic logic requires investment in the limiting factors, and this would translate into encouraging the growth of natural capital by investing in projects to relieve pressure on this type of natural capital stock and by increasing the end-use efficiency of products. This indicates a path to a proper mix of natural and man-made capital. It is business enterprises that produce this mix – by building a dam on a river, by drilling water holes, by cutting trees and reforesting, by mining in woodlands and consequential recultivating.

This view on the relation between business and nature concludes the discussion of responsible dialogues with stakeholders. The next chapter will consider what is meant to be a moral person, a moral leader and a moral organization and how they are tied together. And this may also be viewed at as an issue of implementing human centered management.

Chapter 8

Moral person, moral leader, moral organization

For a leader to be trusted, he or she must, of necessity, be a moral person by character, attitudes and activities. Dealing with others one to one or in a large organization always raises the question of *conditio humana*, which is the concern about human nature and how humans live their lives. The sense of morality and its rationalization need to be adapted to the condition of life: there will always be an interplay between morality and the characteristics, key events, and situations which compose the essentials of human existence. In this, morality and law, which also governs how we live, are closely related. Both deal with questions of justice and want to establish a just world in accordance with their precepts (Weinberger 1991). Also, a sense of morality must consider that each individual possesses dignity and is endowed with liberty, which is how a person expects to be treated by others. Corporate leaders face the challenge of having to be fair to these sides of human nature, with a view to others as well as introspectively. They need to deal with expectations – those of others as well as their own.

The discernment of expectations is a decisive factor in decision-making at all levels of institutions. On a level that is very familiar to the practitioner, this human side has been aptly described by Chris Argyris in his book *The Impact of Budgets on People* (Argyris 1952),[1] where the title says it all. Anyone who has had to set up a budget or assess the content of a budget in any organization has become familiar with people's propensity to overstate or understate in order to be "on the safe side." Employing a budget as a control device will unnecessarily have these consequences. Budgets should rather be seen as a guide to enable future decision-making.

Responsible leaders should pay attention to the moral experiences and expectations of their followers. As with Douglas McGregor's Theory X, that workers tend to be positively engaged towards their work and their fellows (see section 3.1), leaders should first assume that their employees care for each other. But they should also be on the lookout for individuals who intend to outmaneuver their peers. Some of this may lie in an intrinsic feature of humans that has been eradicated through positive experience in most of us, but not in all, and which has been called Social Darwinism. The connotation of "Social

Darwinism" is to apply Charles Darwin's (1809–1882) theories on natural selection to economics (where it supports laissez-faire theory) and to human behavior. It is associated with the phrases "survival of the fittest," attributed to Herbert Spencer (1820–1903), and "root, hog, or die," an old country catch-phrase taken on by sociologist William Graham Sumner (1840–1910). Things have changed since the times of these scholars, but there are certainly people around who act by the principle, even if subconsciously.

The opposite of *Social Darwinism* is altruism – disinterested and selfless concern for the well-being of others. William MacAskill, a professor of philosophy at Lincoln College, Oxford, and a founder of the Effective Altruism movement, has spelled out five key questions that help guide our altruistic decisions (MacAskill 2015): how many people benefit, and by how much? Is this the most effective thing I can do? Is this area neglected? What would have happened otherwise? What are the chances of success, and how good would success be? Applying these questions to real-life scenarios, where leaders often have to determine which causes are the most important ones to be addressed, connects the personal sphere to the sphere of leadership in organizations.

This brings us to the question of whether a person or a leader can always abide by reasoning, abiding by, for example, the Kantian imperative and faith-based convictions? Or are there situational influences on how a person makes decisions? Crane and Matten (2004, pp. 128 ff.) identify two main types of situational influences: issue-related factors and context-related factors. With issue-related factors, they consider the nature of the ethical issue itself, and, in particular, its degree of moral intensity, that is, how important the issue is to the decision-maker. And they consider the issue's moral framing: how that issue is actually represented within an individual's personal environment or within the organization, where some moral issues will be deemed as important and others not.

Issues-related argumentation is not very far from the five questions asked by MacAskill, as it relates to the magnitude of consequences, the probability and the concentration of the effect, the temporal immediacy, the proximity that the decision-maker has to those impacted by his or her decision, and the question of whether there is a social consensus on the ethics of the problem in question.

Context-related factors, while certainly affecting decision-making in the personal sphere, are more apparent in the setting of organizations. We are back again with the very human feature of experience and expectation:

- People expect to be rewarded for what they do – and we take it for granted that they are likely to do what they are rewarded for. Therefore, decision-making is influenced by the systems of reward for moral behavior that people see operating in their workplace. If expectations fail in this context, decision-makers will change their criteria.
- People expect authority from their leaders. People don't just do what gets rewarded; they do what they are told to do, or, perhaps more correctly,

what they think they are being told to do. Leaders may not be directly instructing employees to do something ethical, but their instructions to the employees may appear to leave little option but to act in a moral manner.

- People expect that an organization works well. This brings us back to Max Weber's and Paul du Gay's advocacy of the advantages of good bureaucracy. Bureaucracy organizes the influence of rewards, punishments and authority. To get the best effect for moral decision-making, bureaucracy should stimulate, not suppress, moral autonomy. The functionality of specific rules and roles in the bureaucratic organization must leave enough freedom for thinking and not make the employees act as "moral robots." The author of this book, at the start of his business career in a very large organization, heard the CEO spell out the maxim that job descriptions must never be so tight as to obstruct autonomy and never be so wide that a weak leader can hide behind them. This is a groundwork of not just effective but also moral and responsible leadership.

The term *Groundwork for Moral and Responsible Leadership* brings us to the theme of the moral enterprise. Moral business practices stem from moral culture, and moral culture creates moral organizations. In the 1980s, ethics professor Patrick E. Murphy would restrict the means for creating the moral organization to "corporate credos, programs such as training and ethics audits and codes tailored to the specific needs of a functional area" (Murphy 1989, p. 81), but there is a much wider spectrum nowadays. And we have long surpassed Milton Friedman's dogma that "only people can have responsibilities; a corporation is an artificial person, and, in this sense, may have artificial responsibilities, but business as a whole cannot be said to have responsibilities" (Friedman 1970, p. SM 12). Today, corporations have accepted the double responsibility for "doing good" and "avoiding bad." Most of them are aware that they need to prevent corporate social irresponsibility, such as cheating customers, violating human rights or damaging the environment not just in their own firms but far beyond (Lin Hi and Müller 2013).

We have seen very positive developments since the corporate scandals of the 1990s (if it were not for the criminal acts effected by Volkswagen in 2015 and further misconduct of the same firm in August 2016 with regard to squeezing small suppliers; see Rauwald 2016). There were always "high-ethics, high-profit" firms: Motorola, 3M, Cadbury Schweppes, Northern Chemical, Apple, to name just a few recorded by Pastin (1986). Some 30 years later, most of these and many more appear in *Firms of Endearment* by Sisodia, Wolfe, and Sheth (2014). The authors describe these "firms of endearment" (FoEs) as fueled by passion and purpose instead of cash, and say that FoEs view society and their workers as the ultimate stakeholders. They are "humanistic companies" where the stakeholders (customers, employees, suppliers, business partners, society and investors) develop an affectionate connection to their company, and where the companies seek to maximize their value to society as a whole.

One might ask how "passionate commitment" of the firm translates to profits, but results are amazing: in comparison to "Good to Great" companies (Jim Collins's pivotal research; Collins 2001) and to the S&P 500, FoEs dramatically outperformed these companies over the last 10 and 15 years. When using share value as the performance measure, the increase over the 15-year period ending in 2014 was 1,681.11% for US FoEs and 1,180.17% for international FoEs compared to 262.91% for Good to Great companies and 117.64% for the S&P 500 companies. The spread has widened drastically in the last five years of this 15-year period: for the 10 years ending in 2009, the figures were 409.66% for US FoEs, 512.04% for international FoEs, 175.80% for Good to Great Companies and 107.03% for the S&P 500 companies (Sisodia, Wolfe and Sheth 2014, p. 114).

What makes a firm a moral organization – "a firm of endearment"? Sisodia, Wolfe and Sheth (2014, pp. 8f.) list the following:

- They subscribe to a purpose for being that is different from and goes beyond making money.
- They actively align the interests of all stakeholder groups and not just balance them.
- Their executive salaries are relatively modest.
- They operate at the executive level with an open-door policy.
- Their employee compensations and benefits are significantly higher than the standard for the company's category.
- They devote considerably more time than their competitors to employee training.
- Their employee turnover is far lower than the industry average.
- They empower employees to make sure that customers leave every transaction experience fully satisfied.
- They make a conscious effort to hire people who are passionate about the company and its products.
- They view their suppliers as true partners.
- They honor the spirit of the law rather than merely following the letter of the law.

The list corresponds to what has been said in this book about conducting stakeholder relations responsibly. And there are more novel concepts of morality that are beginning to be practiced in business. The titles of two recent books say it all: *Everybody Matters. The Extraordinary Power of Caring for Your People Like Family* (Chapman and Sisodia 2015) and *Connect: How Companies Succeed by Engaging Radically With Society* (Browne, Nuttall, and Stadlen 2015).

This is an optimistic outlook: all those positive examples seem to prove that companies cannot be great unless they are good. An even more positive point of view has been given by the authors of *Good Company: Business Success in the Worthiness Era* (Bassi et al. 2011). Worthiness means pursuing a purpose that goes beyond making money, incorporating the interests of all stakeholders, and being a good steward throughout. Bassi et al. have ventured to rank the US Fortune 100 companies on their qualities of reciprocity, connectivity, transparency, balance and courage. All these are human centered to a very high degree.

The ranking list of Bassi et al. (2011, pp. 108 f.) has Walt Disney and FedEx with the highest scores, followed by Cisco, IBM and Intel. Walmart, which has so often been criticized for treating employees badly, comes up with a rank not at the lower end but in the middle of the score, as a positive evolvement was happening there in 2011 when the list was set up. This evolvement has continued, and the steps taken by the company to improve working conditions, care for the natural environment and continue to act as a steward for lower-income customers have been widely acknowledged, affecting both reputation and revenue: while other retail chains suffered drawbacks in the first half of 2016, Walmart reported on August 18, 2016, that sales in existing US stores rose for the eighth consecutive quarter, up 1.6% as more customers visited, providing a stark contrast to other retailers (www.wsj.com/articles/wal-mart-lifts-profit-outlook-as-sales-grow-1471519843). So, worthiness obviously pays off. Media stories on Walmart have very rapidly changed from reports on discriminatory events and exceptionally low wages posted on the class action website set up by a law firm (www.walmartclass.com) to a ranking in Fortune's "Best Companies to Work For" list (http://fortune.com/best-companies).

Big firms must set examples, and most of them clearly do. But it is the moral leader who makes it happen, such as Walmart CEO Doug McMillon, who took the helm on February 1, 2014, and has been widely acclaimed for his achievements to make this huge organization become a good employer, increase awareness of ecological concerns, inclusive growth and a respected corporate citizen. "We are a retailer – we are a merchant," he said in an interview, "that is our business. But we do not want to sell anything that offends people, and we look for places to make a positive difference" (www.bloomberg.com/news/articles/2015-06-23/wal-mart-ceo-sees-chance-to-make-a-difference-with-social-issues). Doug McMillon's philosophy has taken up what was said by Paul Camenisch, theology professor at DePaul University in Chicago, at a business ethics workshop in 1985 (as quoted in the introduction to Walton 1988, p. iii): "It is impossible and undesirable to speak of human centered management *within* business without speaking of human centered management *by* business in the larger society."

"Business *and* the society at large" is a wording that might have been commonly used in the 1980s, but it is not to the point any more. The contemporary understanding is that business is "*in* society," as elucidated, among others, by the organizations that bear this name: Business in Society LLC (http://businessinsociety.net) and the Academy of Business in Society (www.abis-global.org) which were referred to in Chapter 1 in conjunction with the UN Global Compact. Human centered management, whether it is exercised in a business firm or in a public institution must be directed towards the common good of all – beyond the stakeholders of a firm or the constituency of a government authority. This has garnered momentum through the United Nations Agenda 2030:[2] the agenda's 17 Sustainable Development Goals are interlinked with each other, and their implementation requires efforts from all members of society:

> Ending poverty (1) and hunger (2), ensuring healthy lives (3) and quality education (4), achieving gender equality, providing access to water (6) and energy (7), providing decent work through sustained, inclusive and sustainable economic growth (8) and a resilient infrastructure (9) – these commitments demand large-scale collaborative action of public authorities, businesses and civil organizations.
>
> Likewise, reducing inequality (10), making cities safe and resilient (11), making consumption and production sustainable (12), fighting against climate change (13) conserving the oceans (14) and the terrestrial ecosystems (15) building peace, justice and strong institutions (16) and building global partnerships for finance, technology, capacity-building and trade (17) – all this necessitates multi-stakeholder collaborations between governments and their citizens, the business sector and the scientific community and supra-national organizations.

With its resources, both financial and intellectual, the business sector can contribute profoundly to support the processes of goal-implementation, and, to quote from the resolution adopted by the UN General Assembly on September 25, 2015, this "will stimulate action over the next 15 years in areas of critical importance for humanity and the planet" (United Nations 2015, p. 1). Business managers and managers in public entities have to become acquainted with the goals and the strategies of implementation and what this all requires. There is an obvious connection to the UN Principles for Responsible Management Education (PRME), and certainly, a nexus to executive training on human centered management. So, the final chapter of this book will recommend how to create responsible management by teaching the human centered paradigm.

Notes

1 Accounting professor Michael Schiff has termed this the other way round ("The impact of people on budgets"), with the same findings (Schiff and Lewin 1970).
2 www.un.org/sustainabledevelopment/development-agenda

Chapter 9

Recommendations for teaching human centered management

The quote from the 1985 business ethics workshop that was given in the previous chapter replicates what educators were concerned with when business ethics teaching was in its infancy. Here is another reference from that time (Harris et al. 1996, pp. 94 ff., quoting Callahan 1980):

> Too often . . . young professionals get caught by surprise when faced with an ethical problem in their professional practice. Never having seriously thought about such a problem, they may not handle it well. . . . Although a conflict of interest may be lurking around the corner, it may not announce itself to the involved parties until matters have gone too far . . . Many of the ethical concepts are "messy." They resist the sort of precise definition which students might want . . . They must learn to deal with ethical disagreement, ambiguity, and vagueness. The trick is to acknowledge that some disagreement and uncertainty can be expected and should be tolerated, but to refuse to accept the view that everyone's opinion is as good as anyone else's when it comes to ethics.

Today, about 500 business schools in the US have executive training programs on business ethics. The scope of the training differs, and so does the content. Recent surveys show that the content on compliance seems to overwhelm, according to Ronald R. Sims, who has taught top-ranked executive education in the area of business ethics for many years in the Raymond A. Mason School of Business at the College of William and Mary in Virginia (Sims 2017). Compliance is mainly a technical concept, and this type of knowledge must indeed be taught. But there should as well be an emphasis on educating the whole person. This holistic approach would have to be similar to the one described in the introduction of this book when referring to the building blocks for multi-stakeholder dialogues (section 1.2.2). Based on that approach, the recommendations for educational programs are as follows.

9.1 A principles-based education on business ethics

Holistic training programs should integrate the views on personal and inter-personal goals, societal objectives and the elements of the sustainable develop-ment. The training must not be isolated or focus only on techniques. It must be connected to a principle-driven and value-creating culture. A holistic view of education requires an encompassing view that integrates multiple layers of meanings and experiences to help learners recognize their mental models and the paradigm shift from a mechanistic mindset to a dynamic perspective. "It is through mental models that we interpret and make sense of the world around us, and in business and social systems mental models shape decisions and actions" (Morecroft 2004, p. 104). The more powerful the mental models the easier it is for managers to understand changes in the external environment to improve decision-making strategies. Mental models can be included in these five learning objectives (see Khan 2010):

1   Learning core values in global ethics
2   Critical ethical executive thinking
3   Interdisciplinary and intercultural thinking
4   Oral rhetorical communication for ethical management
5   Business writing across the globe using technology and information lit-eracy conforming to global business ethics.

Principles-based education will connect all this to basic standards of thought for which it may suffice here to transcribe the Caux Round Table principles for human centered management (see Table 2.1):

•   Respect for all stakeholders, including nature
•   Sincerity, candor, truthfulness
•   Abiding by rules, abstaining from and eliminating illicit operations
•   Contributing to justice and social development
•   Promoting free trade.

Notwithstanding the focus on the global perspective, educational institutions, by nature, will have to take into account the country where they are headquartered and the type of executive they educate. There are major differences between Europe and the US, to consider just the two areas, in the practical implementa-tion of what is taught. In most European countries, there is quite a dense network of regulation on most of the ethically important issues for business. Workers' rights, social and medical care, and environmental issues are only a few examples where European companies have traditionally not had to consider what should guide their decisions because most of this has been tackled by the government in setting up a tight institutional framework for businesses. Examples range from the Scandinavian welfare state, to the German co-habitation system and the strong

Table 9.1 Key actors in business ethics

	US	Europe
Who is responsible for ethical conduct in business?	The individual	Social control by the collective
Who is the key actor in business ethics?	The corporation	Government, trade unions, corporate associations
What are the key guidelines for ethical behavior?	Corporate codes of ethics	Negotiated legal framework of business
What are the key issues in business ethics?	Misconduct and immorality in single decision situations	Social issues in organizing the framework of business

Source: Adapted from Crane and Matten (2004), p. 320

position of trade unions and workers' rights in France. In Europe, governments, trade unions and corporate associations have therefore been key actors in ethical themes. By contrast, in most of these areas, US official institutions do not regulate these themes and so the key actor has tended to be the corporation. Table 9.1 gives a comprehensive view of the key actors in both regions.

These differences must be taken into account when viewing the following examples for curricula, which the author thinks correspond to the recommendations on principles-based education for human centered management.

9.2 Two sets of exemplary business ethics curricula

The first set is an enumeration of learning objectives found in the English language versions of the websites of two German executive education institutions, *Wissenschaftliche Hochschule für Unternehmensführung* (WHU – Otto Beisheim School of Management; www.whu.edu) and Wittenberg Center for Global Ethics (WCGE; www.wcge.org).

WHU lists the following key objectives:

- Provide an engaging journey of learning, combining theory with practice
- Understand how the view on emerging markets has changed
- Analyze current challenges and opportunities of emerging markets
- Explore links between strategy, leadership and innovation
- Promote awareness on cultural differences and need to internationalize
- Develop and leverage personal networks and engage in trusting dialogue
- Reflect on the challenges that lie ahead and own role of leadership.

WCGE posts the following on its English website:

- An introduction to the principles of global ethics and value-oriented management

- Knowledge and tools which help to identify and analyze ethical challenges
- (Reflective competences), to develop solutions (constructive competencies) and to communicate these approaches (communication competencies).

The focus is on these topics:

> The basics of ethics – the moral quality of market economy – corporations and their responsibilities – the management of values – applied ethics in management practice.

The second set of examples presents content for regular curriculum courses in two German business schools (English version of their websites):

The Frankfurt School of Finance and Management (www.frankfurt-school. de) offers two modules: "Leading Intercultural Teams" and "People Working Across Boundaries" with the following contents:

> Motivation, trust, relationship-building, networking
> Developing awareness of critical situations
> Extrapolating beliefs, views and values
> Cross-cultural understanding of each team member
> Leadership – leading virtual teams:
> What do your team members expect and what kind of support do they need?
> Organizational and international diversity
> Developing individual and team goals
> Appropriate use of technology: "connecting" rather than "disconnecting."

And the European School of Management and Technology, Berlin (www.esmt. org) displays a module on "Integrative Leadership in Action" where the content is:

> Leaders, leadership, and followers
> Leading organizations through change
> Ethical dilemmas in leadership
> Corporate governance
> Managing across cultures
> Executive careers and transitions
> Leading and reinventing yourself
> Managing your back-to-the-job agenda
> Executive communication.

Other examples can be found in some other business schools or executive education institutions throughout the world. But not all of them list program contents in their websites or offer English versions. They obviously expect prospective students to trust the reputation of a highly renowned institution or to request detailed information directly. Another aspect, which may explain why large executive education institutions in the US expect participants or their organizations to first establish contact with the institution and request information, is that often executives must have a needs assessment or "philosophical coaching" to understand and capture the importance of principles-based "soft skills" training.

The two topics of leadership and morality have to be taught together as they have to be applied together in real life. There is an extensive body of published thought that examines the topics separately. The literature presumes that managers, leaders and organizations need one topic as much as the other and so would their stakeholders. Some writings raise the expectation that ethics and morality are instrumental in leading to a more profitable enterprise, and it helps organizations to stay out of trouble. Leadership writing is often more centered on accomplishing organizational objectives through people and teams, with the emphasis more on techniques and outcomes. Carroll (2003), examining the major articles of the 1990s and the early 2000s, found out that most of their authors pay little attention to the moral dimension of leadership. Only more recently, Carroll says, have the topics and literatures of ethics/morality and leadership begun to be integrated. It is hoped, then, that this book makes a difference.

9.3 Six teaching blocks

A considerable amount of higher education management programs advertises and claims to integrate moral, social and ecological contents into their curriculums. Some scholars express hope that this will help to eradicate greedy and unethically business practices (Wankel and Stachowitz-Stanusch 2011); it is therefore in the interest of scholars and practitioners alike to further improve this perspective of management education and training programs. The view that ethical leadership pays off in the long run is not new: A 1963 OECD publication quotes John Ulric Nef, co-founder of the University of Chicago's Committee on Social Thought, saying: "The future of industrial civilization in the decades and centuries which lie ahead of us is likely to depend less on the scientist, the engineers and the economists, than upon a renewal of the search for the perfection of the human personality" (OECD 2013). Half a century later, and after a series of economic crises partially attributed to opportunistic behaviors and unethical leadership, it looks like we still have lessons to learn. What learners need is teaching content that connects their experience and expectations. The purpose of this final section is to show avenues for conceptualizing content that has a nexus to practice.

As criticism on business education often highlights what is missing, but fails to offer constructive ideas for improvement, practitioners turn away from training programs when they find them to be overburdened with triviality or pure philosophy. They look for practical application which can solve the problems that business executives face daily. The proposal set forth in the following sections exhibits a Teaching Blocks construct directed to balance reflective, self-aware and practice-based learning which should help executive program faculty and executive program participants to advance social transformation in organizations and contribute to the common good.

The Teaching Blocks are grounded on functional aspects of management and relate each topic to experiences which most executives have encountered in their careers. The respective teaching contents are destined to

- Foster ethical leadership associated with accountability
- Guide leaders and the people they supervise to achieve job satisfaction and high performance as individuals, teams and organizations.

Leadership always pursues predictable or expected outcomes. So, the question about "what and how to teach" in an executive or leadership course or program inevitably connects ethical principles with organizational performance. Consequently, each of the six Teaching Blocks (TBs) described next connects to practical aspects of business. They show how strengthening human centered management produces perceptible outcomes:

1 *Capacity building*: What do executives consider to be leadership capacity?
2 *The "moral market" axiom*: Does the free market system corrode or construct moral character?
3 *Systems thinking and cause–effect relationships*: Are there (tangible) benefits from morality?
4 *Ethical leadership impact on business processes*: Does morality improve efficiency?
5 *The role model perspective*: Is there a visible effect of ethical behavior on the workplace and beyond?
6 *Ethical stakeholder-relationship management*: Can human centered management transcend to all the organization's constituencies and the external social environment?

TB 1. Capacity building

There is continuous debate whether a person's attitudes and values change learning new things. Even though obtaining insight in issues of morality and ethics goes beyond simple learning, the question remains if ethical judgment can be affected by a business course or the faculty/instructors who teach it. Some studies give an affirmative response (Glenn 1992; Desplaces et al. 2007; Jones 2009). And when research claims (e.g., Bass 1999) that leaders can inspire followers to change perceptions and motivations, this indicates that leadership values can therefore be taught and learned.

A survey conducted by Ahn, Ettner, and Loupin (2012) among senior executives in business, non-profit and government uncovered the following *eight value-driven determinants of leadership* in order of importance:

- Integrity (adherence to moral and ethical codes)
- Good judgment (flexibility and situation awareness)
- Leadership by example (collective actions, decisions, general behavior)
- Ethical decision-making (adherence to the principle of "do no harm")
- Trust (reliance between leader and followers)
- Justice/fairness (impartiality and equal treatment)
- Humility (lack of arrogance, capacity to listen carefully, understand deeply)
- Sense of urgency (immediacy, action orientation to achieve results).

The results of the survey are shown in Exhibit 9.1.

The graph shows that Integrity is valued highest among this group of executives, followed by Good judgment and Leadership by example, while Sense of urgency and Humility are ranked lowest. Although it would be provocative to

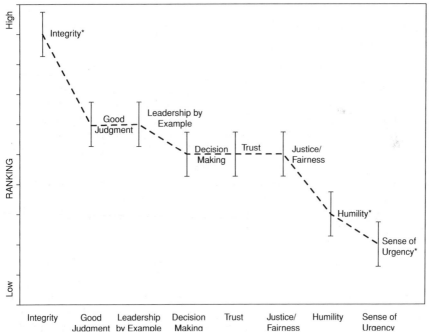

Exhibit 9.1 Rankings of values by multinational leaders

Source: Ahn, Ettner, and Loupin (2012), p. 126

debate these findings, there is almost consensus that leaders need to have the right combination of patience and impatience (Ahn, Ettner, and Loupin 2012, p. 124). And with respect to Humility, it is apparent that a leader needs to live through an ordeal first to grasp its meaning and learn a lesson. Jeffrey Immelt, CEO of General Electric, has said that instead of blaming economic conditions for poor performance during the 2008 crisis, it was indeed the crisis that made General Electric stronger: I am "humbler and hungrier because after the crisis I learned I need to be a better listener. It would have helped me very much to anticipate the radical changes that occurred" (Glader 2009, p. B2). Immelt's lesson in humility validates leaders' needs to cope with contingencies in a way that puts accomplishments and talents in proper perspective to enhance authenticity and credibility (Van Dierendonck 2011; Kanungo 2001).

When there is a consensus on the ingredients of moral capacity, and when managers can be taught to reflect these with their own (moral) behavior, will this eliminate management anomalies, like fraud, conspiracy, negligence and disrespect? It obviously does not suffice. So, having some *moral managers* in the market is not enough; it is the market that needs to be moral. The *moral market* construct (Boatright 1999; Smith 2005) is inextricably linked to human centered management, and the assumption is growing increasingly strong that this lies at the center of potential solutions in the 21st century.

TB 2. Connecting individual capacity to the theory of "moral markets"

The "moral market" construct (Boatright 1999) focuses on economic mechanisms that advance ethical ends that deter and punish immoral behavior. The axiom states clearly that the main objective of markets and competition is to serve human beings. And this is the morale of "doing good": competition and markets guarantee and enhance opportunities for all individuals to attain a better life, and everybody is free to choose which opportunity to pursue. This freedom of choice explains what buyers prefer, which provides a feedback to the producers. A market, thus, corrects itself and, in its purest manifestation, should not give room to lawfulness or immorality. But there is the counter-argument that competitive markets reward selfishness instead of cooperative activity (Hart 2010). The answer lies in the concept of freedom: freedom allows for human imperfections, and markets are human communities. Illegal activities do happen in market societies when opportunistic people and leaders choose short-sighted, self-serving decisions, instead of long-term social solutions.

But when the question arises if free markets corrode moral character, as the Templeton Foundation did (Bogle 2008), it is too nearsighted to accept for an answer what Nobel laureate Joseph E. Stiglitz has stated: "the market may result in a distribution of income that does not comport with any system of social justice" (Stiglitz 2007, p. 487). The proper answer would be that the incompatibility of profits and social justice is not the cause of social injustice, but a corollary: business history shows that corporate managers who have hold control of giant publicly held business enterprises – without holding significant ownership stakes – were lured into all sorts of aberrations hindering their companies (from Enron to WorldCom to Siemens, etc.). But the economic and business landscape is not dominated by these irresponsible few. The system is led by leaders who, while pursuing a reasonable self-interest, exhibit distinguished positive character traits of prudence, initiative and self-reliance to advance the interests of their corporations aligned with the well-being of the local and global community (Bogle 2008). And the corrective system, at the end, worked to expectations. The then culprits of Enron, WorldCom, and Siemens were punished and no longer lead these corporations. From there we get to TB 3, the cause–effect relations.

TB 3. Systems thinking and cause–effect relationships

Human centered managers should learn to identify, assess, diagnose and analyze ethical issues. This type of analysis implies and reveals that morally enhanced attitudes increase the validity of business decisions and consequences. Any experienced manager will have learned that trust and reciprocity yield benefits and that openness produces more success than the withholding of information. This applies to tangible effects like smooth course of action in a supply chain (Capó-Vicedo, Mula, and Capó 2011) or when developing new products in distributive collaboration (Wang 2013), but there are also soft outcomes in cause–effect relations. Brown and Treviño (2006) identify soft outcomes as effects that cannot easily be measured in ethical leadership. These authors identify the following four types of soft outcome in their study:

- Ethical decision-making of leader's followers
- Level of satisfaction, motivation and commitment of leader's followers
- Prosocial behavior (going above and beyond the call of duty)
- Counterproductive behavior (a negative correlation).

The study is based on a multi-sample field survey by Turner et al. (2002), and the results show that persons with higher levels of moral reasoning are more likely to influence their followers to make decisions based on moral principles, demonstrate more concern for the rights of others, and value fairness. A corrective effect has also been reported. Employees' behavior that is harmful to the organization or to other employees decreases when ethical leaders clearly communicate performance expectations and standards of appropriate conduct and spell out consequences associated with rule violations (Brown and Treviño 2006, p. 607).

Contradictory results also exist. Abusive supervision using power and authority to humiliate, ridicule, and mistreat subordinates decreases social-citizenship behavior (Zellars, Tepper, and Duffy 2002) perpetuates detrimental behavior that induces retaliation and aggression (Mitchell and Ambrose 2007). A deeper analysis exhibits a two step-relation: an intangible input (abusive supervision), an intangible outcome (counterproductive behavior) and tangibly deficient organization performance. Twofold cause–effect relations like this require systems thinking.

Cause–effect relations and systems thinking can be taught more effectively when showing that managers often deal with issues where merely solving a problem does not improve the situation and they need to learn to see behind the problem, why it evolved and how it is connected to other issues (Heracleous and Rao 2008). Systems thinking, here, helps to solve interconnected issues through analyzing one by one in isolation. So, for instance, a manager can become aware that customer satisfaction, employee capacity, and competitive technologies are entwined with each other. But from the logic of division of work, solutions for each of these different issues may not be closely intertwined. In systems thinking, the three issues would be viewed as complements that are constitutive to the system of a business operation.

TB 4. The process perspective

M.L. Emiliani, a management educator of Central Connecticut University, assesses that "As educators, we should teach students that improvement is a human centered activity, and it is impossible to innovate and improve processes when managers penalize employees trying new ideas that have potential to fail" (Emiliani 2006, p. 370). Practitioners would translate this into the many cases where abusive supervision, jealous bosses, lack of understanding and the inability to listen to employees cause significant damage to business processes. In opposition, teamwork and the ability to collaborate in a frank and non-opportunistic way is more important to innovation than individual talent and boosts employees' performance and loyalty (Subramaniam and Youndt 2005; Burt and Ronchi 2007).

A 2005 McKinsey report indicates that while companies with high collaborative management achieve superior financial performance, only 25% of senior executives described their organizations as effective at sharing knowledge across boundaries. But nearly 80% acknowledged that collaboration was crucial to growth (McKinsey 2005). An update of this report, five years later, found that management still relies on a few of the same strategies to improve: organization restructuring, business-process reengineering, cross-unit incentives, teamwork training. Despite evidence that many fail because they generate unintended consequences or overlook underlying issues that provide formidable obstacles for people to change behavior and advance (Aiken et al. 2009).

A critical issue is effective collaboration. Collaboration is based on a common purpose that also requires common trust. And instigating trust is a most critical leadership task. There is much research on trust *in* leadership (Yang and Mossholder 2010; Norman, Avolio, and Luthans 2010), but there is much less research and literature on how ethical leaders ensure that trust prevails in their organizations and among their followers (van den Akker et al. 2009). Tschannen–Moran (2004) identifies five dimensions of trust that support trustworthiness in the workplace:

- Benevolence (I convey my knowledge to you without expecting a reward)
- Honesty (I fully share my ideas with you)
- Openness (I do not have second thoughts)
- Reliability (I will be around when needed)
- Competence (I make sure that my abilities are state-of-the-art).

Ethical practitioners consent that these five dimensions are the roots of "real" trust (Kyte 2007). Collaborating trustfully in the weave of a firm's business processes stimulates the learning process for all the people involved. Collective learning is a natural part of organizational development, but it only works the full through human centered management. Selfishness in this regard sooner or later leads to organizational atrophy with heavy costs for all the people involved.

Even the toughest managers recognize that trust, collaboration and social learning produce useful outcomes. And managers are becoming increasingly concerned when they realize through facts that in the long run there is no useful outcome if they do not set an example.

TB 5. The role model perspective and the "common good"

The process perspective shows that employees, who have a clear perception of their leaders' ethical performance, outline their work context more effectively and deploy behaviors transferred from their leaders such as fair treatment, shared values and integrity in personnel and business transactions. There are many critical statements which say that self-interest rules over altruism. But ignoring the importance of human centered behavior on an organization's performance and outcome (as well as on the structure of markets) runs against the reliability and validity of any unbiased analysis.

The encyclical *Caritas in Veritate* by Pope Benedict XVI explains it this way: "Ethics is deeply integrated into the structure of entrepreneurial and managerial actions such that any attempt at arriving at decisions on merely 'technical' grounds fail" (Grassl and Habisch 2011, p. 44). This statement does not imply that an enterprise should not strive for effectiveness, but that it will never succeed if it is merely technically effective. Technical effectiveness relies on collaboration and teamwork in organizations, with leaders setting role model examples. And it is their duty to counter moral muteness through what may be called "good conversation" (Sims, Brinkmann and Sauser 2016, p. 47). This would as well radiate beyond an organization's boundaries to reach the domain of what is called the common good.

The common good of society is the referential value for all businesses and all government undertakings (Mahon and McGowan 1991). It is a classical humanistic concept in the Aristotelian tradition and Medieval Scholastics, philosophically embedded in natural law theory and assumed into Catholic social thought as a key reference for business ethics (Garriga and Melé 2004). A society attains the common good when its members interiorize the four fundaments of Aristotelian humanism (Wicker 1973):

- Prudence and wisdom, using good judgment, taking counsel.
- Fortitude and courage, perseverance and persistence for "noble" causes.
- Temperance and moderation, humility, acknowledging own limitations.
- Justice and fairness, unselfishness.

All these are entrenched in the leadership capabilities as identified in TB 1.

Another term included in the humanistic perspective is *universal*. In the context of globalization, some critics raise the question if humanism is a universal concept. The answer is that humanism has always been valued worldwide, in both its demeanors of being human centered and of dogma-free reasoning (Kudishina 2005). It expands across developed and developing nations. In sub-Saharan Africa, "Swahili humanism" is embedded in the notion of "*utu*," which means "putting moral knowledge in action" (Kresse 2007, p. 168). In East Asia, it is rooted in Confucian philosophy, principles and values (Wei-Ming. (2008). And even though it is sometimes said that forms of life based on Confucian ethics are different from Western values, its emphasis on humanity, rightness, propriety, wisdom, filial piety and loyalty, stemming from communalism rather than individualism (Pye 1988), are increasingly in sync with Aristotelian and Western values.

TB 6. The stakeholder relation perspective

Human centered management is displayed through interactions inside and outside the corporation. Therefore, it is as important in management that the relationships of corporate managers extend to a multitude of stakeholders. Managers are expected to be accountable to shareholders, but also to all the people in the community who are or will be impacted, directly or indirectly, by corporative decision and business operations, whether economic, environmental or social in nature.

This dimension has a systems perspective, meaning that an impact affecting one stakeholder group also affects all stakeholders at the same or at different levels. There is a growing body of evidence in business literature that demonstrates positive and instrumental links between corporate social performance and financial performance (Freeman 2004; Maak and Pless 2006; Valentine 2014), and this naturally includes effects on stakeholders. And the way to achieve stakeholder value is managing with integrity, and making *profits with principles*.

The concept "profits with principles" was coined by Body Shop founder Anita Roddick (Maak and Pless 2006, p. 100), based on awareness that a significant part of her business success originated in managing stakeholder relations ethically and prudently (Roddick 1991). Her design was taken by the Corporate Social Responsibility Initiative at Harvard Business School. The Harvard concept of "Profits with Principles – Delivering Value with Values" (Jackson and Nelson 2004) places shareholder and social value-added in relation with each other and the creation of social value at par with shareholder value. For both, an organization needs to develop processes, products and services that meet customer requirements and societal requirements, to be compliant to all rules and regulations, to carefully control costs, risks, liabilities and impacts, and to give back to the communities in its environment through community investment and transparent communication.

Building sustainable stakeholder relations, beyond the ethical foundation, requires legitimacy. And legitimacy is rooted in a moral conception. There are several typologies of legitimacy in the literature (e.g., Suchman 1995), including regulative (compliance with laws and regulations) and organizational (conferred to an institution from outside stakeholders).

Leaders can build a legitimacy reservoir through effective communications with the organization's social surroundings, like customers, suppliers, joint venture partners, banks and other organizations in the local, national and international community. A critical consideration for successful stakeholder management is a clear philosophical conception that combines ethical, economic and social considerations.

The six teaching blocks presented in this section aim at meeting the demands of practitioners who wish to delve into clear-cut essentials, and to academics who wish to learn the concerns of practitioners.

A comparison may help here. There is a great book by Louis Coutts titled *The Six Hour MBA* (2013). He does not propose to substitute a regular MBA course by one that lasts only six hours. His intent is to demystify management. In a similar fashion, the six TBs demystify the philosophical content of ethics by exploring morality, which is a basic human (and not a metaphysical) concern, in the context of business concerns. Practitioners will find this more understandable than a theoretical treatise, and it should help them to perceive how issues of responsible leadership are deeply engrained in any business.

Teaching or putting business ethics education into practice cannot be exclusively based on case studies. Effective deployment must be complementary, "moving towards the grounded theory approach" (Maital, Prakhya, and Seshadri 2008). That means, begin with a problem, issue or challenge (a "case"), then avoid jumping to data analysis and solution directly ("action strategies"), but systematically seek causal conditions, context, conditions and consequences in order to understand the process and arrive at the desirable outcome. The six TBs guide faculty and students in this "complementary" direction.

The approach of our six TBs connects to the fundamental human centered principle that the purpose of the firm is not solely to maximize stockholders' wealth; they must deploy their power in a socially responsible manner to line up the competing interests of all stakeholders. This is an equally important responsibility. It has become an adopted position among business leaders that contributing to the well-being of the people in the local, national and global constituencies of their firm will produce a benefit to the firm and its shareholders as well. So, leaders must make their decisions in a way that aligns the complementary and also the competing interests of all stakeholders. Similarly, executive education program providers worldwide need to abide by the same principles.

Advocates of the human centered fundamentals mentioned earlier are increasingly shaping business school curricula and executive education worldwide. Among other agencies, there are the UN Global Compact, the Globally Responsible Leadership Initiative (GLRI), the World Business Council on Sustainable Development (WBCSD), the European Foundation for Management Development (EFMD) and the Academy of Business in Society (ABIS Global). The AACSB (American Association of Collegiate Schools of Business), founded in 1916, has expanded rapidly worldwide after 1997, when it accredited the first foreign business school in a French university. Today, this Tampa, Florida-based accrediting agency of the largest global business schools has accredited over 1,400 business programs in 87 countries, and it is requiring business programs to address ethics in business to attain accreditation. And likewise, this is done by EQUIS (European Quality Improvement System for Universities) and AMBA (the Association of MBAs).

Both for university-based executive education programs and for executive training taking place inside business corporations (which are approximately 50% of the total and growing fast; see Thomas and Wilson 2013), the question remains, with regard to an ethics content, not too much now about "Why," but about "What" and "How." Still, there are always some who argue that "the notion of a socially responsible corporation is an oxymoron because of the conflicted nature of the interests of stakeholders in a corporation" (Littrell 2011, p. 63). But if top management takes up the competing interests of all stakeholders in an ethical fashion to decipher conflicts, then solving these conflicts simply becomes a routine. For this, top management must take up the obligation to train ethical leadership at all levels. In the essence, the "What" and "How" is about teaching human centered management: The simple nexus is that complementing economic profits with people and process improvement has become a necessary condition to rebuilding the basis of corporate business performance (Locke 2013).

Well-trained leaders, who practice what they talk, can revert the notion that business activities always have a private return that is much higher than the perceive social return. This is necessary because business companies contribute substantially to progress, and today it is unequivocal that the only way to achieve this is with ethical leadership. Jordi Canals, one of the prominent proponents of executive education (Canals 2010, p. ix) expresses it this way: "There is a widespread belief that the quality of business leadership can be improved . . . [and that] the sound ethical principles that once were replaced by sheer opportunism and self-interest must return to the boardrooms."

Outlook

The author of this book is confident that it contributes to defeating the claim that morality and self-interest are contradictory and that we live in a "bi-moral society" where people guide their lives by two sets of principles, as argued by John Hendry in *Between Enterprise and Ethics* (Hendry 2004). Why should the set of principles that "emphasizes our duties and obligations to others for treating people honestly and with respect, treating them fairly and without prejudice, helping them and caring for them when needed to" (Hendry 2004, p. 2) *not* guide the decisions of business leaders and of people who lead other organizations? These obligations and what has been called *market morality* are not opposites. The morality of the market is not based just on self-interest; market participants accept they have duties and responsibilities. The vast majority of business people abide by these duties and responsibilities and feel accountable to society, but it is the few outsiders that receive attention in the media and, unfortunately, in academic writings as well. Appeals for managing the tensions of the "bi-moral society" may be well founded, but they accept that conjoinment of morality and the free market is impossible. This book holds that conjoinment of morality and the free market is possible, with continuous dialogue and deliberative forms of engagement with stakeholders, and the book also holds that a moral consensus can always be found if people are following the human centered paradigm.

References

Abed, G.T., and Gupta, S. (eds., 2002). *Governance, Corruption, & Economic Performance*. Washington, DC: International Monetary Fund.

Achbar, M., and Bakan, J. (2003). *The Corporation: A Film*. Frederick, MA: Big Picture Media.

Adler, N.J., and Bird, F.B. (1988). International dimensions of executive integrity: Who is responsible for the world? Srivastva, S., and Associates (eds.), *Executive Integrity: The Search for High Human Values in Organizational Life*. San Francisco, CA: Jossey-Bass.

Aguado, R., and Albareda, L. (2016). A new approach of humanistic management education based on the promotion of justice and human dignity in a sustainable economy. Lepeley, M.T., von Kimakonwitz, E., and Bardy, R. (eds.), *Human Centered Management in Executive Education: Global Imperatives, Innovation and New Directions*. Houndmills: Palgrave Macmillan, pp. 182–201.

Ahn, M.J., Ettner, L.W., and Loupin, A. (2012). Values versus traits-based approaches to leadership: Insights from an analysis of the Aeneid. *Leadership & Organization Development Journal*, Vol. 33 (2), pp. 112–130.

Aiken, C., Keller, S., Lavoie, J., and Weiss, L.M. (2009). *How Do I Drive Effective Collaboration to Deliver Real Business Impact?* New York: McKinsey.

Alavi, M., and Denford, J. (2011). Knowledge management: Process, practice and web 2.0. Easterby-Smith, M., and Lyles, M.A. (eds.), *Handbook of Organizational Learning and Knowledge Management* (2nd ed.). Chichester: Wiley and Sons, pp. 105–124.

Albee, E. (2014). *A History of English Utilitarianism* (Vol. 1). London: Routledge.

Allaway, J. (2005). Our lives are not measured in dollars: The Alaska native claims settlement act unrealized. *Journal of Land, Resources & Environmental Law*, Vol. 25, pp. 139–147.

Allison, J.A. (2015). *The Leadership Crisis and the Free Market Cure: Why the Future of Business Depends on the Return to Life, Liberty and the Pursuit of Happyness*. New York: McGraw Hill Professional.

Anandamurti. (1994). *Discourses on Tantra*. Calcutta: Ananda Marga.

Andriof, J. (2001). Patterns of stakeholder partnership building. Andriof, J., and McIntosh, M. (eds.), *Perspectives on Corporate Citizenship*. Sheffield: Greenleaf, pp. 215–238.

Annas J. (2006). Virtue ethics and social psychology. *A Priori*, Vol. 2, pp. 20–34.

Appiah, K.A. (2008). *Experiments in Ethics*. Cambridge, MA: Harvard University Press.

April, K., Peters, K., Locke, K., and Mlambo, C. (2010). Ethics and leadership: Enablers and stumbling blocks. *Journal of Public Affairs*, Vol. 10 (3), pp. 152–172.

Argyris, C. (1952). *The Impact of Budgets on People*. New York: Controllership Foundation.

Ariely, G. (2005). Intellectual capital and knowledge management. Schwartz, D. (ed.), *Encyclopedia of Knowledge Management*. Hershey, PA: Idea Group, pp. 281–288.

Ashkansay, N.M., Wilderrom, C.P.M., and Peterson, M.F. (2000). *Handbook of Organizational Culture and Climate*. Thousand Oaks, CA: Sage.

Ashman, D. (2001). Civil society collaboration with business: Bringing empowerment back in. *World Development*, Vol. 29 (7), pp. 1097–1113.

Audi, F. (2012). The place of ethical theory in business ethics. Brenkert, G.G., and Beauchamp, T.L. (eds.), *The Oxford Handbook of Business Ethics*. Oxford: Oxford University Press, pp. 46–72.

Bakan, J. (2004). *The Corporation: The Pathological Pursuit of Profit and Power*. New York: Simon & Schuster.

Bamberger, K. A, and Mulligan. D.K. (2013). Privacy in Europe: Initial data on governance choices and corporate practices. *George Washington Law Review*, Vol. 81, pp. 1529–1580.

Bardy, R. (2002). Leadership in the US and in Continental Europe. *Controller-Magazin*, pp. 24–28.

Bardy, R. (2015). Business ethics, intellectual capital and corporate performance: A process management approach. Nelson, K. (ed.), *Business Intelligence, Strategies and Ethics*. Hauppauge, NY: Nova Science, pp. 73–89.

Bardy, R. (2016). Can foreign direct investment contribute to restoring social order? *University of St. Thomas Law Journal*, Vol. 12, pp. 249–270.

Bardy, R., and Rubens, A. (2010). Is there a transatlantic divide? Reviewing Peter F. Drucker's thoughts on ethics and leadership of US and European managers. *Management Decision*, Vol. 48 (4), pp. 528–540.

Bardy, R., Drew, S.A.W., and Kennedy, T. (2012). Foreign investment and ethics: How to contribute to social responsibility by doing business in less-developed countries. *Journal of Business Ethics*, Vol. 106 (3), pp. 267–282.

Bardy, R., and Massaro, M. (2013). Stakeholder dialogues in transition economies: educating and training leaders to build relations between investors and local communities. Alon, I., Jones, V., and McIntyre, J.R. (eds.). *Business Education in Emerging Market Economies: Perspectives and Best Practices*. Houndmills: Palgrave Macmillan, pp. 162–180.

Bar-Gill, O., and Ferrari, F. (2010). Informing consumers about themselves. *Erasmus Law Review*, Vol. 3 (2), pp. 93–119.

Bartley, W.W. (ed., 2011). *The Collected Works of F.A. Hayek*. Chicago: University of Chicago Press.

Bass, B.M. (1999). Two decades of research and development in transformational leadership European *Journal of Work and Organizational Psychology*. Vol. 8 (1), pp. 9–32.

Bassi, L., Frauenheim, E., and McMurrer, D. (2011). *Good Company: Business Success in the Worthiness Era*. Oakland, CA: Berrett-Koehler.

Basu, K. (1999). Child labor: Cause, consequence, and cure, with remarks on international labor standards. *Journal of Economic Literature*, Vol. 37, pp. 1083–1119.

Bauman, Z. (1993). *Postmodern Ethics*. Oxford: Blackwell.

Baumhart, R.C. (1962). *Ethics of the Businessman*. New York: America Press.

Behrman, J.N. (1981). *Discourses on Ethics and Business*. Cambridge, MA: Oelgeschlager, Gunn & Hain.

Belal, A.R. (2002). Stakeholder accountability or stakeholder management: A review of UK firms' social and ethical accounting, auditing, and reporting practices. *Corporate Social Responsibility and Environmental Management*, Vol. 9 (1), pp. 8–25.

Bell, N. (2004). The exploitation of migrants in European agriculture. Michele LeVoy, M., Verbruggen, N., and Wets, J. (eds.), *Undocumented Migrant Workers in Europe*. Brussels: European Parliament, pp. 41–46.

Bendell, J. (ed., 2000). *Terms for Endearment: Business, NGOs and Sustainable Development*. Sheffield: Greenleaf.

Benhabib, S. (1993). *Situating the Self: Gender, Community and Postmodernism in Contemporary Ethics*. New York: Psychology Press.

Bennett, S.J. (1991). *Ecopreneuring: The Complete Guide to Small Business Opportunities From the Environmental Revolution*. New York: John Wiley.

Benson, E., and Dodds, F. (2010). *The Stakeholder Empowerment Project*. Geneva: Stakeholder Forum.

Berman, S.L., Wicks, A.C., Kotha, S., and Jones, T.M. (1999). Does stakeholder orientation matter? The relationship between stakeholder management models and firm financial performance. *Academy of Management journal*, Vol. 42 (5), pp. 488–506.

Bierstaker, J.L., Brody, R.G., and Pacini, C. (2006). Accountants' perceptions regarding fraud detection and prevention methods. *Managerial Auditing Journal*, Vol. 21 (5), pp. 520–535.

Bishop, P., and Preston, N. (2000). *Local Government, Public Enterprise and Ethics*. Leichhardt, NSW: Federation Press.

Boatright, J.R. (1999). Does business ethics rest on a mistake? *Business Ethics Quarterly*, Vol. 9 (4), pp. 583–591.

Boatright, J.R. (2013). *Ethics in Finance* (3rd ed.). Chichester: John Wiley and Sons.

Boddy, C.R. (2005). The implications of corporate psychopaths for business and society: An initial examination and a call to arms. *Australasian Journal of Business and Behavioural Sciences*, Vol. 1 (2), pp. 30–40.

Bogle, J.C. (2008). *Does the Free Market Corrode Moral Character?* Templeton Foundation Series of Conversations No. 4. Available at www.templeton.org/market. Accessed September 22, 2017.

Bohm, D. (1980). *Wholeness and the Implicate Order*. London: Routledge & Kegan Paul.

Boiral, O., Baron, C., and Gunnlaugson, O. (2014). Environmental leadership and consciousness development: A case study among Canadian SMEs. *Journal of Business Ethics*, Vol. 123 (3), pp. 363–383.

Bok, S. (2002). *Common Values*. Columbia: University of Missouri Press.

Bollier, D. (1996). *Aiming Higher. 25 Stories of How Companies Prosper by Combining Sound Management and Social Vision*. New York: AMACOM, Division of American Management Association.

Bolton, S.C., Kim, R.C.H., and O'Gorman, K.D. (2011). Corporate social responsibility as a dynamic internal organizational process: A case study. *Journal of Business Ethics*, Vol. 101 (1), pp. 61–74.

Bontis, N. (1998). Intellectual capital: An exploratory study that develops measures and models. *Management Decision*, Vol. 36 (2), pp. 63–76.

Bowie, N.E. (1999). *Business Ethics: A Kantian Perspective*. Malden, MA: Blackwell.

Bowie, N.E. (2013). *Business Ethics in the 21st Century*. New York: Springer Books.

Bowie, N.E., and Werhane, P.H. (2004). *Management Ethics*. Malden, MA: Wiley-Blackwell.

Brand, A. (1990). *The Force of Reason: An Introduction to Habermas' Theory of Communicative Action*. Sydney: Unwin Hyman.

Brenkert, G.G., and Beauchamp, T.L. (eds., 2010). *The Oxford Handbook of Business Ethics*. Oxford: Oxford University Press.

Brown, M.E., and Treviño, L.K. (2006). Ethical leadership: A review and future directions. *Leadership Quarterly*, Vol. 17, pp. 595–616.

Brown, M.E., Treviño, L.K., and Harrison, D.A. (2005). Ethical leadership: A social learning perspective for construct development and testing. *Organizational Behavior and Human Decision Processes*, Vol. 97, pp. 117–134.

Brown, R. (2001). *Group Processes: Dynamics Within and Between Groups*. Malden, MA: Wiley-Blackwell.

Brown, W. (2002). *The European Union and Africa: The Restructuring of North–South Relations*. London: I.B. Tauris.

Browne, J., Nuttall, R., and Stadlen, T. (2015). *Connect: How Companies Succeed by Engaging Radically With Society*. New York: Random House.

Bruch, H., and Walter, F. (2005). The keys to rethinking corporate philanthropy. *MIT Sloan Management Review*, Vol. 47, pp. 48–56.

Buchholz, R.A., and Rosenthal, S.B. (2005). The spirit of entrepreneurship and the qualities of moral decision making: Toward a contemporary conceptual framework for stakeholder theory. *Journal of Business Ethics*, Vol. 58 (1–3), pp. 137–148.

Buckley, P.J., 2009. The impact of the global factory on economic development. *Journal of World Business*, Vol. 44 (2), pp. 131–143.

Burack, E. (1999). Spirituality in the workplace. *Journal of Organizational Change Management*, Vol. 12 (4), 280–291.

Burchell, J., and Cook, J. (2008). Stakeholder dialogue and organisational learning: Changing relationships between companies and NGOs. *Business Ethics: A European Review*, Vol. 17 (1), pp. 35–46.

Burger, R. (2008). *Aristotle's Dialogue with Socrates: On the Nicomachean Ethics*. Chicago: University of Chicago Press.

Burns, J.M. (1978). *Leadership*. New York: Harper and Row.

Burnside-Lawry, J. (2010). *Participatory Communication and Listening: An Exploratory Study of Organisational Listening Competency*. Ph.D. thesis, RMIT University, Melbourne, Australia. Available at http://researchbank.rmit.edu.au/eserv/rmit:4933/Burnside_Lawry.pdf. Accessed May 23, 2016.

Burt, R.S., and Ronchi, D. (2007). Teaching executives to see social capital. *Social Science Research*, Vol. 36 (3), pp. 1156–1183.

Callahan, D. (1980). Goals in the teaching of ethics. Callahan, D., and Bok, S. (eds.), *Ethics Teaching in Higher Education*. New York: Plenum, pp. 61–80.

Cameron, K. (2012). *Positive Leadership: Strategies for Extraordinary Performance*. San Francisco, CA: Berrett-Koehler.

Campbell, D., Moore, G., and Metzger, M. (2002). Corporate philanthropy in the UK 1985–2000: Some empirical findings. *Journal of Business Ethics*, Vol. 39 (1–2), pp. 29–42.

Canals, J. (2010). *Building Respected Companies*. Cambridge: Cambridge University Press.

Cannon, M.D., and Edmondson, A.C., 2005. Failing to learn and learning to fail (intelligently): How great organizations put failure to work to innovate and improve. *Long Range Planning*, Vol. 38 (3), pp. 299–319.

Capó-Vicedo, J., Mula, J., and Capó, J. (2011). A social network-based organizational model for improving knowledge management in supply chains. *Supply Chain Management: An International Journal*, Vol. 16 (4), pp. 284–293.

Carey, C. (1999). Unocal corporation can be liable for human rights abuses in Burma. *Human Rights Brief*, Vol. 7 (1), pp. 4–9.

Carnevale, A.P. (2000). *Community Colleges and Career Qualifications*. Washington, DC: American Association for Community Colleges.

Carpenter, M.A., Bauer, T., and Erdogan, B. (2009). *Principles of Management*. Washington, DC: Flat World Knowledge.

Carr, A. (1968). Is business bluffing ethical? *Harvard Business Review* (Jan.-Feb.), pp. 143–155.

Carr, M. (2004). *Chains of Fortune: Linking Women Producers and Workers With Global Markets*. London: Commonwealth Secretariat.

Carroll, A.B. (1991). The pyramid of corporate social responsibility: Toward the moral management of organizational stakeholders. *Business Horizons*, Vol. 34 (4), pp. 39–48.

Carroll, A.B. (1996). *Business and Society: Ethics and Stakeholder Management* (3rd ed.). Cincinnati, OH: Southwestern.

Carroll, A.B. (2003). Ethical leadership: From moral manager to moral leader. Ferrell, O.C., True, S.L., and Pelton, L.E. (eds.), *Rights, Relationships & Responsibilities: Business Ethics and Social Impact Management*, Vol. 1, pp. 7–17.

Carroll, A.B., and Shabana, K.M. (2010). The business case for corporate social responsibility: A review of concepts, research and practice. *International Journal of Management Reviews*, Vol. 12 (1), pp. 85–105.

Case, J. (1995). *Open Book Management*. New York: HarperCollins.

Cassin, R.L. (2009). *Bribery Everywhere: Chronicles From the Foreign Corrupt Practices Act*. Raleigh, NC: lulu.com.

Casson, M. (2006). Culture and economic performance. Ginsburgh, V.A., and Throsby, D. (eds.), *Handbook of the Economics of Art and Culture*, Vol. 1. Amsterdam: Elsevier, pp. 359–397.

Castka, P., and Balzarova, M.A. (2008). ISO 26000 and supply chains – On the diffusion of the social responsibility standard. *International Journal of Production Economics*, Vol. 163 (11), pp. 274–286.

Cavanagh, G.F. (2006). *American Business Values: A Global Perspective* (5th ed.). Trenton, NJ: Upper Saddle River.

Chandler, B.D. (2011). *Organizations and Ethics: Antecedents and Ethics and Compliance Officers Association Consequences of the Implementation of the Ethics and Compliance Officer Position*. Dissertation Presented to the Faculty of the Graduate School of the University of Texas at Austin.

Chapman, B., and Sisodia, R. (2015). *Everybody Matters. The Extraordinary Power of Caring for Your People Like Family*. New York: Portfolio/Penguin.

Charter, M., Peattie, K., Ottman, J., and Polonsky, M.J. (2002). *Marketing and Sustainability*. Farnham: Centre for Sustainable Design.

Chatterjee, A. (2008). Social compliance, social accountability and corporate social responsibility. *Mainstream Weekly*, April 19.

Chatterji, A.K., Levine, D.I., and Toffel, M.W. (2009). How well do social ratings actually measure corporate social responsibility? *Journal of Economics & Management Strategy*, Vol. 18 (1), pp. 125–169.

Chen, M.-C., Cheng S.-J., and Hwang, Y. (2005). An empirical investigation of the relationship between intellectual capital and firms' market value and financial performance. *Journal of Intellectual Capital*, Vol. 6 (2), 159–176.

Chia, R., and Morgan, S. (1996). Educating the philosopher-manager de-signing the times. *Management Learning*, Vol. 27 (1), pp. 37–64.

Chiappero-Martinetti, E., Egdell, V., Hollywood, E., and McQuaid, R. (2015). Operationalisation of the capability approach. *Technical and Vocational Education and Training: Issues, Concerns and Prospects*, Vol. 20, pp. 115–139.

Chirilă, M. (2009). Remarks on the impact of cultural differences relating to business ethics and tourist behaviour of service suppliers and consumers in Romania. *The Annals of "Dunarea de Jos" University of Galati Fascicle I: Economics and Applied Informatics*. Vol. 15 (2), pp. 503–506.

Choi, J., and Wang, H. (2009). Stakeholder relations and the persistence of corporate financial performance. *Strategic Management Journal*, Vol. 30 (8), pp. 895–907.

Chorafas, D.N. (2015). *Business Efficiency and Ethics: Values and Strategic Decision Making*. New York: Palgrave Macmillan.

Choudhary, A. (2013). Anatomy and impact of Bribery on Siemens AG. *Journal of Legal, Ethical and Regulatory Issues*, Vol. 16 (2), pp. 131–142.

CIPS (Chartered Institute of Purchasing and Supply). *Corporate Code of Ethics*. Available at: www.cips.org/cips-for-business/supply-assurance/corporate-ethical-procurement-and-supply/corporate-code-of-ethics/

Ciulla, J.B. (2004). *Is Good Leadership Contrary to Human Nature?* Presentation at the Gallup Leadership Institute Summit, Lincoln, NE.

Ciulla, J.B. (2013). *Leadership Ethics*. Hoboken, NY: Blackwell.

Claeys, G. (2014). *Thomas Paine: Social and Political Thought*. Durham, NC: National Humanities Center.

Clarke, M., Seng, D., and Whiting, R.H. (2010). *Intellectual Capital and Firm Performance in Australia*. University of Otago Department of Accountancy and Business Law, Working paper series No 12–2010. Dunedin, New Zealand.

Clarkson, M.B.A. (1995). A stakeholder framework for analyzing and evaluating corporate social performance. *Academy of Management Review*, Vol. 20 (1), pp. 92–117.

CMA (UK Competition and Markets Authority, 2016). *2010 to 2015 Government Policy: Business Regulation*. London: CMA, Department for Business, Innovation & Skills.

Code of Ethical Principles and Economic Rules of the Russian Orthodox Church (2004). *Pravoslavnaya Beseda Journal*, Vol. 15.

Coen, D., and Richardson, J. (2009). *Lobbying the European Union: Institutions, Actors, and Issues*. Oxford: Oxford University Press.

Cohen, B. (2006). Sustainable valley entrepreneurial ecosystems. *Business Strategy and the Environment*, Vol. 15 (1), pp. 1–14.

Coleman, J.S. (1988). Social capital in the creation of human capital. *American Journal of Sociology*, Vol. 94, pp. S95–S120.

Collier, P. (2007). *The Bottom Billion: Why the Poorest Countries are Failing and What Can Be Done About It*. Oxford: Oxford University Press.

Collins, J.C. (2001). *Good to Great: Why Some Companies Make the Leap – and Others Don't*. New York: Random House.

Connor, D., Evans, D., and Brink, B. (2011). Private sector: New ways of doing business. Low-Beer, D. (ed.), *Innovative Health Partnerships: The Diplomacy of Diversity*. Singapore: World Scientific, pp. 333–348.

Conway, J.E. (2011). *The Political Bargaining Model as a Framework for Political Risk Management: The Uranium Industry in Kazakhstan*. Proceedings of the 37th EIBA Conference, Bucharest. Brussels: EIBA (European International Business Academy).

Cory, J. (2002). *Activist Business Ethics*. Boston, MA: Kluwer.

Coulter, C. (2015). *Bush Wives and Girl Soldiers: Women's Lives Through War and Peace in Sierra Leone*. Ithaca, NY: Cornell University Press.

Coutts, L.A. (2013). *The 6-Hour MBA*. Bhopal: Manjul.

Covey, S.R. (1989). *The 7 Habits of Highly Effective People*. New York: Free Press.

Covey, S.R. (1992). *Principle-Centered Leadership*. New York: Simon & Schuster.

Coward, H., Neufeldt, R., and Neumaier, E.K. (eds., 2007). *Readings in Eastern Religions* (2nd ed.). Waterloo, ON: Wilfrid Laurier University Press.

Cox, D., La Caze, M., and Levine. M (2005). Integrity. Zalta, E.N. (ed.), *The Stanford Encyclopedia of Philosophy* (Fall Edition). Available at: http://plato.stanford.edu/archives/fall2005/entries/integrity/, accessed May 9, 2016.

Crane, A., and Matten, D. (2004). *Business Ethics. A European Perspective: Managing Corporate Citizenship and Sustainability in the Age of Globalisation*. Oxford: Oxford University Press.

Cremers, M., and Ferrell, A. (2014). Thirty years of shareholder rights and firm value. *Journal of Finance*, Vol. 69 (3), pp. 1167–1196.

Criteria for Performance Excellence (2004). *Malcolm Baldrige National Quality Award*. Gaithersburg, MD: US Department of Commerce, Technology Administration, National Institute of Standards and Technology.

Curtis, V.A., Garbrah-Aidoo, N., and Scott, B. (2007). Ethics in public health research: Masters of marketing: Bringing private sector skills to public health partnerships. *American Journal of Public Health*, Vol. 97 (4), pp. 634–641.

Daboub, A.L., and Calton, J.M. (2002a). Stakeholder learning dialogues: How to preserve ethical responsibility in networks. *Journal of Business Ethics*, Vol. 41 (1), pp. 85–98.

Daboub, A.L., and Calton, J.M. (2002b). *World Trade and Anti-Globalization: Ethical Implications*. Proceedings of the Seventh Annual Conference "Free Trade in the Western Hemisphere: The Challenges and The Future," Laredo, TX, April 11–12, 2002.

Dacey, A. (2008). *The Secular Conscience: Why Belief Belongs in Public Life*. Amherst, NY: Prometheus Books.

Dahan, N.M., Doh, J.P., Oetzel, J., and Yaziji, M. (2010). Corporate-NGO collaboration: Co-creating new business models for developing markets. *Long Range Planning*, Vol. 43 (2), pp. 326–342.

Dalai Lama XIV, and Piburn, S.D. (ed., 1990). *The Dalai Lama: A Policy of Kindness: An Anthology of Writings By and About the Dalai Lama*, Ithaca, NY: Snow Lion.

Daly, H.E. (1990). Toward some operational principles of sustainable development. *Ecological Economics*, Vol. 2 (1), pp. 1–6.

D'Amato, A., Henderson, S., and Florence, S. (2009). *Corporate social responsibility and Sustainable Business. A Guide to Leadership Tasks and Functions*. Greensboro, NC: Center for Creative Leadership.

Davidson, R.J., and Irwin, W. (1999). The functional neuroanatomy of emotion and affective style. *Trends in Cognitive Sciences*, Vol. 3 (1), pp. 11–21.

Davis, J.H., Schoorman, F.D., & Donaldson, L. (1997). Toward a stewardship theory of management. *Academy of Management Review*, Vol. 22 (1), pp. 20–47.

De Borchgrave, R. (2006). *Le Philosophe et le Manager*. Bruxelles: De Boeck Université.

De Bres, H. (2012). The many, not the few: Pluralism about global distributive justice. *Journal of Political Philosophy*, Vol. 20 (3), pp. 314–340.

De Cremer, D., and Tenbrunsel, A.E. (eds., 2012). *Behavioral Business Ethics: Shaping an Emerging Field*. New York: Routledge.

Deigh, J. (1999). Ethics. Audi, R. (ed.), *The Cambridge Dictionary of Philosophy* (2nd ed.). Cambridge: Cambridge University Press, pp. 284–289.

De Kok, J., Deijl, C., and Veldhuis-Van-Essen, C. (2013). *"Is Small Still Beautiful?" Literature review of recent empirical evidence on the contribution of SMEs to employment creation*. Berlin: German Ministry for Economic Cooperation and Development.

Demmke, C., Bovens, M., Henökl, T., Van Lierop, K., Moilanen, T., Pikker, G., and Salminen, A. (2007). *Regulating Conflicts of Interest for Holders of Public Office in the European Union*. Maastricht, Netherlands: European Commission Bureau of European Policy Advisers.

Demuijnck, G. (2008). Is P2P sharing of MP3 files an objectionable form of free riding? Gosseries, A., Marciano, A., and Strowel, A. (eds.), *Intellectual Property and Theories of Justice*. Houndmills, Basingstoke: Palgrave Macmillan, pp. 141–159.

Demuijnck, G., and Ngnodjom, H. (2013). Responsibility and informal CSR in formal Cameroonian SMEs. *Journal of Business Ethics*, Vol. 112 (4), pp. 653–665.

De Oliveira, J.A.P., and Jabbour, C.J.C. (2017). Environmental management, climate change, CSR, and governance in clusters of small firms in developing countries toward an integrated analytical framework. *Business & Society*, Vol. 56 (1), pp. 130–151.

De Ruiter, H., and Souër, J. (2005). An investor's view on executive compensation plans. *Corporate Social Responsibility Newsletter*, pp. 8–15, accessed August 20, 2015.

De Schutter, O. (2008). Corporate social responsibility European style. *European Law Journal*, Vol. 14, pp. 203–236.

De Schutter, O., Eide, A., Khalfan, A., Orellana, M., Salomon, M., and Seiderman, I (2012). Commentary to the Maastricht principles on extraterritorial obligations of states in the area of economic, social and cultural rights. *Human Rights Quarterly*, Vol. 34 (4), pp. 1084–1116.

De Soto, H. (2000). *The Mystery of Capital: Why Capitalism Triumphs in the West and Fails Everywhere Else*. New York: Basic Books.

Desplaces, D. E., Melchar, D. E., Beauvais, L. L., and Bosco, S. M. (2007). The impact of business education on moral judgment competence: An empirical study. *Journal of Business Ethics*, Vol. 74, (1), pp. 73–87.

De Waal, F. (2006). The tower of morality. De Waal, F. (ed.), *Primates and Philosophers: How Morality Evolved*. Princeton, NJ: Princeton University Press, pp. 161–181.

Dewey, J. (1984). The public and its problems. Boydston, J.A. (ed.), *The Later Works* (Vol. 2). Carbondale: Southern Illinois University Press.

Dherse, J.L., and Minguet, H. (1998). *L'éthique ou le chaos?* Paris: Presses de la Renaissance.

Dill, A. (2016). *World Social Capital Monitor. United Nations Partnerships for SDGs Action #11706*. https://sustainabledevelopment.un.org/partnership/?progress&id=16

D'Iribarne, P. (2003). *The Logic of Honor: National Traditions and Corporate Management*. New York: Welcome Rain.

D'Iribarne, P., with Henry, A. (2007). *Successful Companies in the Developing World Managing in Synergy with Cultures*. Paris: Agence Française de Développement Research Department.

Donaldson, T., and Dunfee, T.W. (1999). *Ties That Bind: A Social Contracts Approach to Business Ethics*. Boston, MA: Harvard Business School Press.

Donaldson, T., and Preston, L.E. (1995). The stakeholder theory of the corporation: Concepts, evidence, and implications. *Academy of Management Review*, Vol. 20 (1), pp. 65–91.

Doorn, N. (2009). Applying Rawlsian approaches to resolve ethical issues: Inventory and setting of a research agenda. *Journal of Business Ethics*, Vol. 91 (1), pp. 127–143.

Dorasamy, N. (2010). From self interest to public interest: Promoting higher levels of business ethics. *African Journal of Business Management*, Vol. 4 (1), pp. 49–55.

Doris, J. (2002). *Lack of Character: Personality and Moral Behaviour*. Cambridge: Cambridge University Press.

Dottridge, M. (2005). Types of forced labour and slavery-like abuse occurring in Africa Today. *Cahiers d'études africaines*, Vol. 179–180, pp. 689–712.

Drucker, P.F. (1954/2006). *The Practice of Management*. New York: Collins.

Drucker, P.F. (1974). *Management: Tasks, Responsibilities, Practices*. New York: Harper and Row.

Drucker, P.F. (1995). *Managing the Non-Profit Organization: Practices and Principles*. Oxford: Butterworth-Heinemann.

Du Gay, P. (2000). *In Praise of Bureaucracy: Weber-Organization-Ethics*. London: Sage.

Du Plessis, J.J., Hargovan, A., and Bagaric, M. (2010). *Principles of Contemporary Corporate Governance*. Cambridge: Cambridge University Press.

Dunfee, T.W. (1999). Corporate governance in a market with morality. *Law and Contemporary Problems*, Vol. 62 (3), pp. 129–157.

Dunning, J., and Lundan, S.M. (2008). *Multinational Enterprises and The Global Economy* (2nd ed.). Cheltenham: Edward Elgar.

Dyck, A., Morse, A., and Zingales, L. (2010). Who blows the whistle on corporate fraud? *Journal of Finance*, Vol. 65 (6), pp. 2213–2253.

Earl, P., and Littleboy, B. (2014). *GLS Shackle*. Basingstoke: Palgrave Macmillan Springer.

Edmondson, A.C. (2011). Strategies for learning from failure. *Harvard Business Review*. Vol. 89 (4), pp. 48–55.

Edvinsson, L., and Malone, M. (1997). *Intellectual Capital*. New York: HarperBusiness.

Elson, C.M., Ferrere, C.K., and Goossen, N.J. (2015). The bug at Volkswagen: Lessons in co-determination, ownership, and board structure. *Journal of Applied Corporate Finance*, Vol. 27 (4), pp. 36–43.

Emiliani, M.L. (2006). Improving management education. *Quality Assurance in Education*, Vol. 14 (4), pp. 363–384.

EPA (US Environmental Protection Agency, 2015). *Notice of Violation of the Clean Air Act to Volkswagen AG, Audi AG, and Volkswagen Group of America*. Accessed September 18, 2015.

Epstein, M.J., and Buhovac, A.R. (2014). *Making Sustainability Work: Best Practices in Managing and Measuring Corporate Social, Environmental, and Economic Impacts*. San Francisco, CA: Berrett-Koehler.

Erkutlu, H., and Chafra, J. (2013). Effects of trust and psychological contract violation on authentic leadership and organizational deviance. *Management Research Review*, Vol. 36 (9), pp. 828–848.

Etzioni, A. (1998). *The New Golden Rule: Community and Morality in a Democratic Society*. New York: Basic Books.

European Union (2016). *African Peace Facility 2015 Annual Report*. Luxembourg: Publications Office of the European Union.

Evan, W.M., and Freeman, R.E. (1988). A stakeholder theory of the modern corporation: Kantian capitalism. Beauchamp, T., and Bowie, N. (eds.), *Ethical Theory and Business* (2nd ed.). Englewood Cliffs, NJ: Prentice Hall, pp. 75–93.

Evans, M.D.R., Kelley, J., and Peoples, C.D. (2010). Justifications of inequality: The normative basis of pay differentials in 31 nations. *Social Science Quarterly*, Vol. 91 (5), pp. 1405–1431.

Ezekiel, Z. (2006). *The Evolving Role of the Ethics and Compliance Officer*. Conference Board of Canada Report. Ottawa, Canada.

Fairley, C.G. (2006). *Global Harms, Local Responsibilities: Obligations to the Distant Needy and the Duty Not to Harm*. Doctoral dissertation, University of British Columbia.

Falkner, G. (2002). How intergovernmental are intergovernmental conferences? An example from the Maastricht treaty reform. *Journal of European Public Policy*, Vol. 9 (1), pp. 98–119.

Fathers of the English Dominican Province. (1952). Thomas Aquinas' summa theologica. Hutchins, R.M. (ed.), *Great Books of the Western World*. Chicago: Encyclopedia Britannica.

Fernandes, A. N. (2009). Ethical Considerations of the Public Sector Lobbyist. *McGeorge Law Review* Vol. 421 (1), pp. 183–202.

Ferrell, O.C., and Fraedrich, J. (2014). *Business Ethics: Ethical Decision Making & Cases* (10th ed.). Boston, MA: Cengage Learning.

Fichman, P., and Sanfilippo, M.R. (2016). *Online Trolling and Its Perpetrators: Under the Cyberbridge*. Lanham, MD: Rowman & Littlefield.

Firer, S., and Williams, M. (2003). Intellectual capital and traditional measures of corporate performance. *Journal of Intellectual Capital*, Vol. 4 (3), pp. 348–360.

Fisher, C.M., and Lovell, A. (2003). *Business Ethics and Values*. Harlow: Prentice Hall.

Fitzpatrick, B. (1992). Community social law after Maastricht. *Industrial Law Journal*. Vol. 21 (3), pp. 199–238.

Flew, A. (ed., 1979). Golden rule. *A Dictionary of Philosophy*. London: Pan Books in association with Macmillan Press.

Fornieri, J.R. (2014). *Abraham Lincoln, Philosopher Statesman*. Carbondale: Southern Illinois University Press.

Foster, D., and. Jonker, J. (2005). Stakeholder relationships: The dialogue of engagement. *Corporate Governance*, Vol. 5, (5), pp. 51–57.

Foster, V., and Briceño-Garmendia, C. (2009). *Africa Infrastructure Country Diagnostic*. Washington, DC: World Bank.

Frankfurt, H. (1987). Identification and wholeheartedness. Schoeman, F. (ed.), *Responsibility, Character, and the Emotions: New Essays in Moral Psychology*. New York: Cambridge University Press, pp. 27–45.

Fransen, L.W., and Kolk, A. (2007). Global rule-setting for business: Critical analysis of multi-stakeholder standards. *Organization*, Vol. 14 (5), pp. 667–684.

Freeman, R.E. (1984). *Strategic Management: A Stakeholder Approach*. Boston, MA: Pitman.

Freeman, R.E. (2004). Ethical leadership and creating value for stakeholders. Peterson, R.A., and Ferrell, O.C. (eds.), *Business Ethics: New Challenges for Business Schools and Corporate Leaders*. Armonk, NY: M.E. Sharpe, pp. 82–97.

Friberg-Fernros, H., and Schaffer, J.K. (2014). The consensus paradox: Does deliberative agreement impede rational discourse? *Political Studies*, Vol. 62 (1 suppl.), pp. 99–116.

Friedman, A.L., and Miles, S. (2004). Stakeholder theory and communication practice. *Journal of Communication Management*, Vol. 9 (1), pp. 89–97.

Friedman, M. (1970). The social responsibility of business is to increase its profits. *New York Times Magazine*, September 13, 1970, pp. SM 17–SM 20.

Friedrich, C.J. (1961). Political leadership and the problem of the charismatic power. *Journal of Politics*, Vol. 23 (01), pp. 3–24.

Frost, S. (2008). *Lessons From a Materialist Thinker: Hobbesian Reflections on Ethics and Politics*. Stanford, CA: Stanford University Press.

Gable, C., and Shireman, B. (2005). Stakeholder engagement: A three-phase methodology: Learning to manage your relationships with stakeholders. *Environmental Quality Management*, Vol. 14 (3), pp. 9–24.

Galie, P.J., and Bopst, C. (2006). Machiavelli & modern business: Realist thought in contemporary corporate leadership manuals. *Journal of Business Ethics*, Vol. 65 (3), pp. 235–250.

Gallagher, A. (2004). The situation of undocumented persons in the US: A practical overview. Michele LeVoy, M., Verbruggen, N., and Wets, J. (eds.), *Undocumented Migrant Workers in Europe*. Brussels: European Parliament, pp. 67–80.

Garriga, E., and Melé, D. (2004). Corporate social responsibility theories: Mapping the territory. *Journal of Business Ethics*, Vol. 53 (1–2), pp. 51–71.

Gary, I., and Karl, T.L. (2003). *Bottom of the Barrel. Africa's Oil Boom and the Poor*. Catholic Relief Services Report, June.

Gates, B. (2008). Making Capitalism More Creative. *Time*, July 31, 2008. Accessed on July 22, 2016. Available at www.time.com/time/business/article/0,8599,1828069,00.html

Gibson, K. (2007). *Ethics and Business: An Introduction*. Cambridge: Cambridge University Press.

Gilsing, V. (2006). *The Dynamics of Innovation and Interfirm Networks*. Cheltenham: Edward Elgar.

Gini, A. (1997). Human centered management: An overview. *Journal of Business Ethics*, Vol. 16 (4), pp. 323–330.

Giorgetti, C. (2013). Mass tort claims in international investment proceedings: What are the lessons from the Ecuador–Chevron Dispute? *University of Pennsylvania Journal of International Law*, Vol. 34 (4), pp. 787–818.

Gitlow, A.L. (2005). *Corruption in Corporate America: Who is Responsible? Who Will Protect the Public Interest?* Lanham, MD: University Press of America.

Glader, P. (2009). Corporate news: GE's Immelt to cite lessons learned. *Wall Street Journal*, Dec. 14, p. B2.

Glenn, J.R., Jr. (1992). Can a business and society course affect the ethical judgment of future managers? *Journal of Business Ethics*, Vol. 11 (3), pp. 217–223.

Goldman, A.I. (1979). What is justified belief? Pappas, G.S. (ed.), *Justification and Knowledge*. Dordrecht: D. Reidel, pp. 1–23.

Goodpaster, K.E. (2004). Ethics or excellence? Conscience as a check on the unbalanced pursuit of organizational goals. *Ivey Business Journal*, Vol. 68 (4), pp. 1–8.

Goodpaster, K.E., and Matthews, J.B. (1982). Can a corporation have a conscience. *Harvard Business Review*, Vol. 60 (1), pp. 132–141.

Gore, A., and Blood, D. (2012). A manifesto for sustainable capitalism with commentary. *Sustainability: The Journal of Record*, Vol. 5 (2), pp. 66–69.

Gough, I., and McGregor, J.A. (eds., 2007). *Wellbeing in Developing Countries. From Theory to Research*. Cambridge: Cambridge University Press.

Graafland, J.J. (2002). Modeling the trade-off between profits and principles. *De Economist*, Vol. 150 (2), pp. 129–154.

Graafland, J., Kaptein, M., and Mazereeuw, C. (2010). *Motives of Socially Responsible Business Conduct*. Discussion paper No. 2010–74. Tilburg University Center, Tilburg, Netherlands.

Grant, M. (2011). *The Climax of Rome*. London: Orion Publishing Group.

Grassl, W., and Habisch, A. (2011). Ethics and economics: Towards a new humanistic synthesis for business. *Journal of Business Ethics*, Vol. 99 (1), pp. 37–49.

Gray, B. (1989). *Collaborating: Finding Common Ground in Multiparty Problems*. San Francisco, CA: Jossey-Bass.

Gretzel, U., Davis, E., Bowser, G., Jiang, J., and Brown, M. (2014). Creating global leaders with sustainability mindsets. *Journal of Teaching in Travel & and Tourism*, Vol. 14 (2), pp. 164–183.

Gross, M.L. (1995). Moral judgment, organizational incentives and collective action: participation in abortion politics. *Political Research Quarterly*, Vol. 48 (3), pp. 507–534.

Grunig, J., and Hunt, T. (1984). *Managing Public Relations*. Orlando, FL: Cengage Learning.

Gudgin, G., Coutts, K., Gibson, N., and Buchanan, J. (2016). *The Macro-Economic Impact of Brexit: Using the CBR Macro-Economic Model of the UK Economy (UKMOD)*. Centre for Business Research Working Paper No. 483. Cambridge: University of Cambridge.

Guo, K.H. (2011). Knowledge for managing information systems security: Review and future research directions. Alkhalifa, E. (ed.), *E-Strategies for Resource Management Systems*. New York: Hershey, pp. 266–287.

Guo, X., and Lu, J. (2004). Effectiveness of e-government online services in Australia. Huang, W., Siau, K., and Kwok, K.W. (eds., 2004). *Electronic Government Strategies and Implementation*. Hershey, PA: IGI Global, pp. 214–241.

Gupta, J., and Vegelin, C. (2016). Sustainable development goals and inclusive development. *International Environmental Agreements: Politics, Law and Economics*. Vol. 16 (3), pp. 433–448.

Habermas,J. (1982). Reply to my critics.Thompson,J.B., and Held, D. (eds.), *Habermas: Critical Debates*. Cambridge, MA: MIT Press, pp. 219–283.

Haidt,J. (2012). *The Righteous Mind:Why Good People are Divided by Politics and Religion*. New York:Vintage.

Hamilton, N.W., Coulter, M., and Coulter, M. (2015). Professional formation/professionalism's foundation: Engaging each student's and lawyer's tradition on the question 'What Are My Responsibilities to Others?' *University of St. Thomas Law Journal*, Vol. 12 (2), pp. 271–338.

Hannerz, U. (1992). *Cultural Complexity*. New York: Columbia University Press.

Hannes, S. (2013). Managers vs. regulators: Post-Enron regulation and the great depression. *Harvard Business Law Review*,Vol. 3, pp. 279–300.

Harell, A., and Stolle, D. (2010). Reconciling diversity and community? Defining social cohesion in democracies. Hooghe, M. (ed.), *Social Capital and Social Cohesion: Interdisciplinary Theoretical Perspectives*. Brussels: Royal Flemish Academy of Belgium for Science and the Arts, pp. 1–39.

Harris, C.E., Davis, M., Pritchard, M.S., and Rabins, M.J. (1996). Engineering ethics:What? Why? How? And when? *Journal of Engineering Education*,Vol. 85, pp. 93–96.

Hart,J.T. (2010). Health, inequality and commercialisation. *International Journal of Management Concepts and Philosophy*,Vol. 4 (2), pp. 145–153.

Hassink, H., De Vries, M., and Bollen, L. (2007). A content analysis of whistleblowing policies of leading European companies. *Journal of Business Ethics*,Vol. 75 (1), pp. 25–44.

Hayek Friedrich,A.V. (1944). *The Road to Serfdom*. Sydney: Dymocks.

Heath,J. (2004).A market failures approach to business ethics. Hodgson, B. (ed.), *The Invisible Hand and the Common Good*. Berlin Heidelberg: Springer, pp. 69–89.

Heilbroner, R.L. (2008). Capitalism. Durlauf, S.N., and Blume, L.N. (eds.), *The New Palgrave Dictionary of Economics* (2nd ed.). London: Palgrave Macmillan.

Hemmati, M. (2001). United Nations Environment and Development Forum (UNED). *Report on Multi-Stakeholder Processes – A Methodological Framework*. London: United Nations.

Hendry,J. (2004). *Between Enterprise and Ethics: Business and Management in a Bimoral Society*. Oxford: Oxford University Press.

Heracleous, L., and Rao, A.K. (2008). Systems thinking: The missing link in management education? *Effective Executive*,January, pp. 47–49.

Herman, B. (1993). *The Practice of Moral Judgment*. Cambridge, MA: Harvard University Press.

Hernandez, M., Long, C.P., and Sitkin, S.B. (2014). Cultivating follower trust: Are all leader behaviors equally influential? *Organization Studies*,Vol. 35 (12), pp. 1867–1892.

Heugens, P.P., Van Den Bosch, F.A., and Van Riel, C.B. (2002). Stakeholder integration: Building mutually enforcing relationships. *Business & Society*,Vol. 41 (1), pp. 36–60.

Heyne, P. (2008). *Are Economists Basically Immoral?* Indianapolis, IN: Liberty Fund.

Hiebl, M.R. (2015). Family involvement and organizational ambidexterity in later-generation family businesses:A framework for further investigation. *Management Decision*, Vol. 53 (5), pp. 1061–1082.

Hill, S. (2011).An Adamsian theory of intrinsic value. *Ethical Theory and Moral Practice*,Vol. 14 (3), pp. 273–289.

Hitlin, S., and Piliavin, J.A. (2004).Values: Reviving a dormant concept. *Annual Review of Sociology*,Vol. 30 (1), pp. 359–393.

Hobbes (1651/1996). *Of the Rights of Sovereigns by Institution. Leviathan*. Gaskin, G.C.A. (ed.). Oxford: Oxford University Press.

Hofstede, G. (1980a). *Culture's Consequences: International Differences in Work-Related Values.* Beverly Hills, CA: Sage.

Hofstede, G. (1980b). Motivation, leadership, and organization: Do American theories apply abroad? *Organizational Dynamics*, Vol. 9 (1), pp. 42–63.

Hofstede, G. (2007). Asian management in the 21st century. *Asia Pacific Journal of Management*, Vol. 24 (4), pp. 411–420.

Hoggett, P. (2005). A service to the public: The containment of ethical and moral conflicts by public bureaucracies. Du Gay, P. (ed.), *The Values of Bureaucracy*. Oxford: Oxford University Press, pp. 167–189.

Holian, R. (2006). Management decision making, ethical issues and "emotional" intelligence. *Management Decision*, Vol. 44 (8), pp. 1122–1138.

Hollander, E. (2012). *Inclusive Leadership: The Essential Leader-Follower Relationship.* Abingdon-on-Thames: Routledge.

Holt, T.J., and Bossler, A.M. (2015). *Cybercrime in Progress: Theory and Prevention of Technology-Enabled Offenses.* Abingdon-on-Thames: Routledge.

Homann, K. (2006a), *Competition and Morality.* Wittenberg Center for Global Ethics Discussion Paper Nr. 2006–4. Available at: www.wcge.org/download/DP_2006-4_Homann_-_Competition_and_Morality_o.pdf, accessed May 16, 2016.

Homann, K. (2006b), *The Sense and Limits of the Economic Method in Business Ethics.* Wittenberg Center for Global Ethics Discussion Paper Nr. 2006–5. Available at: www.wcge.org/download /DP_2006-5_Homann_-_The_Sense_and_Limits_of_the_Economic_Method_in_Business_Ethics_o.pdf, accessed May 16, 2016.

Homann, K. (2015). Das Können des moralischen Sollens. *ETHICA*, Vol. 23 (3), pp. 243–259, and Vol. 23 (4), pp. 291–314.

Homann, K. (2016). Theory strategies of business ethics. Luetge, C., and Mukerji, N. (eds.), *Order Ethics: An Ethical Framework for the Social Market Economy*. Cham (ZG), Switzerland. Springer International, pp. 37–56.

Hörisch, J., Freeman, R.E., and Schaltegger, S. (2014). Applying stakeholder theory in sustainability management links: Similarities, dissimilarities, and a conceptual framework. *Organization & Environment*, Vol. 27 (4), pp. 328–346.

Hornsby-Smith, M.P. (2006). *An Introduction to Catholic Social Thought.* Cambridge: Cambridge University Press.

Howard, S. (2002). A spiritual perspective on learning in the workplace. *Journal of Managerial Psychology*, Vol. 17 (3), pp. 230–242.

Husted, B.W. (2005). Risk management, real options, corporate social responsibility. *Journal of Business Ethics*, Vol. 60 (2), pp. 175–183.

Iles, P., and Preece, D. (2006). Developing leaders or developing leadership? The Academy of Chief Executives' programmes in the North East of England. *Leadership*, Vol. 2 (3), pp. 317–340.

International Federation of Social Workers, International Association of Schools of Social Work and International Council on Social Welfare (2012). *The Global Agenda for Social Work and Social Development: Commitment to Action.* Available at: www.globalsocialagenda.org, Accessed July 20, 2016.

Isaacs, W. (1999). *Dialogue and the Art of Thinking Together.* New York: Doubleday.

Islahi, A.A. (2009). *Four Generations of Islamic Economists.* MPRA Paper 29557, University Library of Munich, Germany, revised 2010.

ISO (International Organization for Standardization, 2010). *ISO 26000 Project Overview.* Geneva: International Organization for Standardization.

Jackson, E.T. (2013). Evaluating social impact bonds: questions, challenges, innovations, and possibilities in measuring outcomes in impact investing. *Community Development*, Vol. 44 (5), pp. 608–616.

Jackson, I., and Nelson, J. (2004). *Profits With Principles: Seven Strategies for Delivering Value with Values*. New York: Currency Doubleday.

Jamali, D., Lund-Thomsen, P., and Jeppesen, S. (2017). SMEs and CSR in developing countries. *Business & Society*, Vol. 56 (1), pp. 11–22.

Jamali, D., Zanhour, M., and Keshishian, T. (2008). Peculiar strengths and relational attributes of SMEs in the context of CSR. *Journal of Business Ethics*, Vol. 87 (3), pp. 355–377.

Jensen, H., and Yakovleva, N. (2006). Corporate social responsibility in the mining industry: Exploring trends in social and environmental disclosure. *Journal of Cleaner Production*, Vol. 14 (3–4), pp. 271–284.

Jiliberto, H.R. (2004). A holarchical model for regional sustainability assessment. *Journal of Environmental Assessment Policy and Management*, Vol. 6 (4), pp. 511–538.

Jo, H., and Harjoto, M.A. (2011). Corporate governance and firm value: The impact of corporate social responsibility. *Journal of Business Ethics*, Vol. 103 (3), 351–383.

Johns, J. (1998). The ethical dimensions of national security. Kozak, D.C., and Keagle, J.M. (eds.), *Bureaucratic Politics and National Security: Theory and Practice*. Boulder, CO: Lynne Rienner, pp. 3–15.

Johnson, D. (2015). *Ethics at Work. 2015 Survey of Employees: Main Findings and Themes*. London: Institute of Business Ethics.

Johnston, M. (2014). *Corruption, Contention and Reform: The Power of Deep Democratization*. Cambridge: Cambridge University Press.

Jones, B., Bowd, R., and Tench, R. (2009). Corporate irresponsibility and corporate social responsibility: Competing realities. *Social Responsibility Journal*, Vol. 5 (3), pp. 300–310.

Jones, D.A. (2009). A novel approach to business ethics training: Improving moral reasoning in just a few weeks. *Journal of Business Ethics*, Vol. 88 (2), pp. 367–379.

Jones, D.N., and Truell, R. (2012). The global agenda for social work and social development: A place to link together and be effective in a globalized world. *International Social Work*, Vol. 55 (4), pp. 454–472.

Jones, I.W., and Pollitt, M.G. (1998). Ethical and unethical competition: Establishing the rules of engagement. *Long Range Planning*, Vol. 31 (5), pp. 703–710.

Jones, M. (1995). Instrumental stakeholder theory: A synthesis of ethics and economics. *Academy of Management Review*, Vol. 20 (2) pp. 404–437.

Jost, J.T., Blount, S., Pfeffer, J., and Hunyady, G. (2003). Fair market ideology: Its cognitive-motivational underpinnings. *Research in Organizational Behavior*, Vol. 25, pp. 53–91.

Joullié, J.-E. (2014) The philosopher and the manager. *International Journal of Management Concepts and Philosophy* Vol. 8 (4), pp. 197–208.

Joullié, J.-E. (2016). The philosophical foundations of management thought. *Academy of Management Learning & Education*, Vol. 15 (1), pp. 157–179.

Kabasakal, H., and Bodur, M. (2004). Humane orientation in societies, organizations, and leader attributes. House, R., Hanges, P., Javidan, M., Dorfman, P., and Gupta, V. (eds.), *Culture, Leadership, and Organizations: The Globe Study of 62 Societies*. Thousand Oaks, CA: Sage, pp. 564–601.

Kamukama, N., Ahiauzu, A., and Ntayi, J.M. (2010). Intellectual capital and performance: Testing interaction effects. *Journal of Intellectual Capital*, Vol. 11 (4), pp. 554–574.

Kang, S., and Snell, S. (2009). Intellectual capital architectures and ambidextrous learning: A frame-work for human resource management. *Journal of Management Studies*, Vol. 46 (1), pp. 65–92.

Kant, I. Trans. Ellington, J.W. (1785/1993). *Grounding For the Metaphysics of Morals* (3rd ed.). Indianapolis, IN: Hackett.

Kanu, B.S., Salami, A.O., and Numasawa, K. (2014). *Inclusive Growth – An Imperative For African Agriculture.* Tunis-Belvedere: African Development Bank Group.

Kanungo, R.N. (2001). Ethical values of transactional and transformational leaders. *Canadian Journal of Administrative Sciences/Revue Canadienne des Sciences de l'Administration,* Vol. 18 (4), pp. 257–265.

Kaptein, M. (2008). *The Living Code: Embedding Ethics Into the Corporate DNA.* Shipley: Greenleaf.

Kaptein, M., and Schwartz, M.S. (2008). The effectiveness of business codes: A critical examination of existing studies and the development of an integrated research model. *Journal of Business Ethics,* Vol. 77, pp. 111–127.

Kaptein, M., and Van Tulder, R. (2003). Toward effective stakeholder dialogue. *Business and Society Review.* Vol. 108 (2), pp. 203–224.

Kaptein, M., and Wempe, J.F.D.B. (2002). *The Balanced Company: A Theory of Corporate Integrity.* Oxford: Oxford University Press.

Karakas, F. (2010). Spirituality and performance in organizations: A literature review. *Journal of Business Ethics,* Vol. 94 (1), pp. 89–106.

Katz, D., and Kahn, R.L. (1978). *The Social Psychology of Organizations* (2nd ed.). New York: Wiley.

Kavaliauskas, T. (2011). *The Individual in Business Ethics. An American Cultural Perspective.* London: Palgrave Macmillan.

Kelly, M. (2009). Not just for profit. *strategy+ business,* Vol. 54 (1), pp. 1–10.

Kennedy, H. (2012). Perspectives on sentiment analysis. *Journal of Broadcasting & Electronic Media,* Vol. 56 (4), pp. 435–450.

Kernis, M.H. (2003). Toward a conceptualization of optimal self-esteem. *Psychological Inquiry,* Vol. 14, pp. 1–26.

Kesan, J.P. (2002). Cyber-working or cyber-shirking? A first principles examination of electronic privacy in the workplace. *Florida Law Review,* Vol. 54, pp. 289–314.

Kettle, T.M. (1912). The future of private property. *Studies: An Irish Quarterly Review,* Vol. 1 (1), pp. 146–158.

Khan, H. (2010). Responsible design and delivery of global executive development programs. *ESADE Business & Law School Research Yearbook.* Barcelona: ESADE (Escola Superior d'Administració i Direcció d'Empreses), pp. 388–392.

Khanna, T., and Yafeh, Y. (2007). Business groups in emerging markets: Paragons or parasites? *Journal of Economic Literature,* Vol. 45 (2), pp. 331–372.

Kidder, R.M. (2003). *How Good People Make Tough Choices: Resolving the Dilemmas of Ethical Living.* New York: HarperCollins.

King, M., and Lessidrenska, T. (2011). *Transient Caretakers: Making Life on Earth Sustainable.* Sandton: Pan Macmillan South Africa.

Kirshner, Jodie A. (2015). Call for the EU to assume Jurisdiction over extraterritorial corporate human rights abuses, A. *Northwestern Journal of International Human Rights.* Vol. 13 (1), Article 1.

Klein, S. (2000). Drucker as business moralist. *Journal of Business Ethics,* Vol. 28 (2) pp. 121–128.

Kluckhohn, C. (1951). Values and value-orientations in the theory of action: An exploration in definition and classification. Parsons, T., and Shils, E.A. (eds.), *Toward a General Theory of Action,* Cambridge, MA: Harvard University Press, pp. 388–433.

Kohlberg, L. (1981). *The Philosophy of Moral Development.* New York: Harper and Row.

Kohls, R. 1984. *The Values Americans Live By*. Washington, DC: Meridan House.

Köhn, D. (ed., 2014). *Finance for Food*. New York: Springer Open.

Kolk, A., Van Tulder, R., and Kostwinder, E. (2008). Business and partnerships for development. *European Management Journal*, Vol. 26 (4), pp. 262–273.

Korsgaard, C. (2006). Morality and the distinctiveness of human action. De Waal, F. (ed.), *Primates and Philosophers: How Morality Evolved*. Princeton, NJ: Princeton University Press, pp. 98–119.

Korsgaard, C.M. (1996). *Creating the Kingdom of Ends*. Cambridge: Cambridge University Press.

Koskenniemi, M. (2009). The politics of international law – 20 years later. *European Journal of International Law*, Vol. 20, pp. 7–19.

Kramer, M.R. (2011). Creating shared value. *Harvard Business Review*, Vol. 89 (1/2), pp. 62–77.

Krawiec, K.D. (2003). Cosmetic compliance and the failure of negotiated governance. *Washington University Law Review*, Vol. 81 (2), pp. 487–543.

Krebs, D.L., Denton, K., and Wark, G. (1997). The forms and functions of real-life moral decision-making. *Journal of Moral Education*, Vol. 26, pp. 131–146.

Kresse, K. (2007). *Philosophizing in Mombasa: Knowledge, Islam and Intellectual Practice on the Swahili Coast*. Edinburgh: Edinburgh University Press.

Kroeber, A.L., and Kluckhohn, C. (1952). Culture: A critical review of concepts and definitions. *Peabody Museum of Archaeology & Ethnology Papers*. Cambridge, MA: Harvard University, Vol. 47 (1).

Kropotkin, P. (1889/2006). *La morale anarchiste* [1889]. La Tour-d'Aigues: Seuil/Éditeurs.

Kudishina, A. (2005). The development of the humanist movement in Russia. *Humanist Bulletin*, Vol 21 (3); Smirnov, R.K. (2014). On the relation between bourgeois consciousness and humanism. *Life Science Journal*, Vol. 11, pp. 405–408.

Kurland, N.B. (1995). Ethics, incentives, and conflicts of interest: A practical solution. *Journal of Business Ethics*, Vol. 14 (6), pp. 465–475.

Kyte, R. (2007). Balancing rights with responsibilities: Looking for the global drivers of materiality in corporate social responsibility & (and) the voluntary initiatives that develop and support them. *American University International Law Review*, Vol. 23, pp. 559–572.

Labeff, E.E., Clark, R.E., Haines, V.J., and Diekhoff, G.M. (1990). Situational ethics and college: Student cheating. *Sociological Inquiry*. Vol. 60, pp. 191–198.

Laffont, J.J. (1975). Macroeconomic constraints, economic efficiency and ethics: An introduction to Kantian economics. *Economica*, Vol. 42 (168), pp. 430–437.

Laffont, J.J., and Martimort, D. (2009). *The Theory of Incentives: The Principal-Agent Model*. Princeton, NJ: Princeton University Press.

Langan, M. (2013). *The Decent Work Agenda and ACP-EU Relations*. Proceedings of the EUSA Biennial Conference, May 2013. Baltimore, MD.

Lange, D., and Washburn, N.T. (2012). Understanding attributions of corporate social irresponsibility. *Academy of Management Review*, Vol. 37 (2), 300–326.

Langfield-Smith, K., and Greenwood, M.R. (1998). Developing co-operative buyer – supplier relationships: A case study of Toyota. *Journal of Management Studies*, Vol. 35 (3), pp. 331–353.

Lawney, S., and Brooks, N. (2015). The state of ethics in large companies. *A Supplemental Research from the National Business Ethics Survey 2013*. Arlington, VA: Ethics and Compliance Initiative. Available at: http://ethics.org/ecihome/research/nbes/nbes-reports/large-companies

Lee, I.B. (2006). Efficiency and ethics in the debate about shareholder primacy. *Delaware Journal of Corporate Law*, Vol. 31 (2), pp. 533–585.

Leiserowitz, A.A., Maibach, E.W., Roser-Renouf, C., Smith, N., and Dawson, E. (2013). Climategate, public opinion, and the loss of trust. *American Behavioral Scientist*, Vol. 57 (6), pp. 818–837.

Lenox, M. (2008). The prospects for industry self-regulation of environmental externalities. Woods, N. (ed.), *Making Global Regulation Effective: What Role for Self-Regulation*. Oxford: Oxford University Press, pp. 22–43.

Lepoutre, J., and Heene, A. (2006). Investigating the impact of firm size on small business social responsibility: A critical review. *Journal of Business Ethics*, Vol. 67, pp. 257–273.

Letelier, M.F., Flores, F., and Spinosa, C. (2003). Developing productive customers in emerging markets. *California Management Review*, Vol. 45 (4), pp. 77–103.

Leviton, L.C., and Bass, M.E. (2004). Using evaluation to advance a foundation's mission. Braverman, M.T., Constantine, N.A., and Slater, J.K. (eds.), *Foundations and Evaluation: Contexts and Practices for Effective Philanthropy*. New York: John Wiley and Sons, pp. 3–26.

Lewis, C.S. (1952). *Mere Christianity*. London: HarperCollins.

Lewis, C.W., and Catron, B.L. (1996). Professional standards and ethics. Perry, J.L. (ed.), *Handbook of Public Administration* (2nd ed.). San Francisco, CA: Jossey-Bass, pp. 699–712.

Lian, H., Ferris, D.L., Morrison, R., and Brown, D.J. (2014). Blame it on the supervisor or the subordinate? Reciprocal relations between abusive supervision and organizational deviance. *Journal of Applied Psychology*, Vol. 9, pp. 651–664.

Liang, L.H., Lian, H., Brown, D., Ferris, D.L., Hanig, S., and Keeping, L. (2015). Why are abusive supervisors abusive? A dual-system self-control model. *Academy of Management Journal*, amj-2014.

Lin Hi, N. (2008). *Corporate Social Responsibility: An Investment in Social Cooperation for Mutual Advantage*. Wittenberg Center for Global Ethics Discussion Paper Nr. 2008–6. Available at: www.wcge.org/download/DP_2008-6_NickLin-Hi_CorporateSocialResponsibility_final_oo.pdf, accessed December 13, 2014.

Lin, N., Cook, K., and Burt, R.S. (eds., 2001). *Social Capital. Theory and Research* (4th printing 2008). New Brunswick, NJ: Transaction.

Lin Hi, N., and Müller, K. (2013). The corporate social responsibility bottom line: Preventing corporate social irresponsibility. *Journal of Business Research*, Vol. 66 (10), pp. 1928–1936.

Lipinski, E. (2007). Love. Berenbaum, M., and Skolnik, F. (eds.), *Encyclopedia Judaica*. New York: Macmillan Reference USA, pp. 227–250.

Lipman-Blumen, J. (2006). *The Allure of Toxic Leaders: Why We Follow Destructive Bosses and Corrupt Politicians – and How We Can Survive Them*. New York: Oxford University Press.

Littlechild, S.C. (2003). Reflections on George Shackle – Three Excerpts from the Shackle Collection. *Review of Austrian Economics*, Vol. 16 (1), pp. 113–117.

Littrell, R.F. (2011). A proposal for the structure of moral and ethical education of university students and business people. Wankel, C., and Stachowitz-Stanusch, A. (eds.), *Ethically Educating Tomorrow's Business Leaders*, pp. 51–75, Bingley: Emerald Group.

Locke, J. (1698/1988). Laslett, P. (ed.), *Two Treatises of Government* (Student ed.), Cambridge: Cambridge University Press.

Locke, R.M., Qin, F., and Brause, A. (2007). Does monitoring improve labor standards? *Lessons from Nike: Industrial & Labor Relations Review*, Vol. 61 (1), pp. 3–31.

Locke, R.R. (2013). Reassessing the basis of corporate business performance: Modern financial economics' profit control versus integrated people- and process-improvement. *Real-World Economics Review*, Issue No. 64, pp. 110–124.

Logue, N.C. (2005). *Cultural Relativism or Ethical Imperialism: Dealing With Bribery Across Cultures*. Wenham, MA: Gordon College Working Paper.

Loriaux, M. (1992). The realists and Saint Augustine: Skepticism, psychology, and moral action in international relations thought. *iau*, Vol. 36 (4), pp. 401–420.

Luhmann, N. (1995). *Social Systems*. Stanford, CA: Stanford University Press.

Lukes, S. (1997). Social justice: the Hayekian challenge. *Critical Review*, Vol. 11 (1), pp. 65–80.

Lukin, S. (2008). Formation of the orthodox doctrine of social responsibility of business. *Oikonomia. Rivista online della Università Domenicana Internazionale in Roma*, Vol. 7 (2), pp. 7–16.

Lundan, S.M., and Mirza, H. (2011). TNC evolution and the emerging investment-development paradigm. *Transnational Corporations*, Vol. 19 (2), pp. 29–45.

Lütge, C. (2005). Economic ethics, business ethics and the idea of mutual advantages, *Business Ethics: A European Review*, Vol. 14 (2), pp. 108–118.

Lutz, A. (2015). *On Commercial Gluts. Unexpected Affinities Between Jean-Baptiste Say and the Saint-Simonians*. GATE Working Paper 2015–23. Lyon: Groupe d'Analyse et de Théorie Economique (GATE), Centre national de la recherche scientifique, Université Lyon.

Maak, T. (2007). Responsible leadership, stakeholder engagement, and the emergence of social capital. *Journal of Business Ethics*, Vol. 74 (4), pp. 329–343.

Maak, T., and Pless, N.M. (2006). Responsible leadership in a stakeholder society – a relational perspective. *Journal of Business Ethics*, Vol. 66 (1), pp. 99–115.

MacAskill, W. (2015). *Doing Good Better: Effective Altruism and a Radical New Way to Make a Difference*. New York: Faber & Faber.

Machan, T.R. (1987). Advertising: The whole or only some of the truth? *Public Affairs Quarterly*, Vol. 1 (4), pp. 59–71.

Machiavelli, N., trans. Marriott, W.K. (2001). The prince. Manis, J. (ed.), *The Electronic Classics Series*. Hazleton, PA: PSU-Hazleton.

MacIntyre, A. (1988). *Whose Justice? Which Rationality?* London: Duckworth.

Mackenroth, T. (2004). Corporate governance in the Queensland public sector. *Keeping Good Companies*, Vol. 56 (2), pp. 81–84.

MacRae, D., and Becker, G.S. (1978). The sociological economics of Gary S. Becker. *American Journal of Sociology*, Vol. 83 (5), pp. 1244–1258.

Madsen, P., and Shafritz, J.M. (1990). *Essentials of Business Ethics*. New York: Meridian.

Mahon, J.F., and McGowan, R.A. (1991). Searching for the common good: A process-oriented approach, *Business Horizons*, Vol. 34 (4), pp. 79–87.

Mahrt, M. (2010). *Values of German Media Users*. Doctoral thesis, University of Amsterdam. Wiesbaden: VS Verlag für Sozialwissenschaften.

Mair, J., Martí, I., and Ventresca, M.J. (2012). Building inclusive markets in rural Bangladesh: How intermediaries work institutional voids. *Academy of Management Journal*, Vol. 55 (4), pp. 819–850.

Maital, S., Prakhya, S., and Seshadri, D.V.R. (2008). Bridging the chasm between management education, research and practice: Moving towards the 'grounded theory' approach. *Vikalpa*, Vol. 33 (1), pp. 1–18.

Marcoux, A. (2008). Business Ethics. Zalta, E.N. (ed.), *The Stanford Encyclopedia of Philosophy*. Stanford, CA: Metaphysics Research Lab.

Marques, J., Dhiman, S., and King, R. (2007). *Spirituality in the Workplace: What It Is, Why It Matters, How to Make It Work for You*. Manhattan Beach, CA: Personhood Press.

Marschke, M., and Vandergeest, P. (2016). Slavery scandals: Unpacking labour challenges and policy responses within the off-shore fisheries sector. *Marine Policy*, Vol. 68, pp. 39–46.

Matsumoto, D. (1996). *Culture and Psychology*. Pacific Grove, CA: Brooks/Cole.

Mawritz, M.B., Mayer, D.M., Hoobler, J.M., Wayne, S.J., and Marinova, S.V. (2012). A trickle-down model of abusive supervision. *Personnel Psychology*, Vol. 65, pp. 325–357.

McElroy, M.W. (2003). *The New Knowledge Management: Complexity, Learning, and Sustainable Innovation*. Boston, MA: KMCI Press, Butterworth-Heinemann.

McEvily, B., and Tortoriello, M. (2011). Measuring trust in organisational research: Review and recommendations. *Journal of Trust Research*, Vol. 1 (1), pp. 23–63.

McGregor, D. (1966). *The Human Side of Enterprise*. Cambridge, MA: MIT Press.

McKinney, J.A., Emerson, T.L., and Neubert, M.J. (2010). The effects of ethical codes on ethical perceptions of actions toward stakeholders. *Journal of Business Ethics*, Vol. 97 (4), pp. 505–516.

McKinsey. (2005). Global Survey of Business Executives. *The McKinsey Quarterly, web exclusive*, available at www.mckinseyquarterly.com/links/22581

McMahon, T.F. (2004). *Ethical Leadership through Transforming Justice*. Lanham, MD: University Press of America.

Meese, E., III., and Ortmeier, P.J. (2010). *Leadership, Ethics, and Policing: Challenges for the 21st. Century* (2nd ed.). Upper Saddle River, NJ: Pearson/Prentice Hall.

Meltzer, A.H. (2012). *Why Capitalism?* Oxford: Oxford University Press.

Mena, S., Rintamäki, J., Fleming, P., and Spicer, A. (2016). On the forgetting of corporate irresponsibility. *Academy of Management Review*, Vol. 41 (4), pp. 720–738.

Miller, D. (1999). *Principles of Social Justice*. Cambridge, MA: Harvard University Press.

Mirvis, P.H. (2012). Employee engagement and CSR. *California Management Review*, Vol. 54 (4), pp. 93–117.

Mirvis, P.H., and Kanter, D.L. (1991). Beyond demography: A psychographic profile of the workforce. *Human Resource Management*, Vol. 30 (1), pp. 45–68.

Mitchell, L. (2001). *Corporate Irresponsibility: America's Newest Export*. New Haven, CT: Yale University Press.

Mitchell, M.S., and Ambrose, M.L. (2007). Abusive supervision and workplace deviance and the moderating effects of negative reciprocity beliefs. *Journal of Applied Psychology*, Vol. 92 (4), pp. 1159–1178.

Mitchell, R.K., Agle, B.R. and Wood, D. (1997). Toward a theory of stakeholder identification and salience. *Academy of Management Review*, Vol. 22 (4), pp. 853–886.

Mizutani, H. (2007). Whistleblower protection act. *Japan Labor Review*, Vol. 4 (3), pp. 95–119.

Morecroft, J. (2004). Mental models and learning in system dynamics practice. Pidd, M. (ed.), *Systems Modelling: Theory and Practice*. New York: Wiley, pp. 101–126.

Morrell, K. (2009). Governance and the public good. *Public Administration*, Vol. 87 (3), pp. 538–556.

Mosley, L., and Uno, S. (2007). Racing to the bottom or climbing to the top? Economic globalization and collective labor rights. *Comparative Political Studies*, Vol. 40 (8), pp. 923–948.

Mueller, H.M., Ouimet, P.P., and Simintzi, E. (2016). *Within-Firm Pay Inequality*. Cambridge, MA: National Bureau of Economic Research.

Murphy, P.E. (1989). Creating ethical corporate structures. *MIT Sloan Management Review*, Vol. 30 (2), pp. 81–96.

Narayan, D., Pritchett, L., and Kapoor, S. (2009). *Moving Out of Poverty: Success From the Bottom Up* (Vol. 2). Washington, DC: World Bank.

Narveson, J. (2007). *Classics of Political and Social Philosophy*. Waterloo, ON: University of Waterloo.

Nash, L.L. (1981). Ethics without the sermon. *Harvard Business Review*. Vol. 59 (6), pp. 79–90.

National Society of Professional Engineers (NSPE). (1993). NSPE code of ethics for engineers. *Journal of the Minerals, Metals, and Materials Society*, Vol. 45 (4), pp. 14–16.

Nazari, J.A., and Herremans, I.M. (2007). Extended VAIC model: Measuring intellectual capital components. *Journal of Intellectual Capital*, Vol. 8 (4), pp. 595–609.

NCVO (The National Council for Voluntary Organisations, 2014). *How Has the Number of Civil Society Organisations Changed?* UK Civil Society Almanac. Available at https://data.ncvo.org.uk/a/almanac14/fast-facts-3/

Nelling, E., and Webb, E. (2009). Corporate social responsibility and financial performance: The "virtuous circle" revisited. *Review of Quantitative Finance and Accounting*, Vol. 32 (2), pp. 197–209.

Noll, M.A. (2011). *Protestantism: A Very Short Introduction*. Oxford: Oxford University Press.

Nonaka, I. (1994). A dynamic theory of organizational knowledge creation. *Organization Science*, Vol. 5 (1), pp. 14–37.

Nonaka, I., and Takeuchi, H. (1995). *The Knowledge Creating Company: How Japanese Companies Create the Dynamics of Innovation*. New York: Oxford University Press.

Norman, S.M., Avolio, B.J., and Luthans, F. (2010). The impact of positivity and transparency on trust in leaders and their perceived effectiveness. *Leadership Quarterly*, Vol. 21 (3), pp. 350–364.

North, D.C. (1990). *Institutions, Institutional Change and Economic Performance*. Cambridge: Cambridge University Press.

Novak, M. (1996). *Business as a Calling. Work and The Examined Life*. New York: Free Press.

NRTEE (National Roundtable on the Environment and the Economy) of Canada. (1993). *Consensus Guiding Principles*. Quebec: NRTEE.

Nussbaum, M.C. (1992). Human functioning and social justice in defense of Aristotelian essentialism. *Political Theory*, Vol. 20 (2), pp. 202–246.

Nye, J. (2002). Corruption and political development: A cost benefit analysis. Nye, J., Heidenheimer, A.J., and Johnston, M. (eds.), *Political Corruption. Contexts and Concepts*. New Brunswick, NJ: Transaction, pp. 963–983.

Oakley, R.L., and Salam, A.F. (2012). *Cyber Citizens and Cyber Deviance: Exploring Social and Technical Factors as Antecedents to Cyber Deviance and the Implications for Cyber Citizenship*. SIGHCI 2012 Proceedings. Paper # 7.

OECD (Organisation for Economic Co-operation and Development, 1963). *Issues in Management Education*. Paris: OECD.

OECD (Organisation for Economic Co-operation and Development, 1996). *Ethics in the Public Service. Current Issues and Practices*. Paris: OECD.

Oesterle, M.J., Elosge, C., and Elosge, L. (2016). Me, myself and I: The role of CEO narcissism in internationalization decisions. *International Business Review*, Vol. 25 (5), pp. 1114–1123.

Office of Government Ethics. (1992). *Principles of Ethical Conduct for Government Officers and Employees*. Washington, DC: White House, Executive Order 12674.

Ojala, A. (2015). Geographic, cultural, and psychic distance to foreign markets in the context of small and new ventures. *International Business Review*, Vol. 24 (5), pp. 825–835.

Oliver, D. (2009). Engineers and white-collar crime. *Journal of Legal Affairs and Dispute Resolution in Engineering and Construction*, Vol. 1 (1), pp. 32–39.

Onyx, J. (2008). Third sector organisation accountability and performance. Hasan, S., and Onyx, J. (eds.), *Comparative Third Sector Governance in Asia*. New York: Springer, pp. 119–129.

Osajda, M. (2011). *The UK Bribery Act of 2010 Whither the FCPA? World Check White Paper*. London: Global World Check.

Osterwalder, A., and Pigneur, Y. (2011). Aligning profit and purpose through business model innovation. Palazzo, G. (ed.), *Responsible Management Practices For the 21st Century*. Upper Saddle River, NJ: Pearson, pp. 61–75.

Palm, E. (2009). Privacy expectations at work – What is reasonable and why? *Ethical Theory and Moral Practice*, Vol. 12 (2), pp. 201–215.

Parr, R.L., and Smith, G.V. (2013). *Intellectual Property: Valuation, Exploitation, and Infringement Damages*. Cumulative Supplement (11th ed.). Hoboken, NJ: John Wiley and Sons.

Parsons, P.J. (2004). *Ethics in Public Relations: A Guide to Best Practice*. London: Kogan Page.

Parsons, T. (1980). *Social Systems and The Evolution of Action Theory*. New York: Free Press.

Pascal, B. (1670/1966). *Pensees*. Krailsheimer, A.J. (ed.), London: Penguin.

Pastin, M. (1986). Lessons from high-profit, high-ethics companies: An agenda for managerial action. Pastin, M., and Hayward, G. (eds.), *The Hard Problems of Management: Gaining the Ethics Edge*. San Francisco, CA: Jossey-Bass.

Payne, S.L., and Calton, J.M. (2002). Towards a managerial practice of stakeholder engagement: Developing multi-stakeholder learning dialogues. *Journal of Corporate Citizenship*, Vol. 2 (6), pp. 37–53.

Peacock, M. (2010). Obligation and advantage in Hobbes' *Leviathan*. *Canadian Journal of Philosophy*, Vol. 40 (3), pp. 433–458.

Pearce, D., and Atkinson, G. (1993). Capital theory and the measurement of sustainable development: an indicator of "weak" sustainability. *Ecological Economics*, Vol. 8 (2), pp. 103–108.

Peikoff, L. (1991). *Objectivism: The Philosophy of Ayn Rand*. New York: E.P. Dutton.

Pellegrino, E.D. (1989). Character, virtue and self-interest in the ethics of the professions. *Journal of Contemporary Health Law & Policy*, Vol. 5, pp. 53–73.

Peterson, M. (2015). Social enterprise for poverty alleviation in an era of sector convergence. *Journal of Ethics & Entrepreneurship*, Vol. 5 (1), pp. 5–25.

Petty, R.D. (2015). The historic development of modern US advertising regulation. *Journal of Historical Research in Marketing*, Vol. 7 (4), pp. 524–548.

Pfeffer, J. (1994). *Competitive Advantage Through People: Unleashing the Power of the Work Force*. Boston, MA: Harvard Business Press.

Pfeffer, J. (1995). Producing sustainable competitive advantage through the effective management of people. *Academy of Management Executive*, Vol. 9 (1), pp. 55–69.

Pfeffer, J. (1998). Seven practices of successful organizations. *California Management Review*, Vol. 40 (2), pp. 96–124.

Pies, I., Hielscher, S., and Beckmann, M. (2009). Moral commitments and the societal role of business: An ordonomic approach to corporate citizenship. *Business Ethics Quarterly*, Vol. 19 (3), pp. 375–401.

Pimple, M.M. (2012). Business ethics and corporate social responsibility. *Journal of Management Research and Reviews*, Vol. 2 (5), pp. 761–765.

Poliner Shapiro, J., and Stefkovich, J.A. (2016). *Ethical Leadership and Decision Making in Education: Applying Theoretical Perspectives to Complex Dilemmas* (4th ed.). Abingdon-on-Thames: Routledge 2011.

Pope Benedict XVI (2005). *Deus Caritas Est*. Encyclical Letter. The Vatican: Vatican Publishing House.

Pope John Paul II (1991). *Centesimus Annus*. Encyclical Letter. The Vatican: Vatican Publishing House.

Porter, M.E., Kramer, M.R. (2011). Creating shared value: How to reinvent capitalism -and unleash a wave of innovation and growth. *Harvard Business Review*, Vol. 89 (1–2), pp. 62–77.

Post, J.E. (1985). Assessing the Nestlé boycott: Corporate accountability and human rights. *California Management Review*, Vol. 27 (2), pp. 113–131.

Prado-Lorenzo, J.M., García-Sánchez, I.M., and Gallego-Álvarez, I. (2012). Effects of activist shareholding on corporate social responsibility reporting practices: An empirical study in Spain. *Journal of Economics, Finance and Administrative Science*, Vol. 17 (32), pp. 7–16.

Prahalad, C.K. (2010). *The Fortune at the Bottom of the Pyramid: Eradicating Poverty Through Profits*. Revised and Updated 5th Anniversary Edition. Upper Saddle River, NJ: Pearson Education.

Preuss, L. (2001). In dirty chains? Purchasing and greener manufacturing. *Journal of Business Ethics*, Vol. 34 (3), pp. 345–359.

Primbs, M., and Wang, C. (2016). *Notable Governance Failures: Enron, Siemens and Beyond*. University of Pennsylvania Law School Seminar Paper Spring 2016. Penn Law: Legal Scholarship Repository

Principia Cybernetica Web. (1996). *What is complexity?* Available at http://pespmc1.vub.ac.be/complexi.html

Puffer, S.M., and McCarthy, D.J. (1995). Finding the common ground in Russian and American business ethics. *California Management Review*, Vol. 37 (2), pp. 29–46.

Pulic, A. (1998). *Measuring the Performance of Intellectual Potential in Knowledge Economy*. Available at www.vaic-on.net/download/Papers/Measuring_the_ Performance_of_Intellectual_Potential.pdf, accessed July 13, 2016.

Pursey, P., Heugens, A., Kaptein, S.P., and van Oosterhout, J. (2008). Contracts to communities: A processual model of organizational virtue. *Journal of Management Studies*, Vol. 45 (1), pp. 100–121.

PwC. (2014). *PriceWaterhouseCoopers State of Compliance Survey*. Available at www.pwc.com/us/stateofcompliance, accessed December 13, 2014.

Pye, L.W. (1988). The new Asian capitalism: a political portrait. Berger, P.L., and Hsiao, H-H.M. (eds.), *In search of an East Asian Development Model*. New Brunswick, NJ: Transaction, pp. 81–98.

Quinn, D.P., and Jones, T.M. (1995). An agent morality view of business policy. *Academy of Management Review*, Vol. 20 (1), pp. 22–42.

Quinn, M.J. (2014). *Ethics For the Information Age*. Upper Saddle River, NJ: Pearson.

Rachels, J. (1999). *The Elements of Moral Philosophy* (3rd ed.). New York: McGraw-Hill.

Rais, S., and Goedegebuure, R.V. (2009). Stakeholder orientation and financial performance: evidence from Indonesia. *Problems and Perspectives in Management*, Vol. 7 (3), pp. 62–75.

Rao, M., and Sylvester S. (2000). Business and education in transition. *AAHE* (American Association for Higher Education) *Bulletin*, Vol. 52 (8), pp. 1–13.

Rauwald, C. (2016). *VW Holds Emergency Supplier Talks as Production Hold Widens. Bloomberg News Service*. Available at www.bloomberg.com/news/articles/2016-08-22/vw-restarts-talks-as-supplier-feud-expands-to-golf-production

Rawls, J. (2001). *Justice as Fairness: A Restatement*. Cambridge, MA: Harvard University Press.

Reeves-Ellington, R. (2004). What is missing from business education? Meeting the needs of emerging market business education. Alon, I., and McIntyre, J.R. (eds.), *Business Education and Emerging Market Economies. Perspectives and Best Practices*. Norwell, MA: Springer US, pp. 27–48.

Reginster, B. (2007). Nietzsche's new happiness: Longing, Boredom, and the elusiveness of fulfillment. *Philosophic Exchange*, Vol. 37 (1), pp. 17–25.

Reitz, H.J., Wall, J.A., Jr., and Love, M.S. (1998). Ethics in negotiation: Oil and water or good lubrication? *Business Horizons*, Vol. 41 (3), pp. 5–14.

Reitze, A.W. (2016). *The Volkswagen Air Pollution Emissions Litigation*. Environmental Law Reporter,Vol. 46, paper ID 46 ELR 10564.

Resick, C.J., Hanges, P.J., Dickson, M.W., and Mitchelson, J.K. (2006). A cross-cultural examination of the endorsement of ethical leadership. *Journal of Business Ethics*, Vol. 63 (4), pp. 345–359.

Richards, D.L., Gelleny, R.D., and Sacko, D.H. (2001). Money with a mean streak? Foreign economic penetration and government respect for human rights in developing countries. *International Studies Quarterly,*Vol. 45, pp. 219–239.

Roddick, A. (1991). *Body and Soul: Profits With Principles, the Amazing Success Story of Anita Roddick & the Body Shop*. New York: Crown.

Rogers, D.S. (2013). Bringing poor people's voices into policy discussions. *World Social Science Report 2013*, Paris: UNESCO, pp. 362–364.

Rogerson, W.P. (1985). The first-order approach to principal-agent problems. *Econometrica: Journal of the Econometric Society*, pp. 1357–1367.

Rosensweig, J. (1998). *Winning the Global Game: A Strategy For Linking People and Profits*. New York: Simon and Schuster.

Rosenthal, A. (2001). *The Third House: Lobbyists and Lobbying in the States*. Beverly Hills, CA: Sage.

Ross, W.D. (1930). *The Right and the Good*. Oxford: Oxford University Press.

Rost, J.C. (1991). *Leadership For the Twenty-First Century*. New York: Praeger.

Russo, A., and Perrini, F. (2010). Investigating stakeholder theory and social capital: CSR in large firms and SMEs. *Journal of Business ethics,*Vol. 91 (2), pp. 207–221.

Saad, L. (2013). In U.S. *Rise in Religious "Nones."* Available at www.gallup.com/poll/159785/rise-religious-nones-slows-2012.aspx?g_source=spirituality&g_medium=search&g_campaign=tiles.

Saee, J. (2005). Effective leadership for the global economy in the 21st century. *Journal of Business Economics and Management,*Vol. 6 (1), pp. 3–11.

Saisana, M., and Saltelli, A. (2012). *Corruption Perceptions Index 2012 Statistical Assessment*. European Commission Joint Research Centre Scientific and Policy Report: Luxembourg: Publications Office of the European Union.

Salamon, L.M., and Sokolowski, S.W. (2004). *Global Civil Society: Dimensions of the Nonprofit Sector,*Vol. 2. Bloomfield, CT: Kumarian Press.

Sandel, M.J. (2009). *Justice. What's the Right Thing to Do?* New York: Farrar, Straus & Giroux.

Saner, R., Yiu, L., and Søndergaard, M. (2000). Business diplomacy management: A core competency for global companies. *Academy of Management Executive,*Vol. 14 (1), pp. 80–92.

Santos, N.S.J., and Laczniak, G.R. (2008). *Marketing to the Poor. A Justice-Inspired Approach*. 14th Annual World Forum on Business and Education in an Era of Globalization. Colleagues in Jesuit Business Education International Association of Jesuit Business Schools on July 20–23, 2008, Marquette, MI.

Sardar, Z. (2007). *What Do Muslims Believe? The Roots and Realities of Modern Islam*. London: Walker Books.

Savage, G.T., Nix, T.W., Whitehead, C.J., and Blair, J.D. (1991). Strategies for assessing and managing organizational stakeholders. *Academy of Management Executive*, Vol. 5 (2), pp. 61–75.

Sayer, A. (2007). Moral economy as critique. *New Political Economy,*Vol. 12 (2), pp. 261–270.

Scharmer, O. (2010). Seven acupuncture points for shifting capitalism to create a regenerative ecosystem economy. *Oxford Leadership Journal,*Vol. 1 (3), pp. 1–21.

Scherhorn, G. (2004). *Sustainability Reinvented*. Working Paper Series In Culture of Consumption and ESRC-AHRB Research Program. London: ESRC-AHRB Research Center.

Schiff, M., and Lewin, A.Y. (1970). The impact of people on budgets. *Accounting Review*, Vol. 45 (2), pp. 259–268.

Schilit, H. (2010). *Financial Shenanigans*. Mumbai: Tata McGraw-Hill Education.

Schminke, M. (ed.). (2010). *Managerial Ethics: Managing the Psychology of Morality*. New York: Routledge.

Schminke, M., Arnaud, A., and Kuenzi, M. (2007). The power of ethical work climates. *Organizational Dynamics*, Vol. 36 (2), pp. 171–186.

Schreck, P. (2011). Reviewing the business case for corporate social responsibility: New evidence and analysis. *Journal of Business Ethics*, Vol. 103 (2), pp. 167–188.

Schumann, P.L. (2001). A moral principles framework for human resource management ethics. *Human Resource Management Review*, Vol. 11 (1), pp. 93–111.

Schütrumpf, E. (2014). Cicero's view on the merits of a practical life in De Republica. *Etica & Politica/Ethics & Politics*, Vol. 16 (2), pp. 395–411. Schwaiger, M. (2004). Components and parameters of corporate reputation – an empirical study. *Schmalenbach Business Review*, Vol. 56 (1), pp. 46–71.

Schwartz, M. (1998). Peter Drucker and the denial of business ethics. *Journal of Business Ethics*, Vol. 17 (15), pp. 1685–1692.

Schwartz, M. (2007). The 'business ethics' of management theory. *Journal of Management History*, Vol. 13 (1), pp. 43–54.

Schwartz, S.H. (1992). Universals in the content and structure of values: Theoretical advances and empirical tests in 20 countries. Zanna, M. (ed.), *Advances in Experimental Social Psychology* (Vol. 25), New York: Academic Press, pp. 1–66.

Scott, R.W. (2004). Institutional theory. Ritzer, G. (ed.), *Encyclopedia of Social Theory*. Thousand Oaks, CA: Sage, pp. 408–414.

Sehgal, K. (2010). *Walk in My Shoes: Conversations Between a Civil Rights Legend and His Godson*. London: Palgrave Macmillan.

Sekerka, L.E. (2016). *Ethics is a Daily Deal. Choosing to Build Moral Strength as a Practice* New York: Springer.

Sen, A. (1985). *Commodities and Capabilities*. Amsterdam: Elsevier.

Sen, A. (2000). *Development as Freedom*. New York: Alfred A. Knopf.

Senge, P.M. (1994). The art and practice of the learning organization. Ray, M., and Rinzler, A. (eds.), *The New Paradigm in Business: Emerging Strategies For Leadership and Organizational Change*. New York: Penguin Books, pp. 126–138.

Shapiro, S.P. (2005). Agency theory. *Annual Review of Sociology*, pp. 263–284.

Sharma, A. (2005). *Modern Hindu Thought: An Introduction*. Oxford: Oxford University Press.

Shaw, W.H., and Barry, V. (1998). *Moral Issues in Business*. London: International Thomson.

Shermer, M. (2004). *The Science of Good and Evil: Why People Cheat, Gossip, Care, Share, and Follow the Golden Rule*. New York: Times Books.

Shimizu, K., Hitt, M.A., Vaidyanath, D., and Pisano, V. (2004). Theoretical foundations of cross-border mergers and acquisitions: A review of current research and recommendations for the future. *Journal of International Management*, Vol. 10 (3), 307–353.

Sialkoti, M. S. (1984). *Morals and Manners in Islam*. Varanasi, Uttar Pradesh, India: Idaratul-Buhoosil Islamia.

Siltaoja, M.E. (2006). Value priorities as combining core factors between CSR and reputation – a qualitative study. *Journal of Business Ethics*, Vol. 68 (1), pp. 91–111.

Simcic Brønn, P., and C. Brønn (2003). A reflective stakeholder approach: Co-orientation as a basis for communication and learning. *Journal of Communication Management*, Vol. 7 (4), pp. 291–303.

Sims, R.R. (2017). *A Contemporary Look at Business Ethics*. Charlotte, NC: Information Age.

Sims, R.R., Brinkmann, J., and Sauser, W.I., Jr. (2016). The C-suite's role in countering moral muteness. Sims, R.R., and Quatro, S.A. (eds.), *Executive Ethics II: Ethical Dilemmas and Challenges for the C Suite*. Charlotte, NC: Information Age, pp. 37–62.

Singer, P. (1972). Famine, affluence, and morality. *Philosophy & Public Affairs*, Vol. 1 (3), 229–243.

Sisodia, R.S. (2011) Conscious Capitalism. *California Management Review*, Vol. 53 (3), pp. 98–108.

Sisodia, R., Wolfe, D., and Sheth, J. (2014). *Firms of Endearment: How World Class Companies Profit From Passion and Purpose* (2nd ed.). Upper Saddle River, NJ: Pearson.

Slim, H. (2002). *By What Authority? The Legitimacy and Accountability of Non-Governmental Organisations*. International Council on Human Rights Policy Meeting in Geneva, January 10–12, 2002. Available at Diario de la Ayuda Humanitaria (JHA), www.jha.ac/articles/a082.htm, accessed August 6, 2016.

Small, M.W. (2004). Philosophy in management: A new trend in management development. *Journal of Management Development*, Vol. 23, pp. 183–196.

Smit, A. (2013). Responsible leadership development through management education: A business ethics perspective. *African Journal of Business Ethics*, Vol. 7 (2), pp. 45–58.

Smith, H., and Novak, P. (2003). *Buddhism: A Concise Introduction*. New York: HarperCollins.

Smith, J.D. (2005). Moral markets and moral managers revisited. *Journal of Business Ethics*, Vol. 61 (2), pp. 129–141.

Snider, J., Hill, R.P., and Martin, D. (2003). Corporate social responsibility in the 21st century: A view from the world's most successful firms. *Journal of Business Ethics*, Vol. 48 (2), pp. 175–187.

Society of European Affairs Professionals. (2007). *SEAP Response to the European Commission Communication: Follow Up to the Green Paper European Transparency Initiative*. Available at www.seap.eu.org/linkdocs/ETI_position_paper.pdf

Solomon, J. (2007). *Corporate Governance and Accountability*. Hoboken, NJ: Wiley.

Sorell, T., and Hendry, J. (1994). *Business Ethics*. Oxford: Butterworth-Heinemann.

Spalding, A.B. (2010). Unwitting sanctions: Understanding anti-bribery legislation as economic sanctions against emerging markets. *Florida Law Review*, Vol. 62, pp. 351–425.

Srivastva, S., and Cooperrider, D.L. (1988). The urgency for executive integrity. *Executive Integrity: The Search For High Human Values in Organizational Life*. San Francisco, CA: Jossey-Bass, pp. 1–28.

St. John, G. (2008). Protestival: Global days of action and carnivalized politics in the present. *Social Movement Studies*, Vol. 7 (2), pp. 167–190.

Stanford Encyclopedia of Philosophy. (2014). *Hobbes's Moral and Political Philosophy*. First published February 12, 2002; substantive revision February 25, 2014. Accessed May 28, 2016. http://plato.stanford.edu/entries/hobbes-moral/

Stanford Law School. (2017). *Foreign Corrupt Practices Act Clearinghouse*. http://fcpa.stanford.edu/statistics-analytics.html

Stanwick, P.A., and Stanwick, S.D. (1998). The relationship between corporate social performance, and organizational size, financial performance, and environmental performance: An empirical examination. *Journal of Business Ethics*, Vol. 17 (2), pp. 195–204.

Stark, A. (1992). What's the matter with business ethics? *Harvard Business Review*, Vol. 71 (3), pp. 38–40. Stiglitz, J.E. (2007). Multinational corporations: Towards principles of cross-border legal frameworks in a globalized world: Balancing rights with responsibilities. *American University International Law Review*, Vol. 23 (3), pp. 451–558.

Stiglitz, J.E., Sen, A., and Fitoussi, J.P. (2010). *Report By the Commission on the Measurement of Economic Performance and Social Progress*. Paris: Commission on the Measurement of Economic Performance and Social Progress.

Strauss, G. (2001). HRM in the USA: Correcting some British impressions. *International Journal of Human Resource Management*, Vol. 12 (6), 873–897.

Stroud, S.R. (2002). Defending Kant's ethics in light of the modern business organization. *Teaching Ethics*, Vol. 2 (2), pp. 29–40.

Stucke, M.E. (2013). In search of effective ethics & compliance programs. *Journal of Corporate Law*, Vol. 39 (4), pp. 769–832.

Subramaniam, M., and Youndt, M.A. (2005). The influence of intellectual capital on the types of innovative capabilities. *Academy of Management Journal*, Vol. 48 (3), pp. 450–463.

Suchanek, A. (2008). *Business Ethics and the Golden Rule*. Wittenberg Center for Global Ethics Discussion Paper 2008–3. Available at: www.wcge.org/download/DP_2008-3_Andreas_Suchanek_-Business_Ethics_and_the_Golden_Rule.pdf

Suchman, M.C. (1995). Managing legitimacy: Strategic and institutional approaches. *Academy of Management Review*, Vol. 20 (3), pp. 571–610. Sullivan, P.H. (2000). *Value-Driven Intellectual Capital*. Hoboken, NJ: Wiley.

Szépesi, S. (2004). *Coercion or Engagement? Economics and Institutions in ACP-EU Trade Negotiations*. European Centre for Development Policy Management Discussion Paper No. 56.

Tafti, A., Mithas, S., and Krishnan, M.S. (2007). Information technology and the autonomy – control duality: Toward a theory. *Information Technology and Management*, Vol. 8 (2), pp. 147–166.

Tavris, C., and Offir, C. (1995). *Psychology in Perspective*. London: HarperCollins College.

Taylor, B.R. (2010). *Dark Green Religion: Nature Spirituality and the Planetary Future*. Berkeley: University of California Press.

Taylor, I. (2010). *The International Relations of Sub-Saharan Africa*. London: Bloomsbury.

ten Bos, R., and Willmott, H. (2001). Towards a post-dualistic business ethics: Interweaving reason and emotion in working life. *Journal of Management Studies*, Vol. 38 (6), pp. 769–793.

Tenbrunsel, A.E., and Messick, D.M. (2004). Ethical fading: The role of self-deception in unethical behavior. *Social Justice Research*, Vol. 17 (2), pp. 223–236.

Thau, S., Bennett, R.J., Mitchell, M.S., and Marrs, M.B. (2009). How management style moderates the relationship between abusive supervision and workplace deviance: An uncertainty management theory perspective. *Organizational Behavior and Human Decision Processes*, Vol. 108 (2), pp. 79–92.

Thomas, H., and Wilson A. (2013). *Promises Fulfilled and Unfulfilled in Management Education: Reflections on the Role, Impact and Future of Management Education: EFMD Perspectives* (3rd ed.). Bingley: Emerald Group.

Tirole, J. (2001). Corporate governance. *Econometrica*, Vol. 69 (1), pp. 1–35.

Torugsa, N.A., O'Donohue, W., and Hecker, R. (2013). Proactive CSR: An empirical analysis of the role of its economic, social and environmental dimensions on the association between capabilities and performance. *Journal of Business Ethics*, Vol. 115 (2), pp. 383–402.

Treviño, L.K., and Nelson, K.A. (2011). *Managing Business Ethics: Straight Talk About How to Do It Right* (5th ed.). Hoboken, NJ: John Wiley.

Trompenaars, F., and Voerman, E. (2009). *Servant Leadership Across Cultures: Harnessing the Strength of the World's Most Powerful Leadership Philosophy*. Oxford: Infinite Ideas.

Tsahuridu, E., and Vandekerckhove, W. (2008). Organisational whistleblowing policies: Making employees responsible or liable? *Journal of Business Ethics*, Vol. 82 (1), pp. 107–118.

Tschannen-Moran, M. (2004). *Trust Matters*. San Francisco, CA: Jossey-Bass.

Turner, N., Barling, J., Epitropaki, O., Butcher, V., and Milner, C. (2002). Transformational leadership and moral reasoning. *Journal of Applied Psychology*, Vol. 87, pp. 304–311.

Turner, R.K., and Fairbrass, J. (2001). Sustainable development policy in the United Kingdom. *Milieu*, Vol. 16 (3), pp. 107–123.

Twenge, J.M. (2006). *Generation Me: Why Today's Young Americans Are More Confident, Assertive, Entitled – and More Miserable Than Ever Before*. New York: Free Press.

Twenge, J.M. (2010). A review of the empirical evidence on generational differences in work attitudes. *Journal of Business and Psychology*, Vol. 25 (2), 201–210.

US Catholic Bishops. (1996). *Economic Justice for All*. Washington DC: US Catholic Conference.

Uddin, M.B., Tarique, K.M., and Hassan, M. (2008). Three dimensional aspects of corporate social responsibility. *Daffodil International University Journal of Business and Economics*, Vol. 3 (1), pp. 199–212.

UN DPI (United Nations Department of Public Information, 2011). *Sustainable Societies – Responsive Citizens*. Declaration of the 64th Annual UN DPI/NGO. Conference. Bonn: United Nations.

UNCTAD (United Nations Conference on Trade and Development, 2011). *Trade Facilitation in Regional Trade Agreements*. New York: United Nations.

United Nations. (1999). *Global Compact*. Available at www.unglobalcompact.org

United Nations. (2015). *Transforming our World: The 2030 Agenda for Sustainable Development*. Resolution adopted by the General Assembly on 25 September 2015, A/RES/70/1. Geneva: United Nations.

UNWTO (United Nations World Tourism Organization, 2016). *Tourism Highlights*. Madrid: United Nations World Tourism Organization.

Ur Rehman, W., Ur Rehman, H., Usman, M., and Ashgar, N. (2012). A link of intellectual capital performance with corporate performance: Comparative study from banking sector in Pakistan. *International Journal of Business and Social Science*, Vol. 3 (12), pp. 313–321.

Useem, M. (1998). *The Leadership Moment: Nine Stories of Triumph and Disaster and Their Lessons for Us All*. New York: Times Business/Random House.

Valentine, S. (ed., 2014). *Organizational Ethics and Stakeholder Well-Being in the Business Environment*. Charlotte, NC: Information Age.

van de Klundert, T. (1999). Economic efficiency and ethics. *De Economist*, Vol. 147 (2), pp. 127–149.

Van den Akker, L., Heres, L., Lasthuizen, K., and Six, F. (2009). Ethical leadership and trust: It's all about meeting expectations. *International journal of Leadership Studies*, Vol. 5 (2), pp. 102–122.

van Dierendonck, D. (2011). Servant leadership: A review and synthesis. *Journal of Management*, Vol. 37 (4), pp. 1228–1261.

van Knippenberg, D., De Cremer, D., and van Knippenberg, B. 2007. Leadership and fairness: The state of the art. *European Journal of Work and Organizational Psychology*, Vol. 16 (2), pp. 113–140.

van Tulder, R., and van der Zwart, A. (2006). *International Business – Society Management: Linking Corporate Responsibility and Globalization*. London: Routledge.

von Bergen, C.W., and Bressler, M.S. (2014). Laissez Faire leadership: Doing nothing and its destructive effects. *European Journal of Management*, Vol. 14 (1), pp. 83–94.

von Hayek, F.A. (1944). *The Road to Serfdom*. London: George Routledge & Sons.

Voronov, M., and Weber, K. (2016). The heart of institutions: Emotional competence and institutional actorhood. *Academy of Management Review*, pp. 456–478.

Vranka, M.A., and Houdek, P. (2015). Many faces of bankers' identity: how (not) to study dishonesty. *Frontiers in Psychology*, Vol. 6, pp. 203–208.

Waddock, S.A., and Graves, S.B. (1997). The corporate social performance-financial performance link. *Strategic Management Journal*, Vol. 18, pp. 303–319.

Wagner-Tsukamoto, S.A. (2012). Updating Adam Smith on business ethics. *Conference Proceedings 4th World Business Ethics Forum (WBEF)*. Hong Kong: Hong Kong Baptist University.

Walker, C. (2016). Fuelling the fire: New coal technologies spell disaster for climate. *Chain Reaction*, Vol. 128 (November), pp. 17–18.

Walton, C.E. (1988). *The Moral Manager*. New York: Harper and Row.

Walumbwa, F.O., Avolio, B.J., Gardner, W.L., Wernsing, T.S., and Peterson, S.J. (2008). Authentic leadership: Development and validation of a theory-based measure. *Journal of Management*, Vol. 34 (1), pp. 89–126.

Walzer, M.W. (1983). *Spheres of Justice: A Defense of Pluralism and Equality*. New York: Basic Books.

Wang, Y. (2013). *Collaboration in Global Distributed Teams: An Interdisciplinary Review.* https://doi.org/10.2139/ssrn.2352798

Wankel, C., and Stachowitz-Stanusch, A. (2011). Management education for integrity; transcending amoral business curricula. *Management Education For Integrity: Ethically Educating Tomorrow's Business Leaders*. Bingley: Emerald Group, pp. 3–12.

Wartick, S., and D. Wood (1999). *International Business and Society*. Oxford: Oxford University Press.

WCED (World Commission on Environment and Development, 1987). *Our Common Future*. Oxford: Oxford University Press.

Weatherbee, T.G. (2010). Counterproductive use of technology at work: information & communications technologies and cyberdeviancy. *Human Resource Management Review*, Vol. 20 (1), pp. 35–44.

Weber, M. (1905/1976). *The Protestant Ethic and the Spirit of Capitalism*. Translated by T. Talcott Parsons. London: George Allen & Unwin.

Weber, M. (1947). *The Theory of Social and Economic Organization*. Translated by A.M. Henderson and T. Parsons. New York: Oxford University Press.

Weber, M. (2008). The business case for corporate social responsibility: A company-level measurement approach for CSR. *European Management Journal*, Vol. 26 (4), pp. 247–261.

Weber, W. (2009). *Interview with C.K. Prahalad*. Available at www.youtube.com/watch?v=NWObwaycIRU

Weber, Y., and Tarba, S.Y. (2012). Mergers and acquisitions process: The use of corporate culture analysis. *Cross Cultural Management: An International Journal*, Vol. 19 (3), pp. 288–303.

Webley, S. (2003). *Developing a Code of Ethics*. London: Institute for Business Ethics.

Wei-Ming, T. (2008). The rise of industrial East Asia: The role of Confucian values. *Copenhagen Journal of Asian Studies*, Vol. 4 (1), pp. 81–97.

Weinberger, O. (1991). The *conditio humana* and the ideal of justice. Weinberger, O. (ed.), *Law, Institution and Legal Politics*. Dordrecht: Springer, pp. 247–259.

Werlin, H.H. (2007). Corruption and democracy: Is Lord Acton right? *Journal of Social, Political, and Economic Studies*, Vol. 32 (3), pp. 359–382.

Wernz, J. (2014). Risk modeling and capital: Operational risk. Wernz, J. (ed.), *Bank Management and Control*. Berlin Heidelberg: Springer, pp. 81–92.

West, C.C. (2002). The Russian Orthodox Church and social doctrine: A commentary on fundamentals of the social conception of the Russian Orthodox Church. *Occasional Papers on Religion in Eastern Europe*, Vol. 22 (2), pp. 3–11.

Whetten, B. (2013). Integrating money and meaning: the role of purpose and profit in integral business. *Journal of Integral Theory and Practice*, Vol. 8 (1 & 2), pp. 149–160.

Whetten, D.A., Rands, G., and Godfrey, P. (2002). What are the responsibilities of business to society? Pettigrew, A., Thomas, H., and Whittington, R. (eds.), *Handbook of Strategy and Management*. London: Sage, pp. 373–408.

WHO (World Health Organization) and ITU (International Telecommunication Union). (2012). *National Health Strategy Toolkit*. Geneva: WHO Press.

Wicker, B. (1973). Humanism and ideology. *New Blackfriars*, Vol. 54 (638), pp. 321–327.

Williamson, O.E. (1989). Transaction cost economics. *Handbook of Industrial Organization*, Vol. 1, pp. 135–182.

Willis Towers Watson (2016). *Employee Health and Business Success: Making the Connections and Taking Action*. Global Research Report Summary. London: Willis Towers Watson. Available at: www.willistowerswatson.com/en/insights/2016/03/stayingatwork-report-employee-health-and-business-successjob, accessed August 15, 2016.

Wilson, R. (2006). Islam and business. *Thunderbird International Business Review*, Vol. 48 (1), pp. 109–123.

Wohl, R. (2005). *The Spectacle of Flight: Aviation and the Western Imagination, 1920–1950*. New Haven, CT: Yale University Press.

Wolf, A. (2000). Symposium on accountability in public administration: reconciling democracy, efficiency and ethics. *International Review of Administrative Sciences*, Vol. 66 (1), pp. 15–20.

Woodstock Theological Center (2002). *The Ethics of Lobbying: Organized Interests, Political Power, and the Common Good*. Washington, DC: Georgetown University Press.

World Bank. (2006). *World Development Report 2006: Equity and Development*. Washington, DC: World Bank.

World Economic Forum. (2002). *Global Corporate Citizenship: The Leadership Challenge for CEOs and Boards*. Geneva: World Economic Forum.

Wray, L.R. (2011). Minsky's money manager capitalism and the global financial crisis. *International Journal of Political Economy*, Vol. 40 (2), pp. 5–20.

Xueming, L., and Bhattacharya, C.B. (2006). Corporate social responsibility, customer satisfaction, and market value. *Journal of Marketing*, Vol. 70 (4), pp. 1–18.

Yamagami, A. (2004). *Consumer Administration in Japan and in Hyogo Prefecture*. Kobe: Life Enhancement Center of Hyogo Prefecture.

Yang, J., and Mossholder, K.W. (2010). Examining the effects of trust in leaders: A bases-and-foci approach. *Leadership Quarterly*, Vol. 21 (1), pp. 50–63.

Young, A.J. (2010). Rebuilding Haiti With Public Purpose Capitalism. *Huffington Post*, Jan. 26, 2010. Available at www.huffingtonpost.com/amb-andrew-j-young/rebuilding-haiti-with-pub_b_437634.html, accessed July 16, 2016.

Young, S.B. (2003). *Moral Capitalism at Work: Reconciling Private Interest With the Public Good*. San Francisco, CA: Berrett Koehler.

Young, S.B. (2006). Moral capitalism at work. Kidd, J.B., and Frank-Jürgen Richter, F.-J. (eds.), *Development Models, Globalization and Economies*. New York: Palgrave Macmillan.

Yukl, G., Mahsud, R., Hassan, S., and Prussia, G.E. (2013). An improved measure of ethical leadership. *Journal of Leadership & Organizational Studies*, Vol. 20 (1), pp. 38–48.

Yukl, Gary A. (2010). *Leadership in Organizations* (7th ed.), Upper Saddle River, NJ: Prentice Hall.

Yunus, M. (2007). *Creating a World Without Poverty: Social Business and the Future of Capitalism.* New York: PublicAffairs.

Zaman, F., Khan Marri, M.Y., Sadozai, A.M., and Ramay, M.I. (2012). Islamic work ethics in contemporary era and its relationship with organizational citizenship behavior: A study based on public sector hospitals and banks in Pakistan. *Interdisciplinary Journal of Contemporary Research in Business,* Vol. 4 (6), pp. 772–779.

Zellars, K.L., Tepper, B.J., and Duffy, M.K. (2002). Abusive supervision and subordinates' organizational citizenship behavior. *Journal of Applied Psychology,* Vol. 87, pp. 1068–1076.

Zhaoming, G. (2007). Institutional ethics and institutional good. *Social Sciences in China,* Vol. 6, p. 4.

Zimbardo, P.G. (1973). On the ethics of intervention in human psychological research: With special reference to the Stanford prison experiment. *Cognition,* Vol. 2 (2), pp. 243–256.

Index

Page numbers in *italics* indicate an exhibit on the corresponding page and page numbers in **bold** indicate a table on the corresponding page.